WHEN THE ETERNAL CAN BE MET

When the Eternal Can Be Met

The Bergsonian Theology of Time in the Works of C. S. Lewis, T. S. Eliot, and W. H. Auden

COREY LATTA

☙PICKWICK *Publications* • Eugene, Oregon

WHEN THE ETERNAL CAN BE MET
The Bergsonian Theology of Time in the Works of C. S. Lewis, T. S. Eliot, and W. H. Auden

Copyright © 2014 Corey Latta. All rights reserved. Except for brief quotations in critical publications or reviews, no part of this book may be reproduced in any manner without prior written permission from the publisher. Write: Permissions, Wipf and Stock Publishers, 199 W. 8th Ave., Suite 3, Eugene, OR 97401.

Pickwick Publications
An Imprint of Wipf and Stock Publishers
199 W. 8th Ave., Suite 3
Eugene, OR 97401

www.wipfandstock.com

ISBN 13: 978-1-62564-421-3

Cataloguing-in-Publication data:

Latta, Corey.

When the Eternal can be met : the Bergsonian theology of time in the works of C. S. Lewis, T. S. Eliot, and W. H. Auden / Corey Latta.

viii + 226 pp. ; 23 cm. Includes bibliographical references.

ISBN 13: 978-1-62564-421-3

1. Bergson, Henri, 1859–1941. 2. Lewis, C. S. (Clive Staples), 1898–1963—Criticism and interpretation. 3. Eliot, T. S. (Thomas Stearns), 1888–1965—Criticism and interpretation. 4. Auden, W. H. (Wystan Hugh), 1907–1973—Criticism and interpretation. 5. Time. I. Title.

B2430.B43 L188 2014

Manufactured in the U.S.A.

I dedicate this book to my wife, Jennifer,
who fills my present with joy, love, and friendship.

To Jameela Lares, Richard Oster, and Troy Miller,
whose examples of scholarship and intellectual integrity
have inspired my habits and animated my thinking.

The time has passed when time doesn't count.
PAUL VALÉRY, "LA CRISE DE L'ESPRIT" (1919)

Humans live in time . . . therefore . . . attend chiefly to two things, to eternity itself and to . . . the Present. For the Present is the point at which time touches eternity . . . in it alone freedom and actuality are offered.
C. S. LEWIS, *THE SCREWTAPE LETTERS* (1942)

Contents

Introduction 1

1 The Task of Theologizing Literature in the Twentieth Century 19

2 Bergsonian Conceptions of Time: Duration, Dualism, Intuition 42

3 Meeting the Eternal in the Present: Bergsonism and the Theology of Present Time in C. S. Lewis's *The Great Divorce* 77

4 T. S. Eliot's Bergsonian "Always Present": Incarnation and Duration in *Four Quartets* 115

5 W. H. Auden's Themes of Time and Dualism: The Bergsonian Theology of "Kairos and Logos" 167

Conclusion 211

Bibliography 217

Introduction

Broadly, this book is about philosophical influence on theological articulations. Specifically, I claim that C. S. Lewis, T. S. Eliot, and W. H. Auden's post-conversion works that have time as a theological theme cannot be completely understood apart from the philosophy of Henri Bergson. Until now there have only been four books devoted exclusively to the relationship between the philosophy of Henri Bergson and twentieth-century literature. Both Paul Douglass in *Bergson, Eliot, and American Literature* (1986) and Tom Quirk in *Bergson and American Culture* (1990) examine Bergson's influence on Anglo-American writers. While Shiv Kumar's *Bergson and the Stream-of-Consciousness Novel* (1963) looks at Bergson's impact on James Joyce and Virginia Woolf, its scope is narrowed to only include a few of Bergson's ideas and their influence on a select group of authors. The most exhaustive study of Bergson, twentieth-century authors, and literary modernism is Mary Ann Gillies's *Henri Bergson and British Modernism* (1996). In Gillies' treatment of Bergson's influence on twentieth-century literature, she focuses on authors such as Conrad, Joyce, Woolf, Richardson, and Eliot. Other works like Michael Levenson's *A Genealogy of Modernism* (1984) and Sanford Schwartz's *Matrix of Modernism: Pound, Eliot and Early Twentieth Century Thought* (1985) have devoted chapters and essays to Bergson's relationship to modernism, twentieth-century currents of thought, and twentieth-century literature. This present work makes only the fifth major attempt to investigate Bergson's influence on twentieth-century literature and the first attempt to examine Bergson's influence on the Christian theology of twentieth-century authors C. S. Lewis, T. S. Eliot, and W. H. Auden.

Bergson was a major philosophical force in the first two decades of the twentieth century, and by the time Lewis, Eliot, and Auden wrote their post-conversion works Bergson's ideas were widely known by twentieth-century philosophers, theologians, and writers.[1] Because of Bergson's influence it is surprising that there is such a scarcity of scholarship on Bergson and the theological literature of important twentieth-century authors. Thus, I seek to fill the holes, while creating some new craters, in scholarship on early- to mid-twentieth century theologized literature and Bergson's influence on important twentieth-century writers by demonstrating a strong dependence on Bergson's ideas by Lewis, Eliot, and Auden.

C. S. Lewis's *The Great Divorce*, T. S. Eliot's *Four Quartets*, and W. H. Auden's "Kairos and Logos" are theological treatments of time that rely on Bergson's theory of time, and particularly on his concept of *duration*. Indeed, without Bergson, Lewis, Eliot, and Auden could not have composed their works, as we now know them and could not have articulated what I will refer to as their theologies of time. There are three reasons why I think the Bergson connection to these twentieth-century Christian writers is important and contributory to studies of Lewis, Eliot, and Auden, as well as to the field of theology and literature. First, one cannot understand the theological agendas in these authors' works without an understanding of Bergsonian duration. Second, not only was Christian theology of the utmost personal importance to each author, but also the promulgation of theology was the controlling idea behind their post-conversion works on time.

Yet another reason is that scholars have missed the theological connections between the three authors. While Lewis, Eliot, and Auden enjoyed successful contemporaneous careers and while they all converted to Christianity roughly within a decade of one another, scholars have failed to see any strong theological connections among them. The fact is that Lewis, Eliot, and Auden share a remarkable theological and thematic relationship that once revealed will situate each writer in a group of authors that shared the common goal of theologizing the theme of time for a twentieth-century audience. Scholarship has created a gulf between these authors, in that Eliot and Auden have been depicted as icons of literary modernism, while Lewis has traditionally been cast as an apologist and creator of the fantastic. This divergent reading of these three authors needs to be altered to accommodate their important theological commonalities.

---

1. For more on Bergson's influence on several twentieth-century thinkers, see Pilkington's *Bergson and His Influence: A Reassessment*.

Introduction

In the area of theology, Eliot and Auden were every bit as interested in promulgating Christianity as Lewis. In fact, like Lewis, whose career is known for popularizing theology to his fellow twentieth-century readers, Eliot and Auden took on the roles of what I will here describe as literary theologians. And the theme of time reveals a theological interest deemed immensely important by each author. Establishing this theological and thematic connection among the authors is thus important for understanding their individual post-conversion careers. It is also a significant thread in their theological constructions that Lewis, Eliot, and Auden all composed Bergsonian works on time. Without a Bergsonian reading, which has yet to be applied to the works studied here, one misses a controlling idea behind their post-conversion works. Lewis, Eliot, and Auden did not choose to write biblically allegorical treatments of time, in the vein of Bunyan's *Pilgrim's Progress* (1678) or like Hannah Hurnard's *Hinds' Feet on High Places* (1955), nor did they mostly rely on a prominent theologian from centuries past or a distinctly religious thinker from their own. Instead, each author looked to and was influenced by the philosophy of twentieth-century philosopher Henri Bergson.

To most fully understand Lewis, Eliot, and Auden's theologies of time and the works that it produced, one must understand that Bergsonian duration is the foundation on which each author built. Some scholars have rightly connected Bergson's ideas with the works of Lewis, of Eliot, and of Auden. However, those scholars are few, and none treat Bergson's influence on all three authors. Furthermore, I have been unable to find another scholar who connects Bergsonian duration to any of these authors' works in which theologized time is a theme, a theme on which I will concentrate. A Bergsonian reading provides an explanation as to how Lewis, Eliot, and Auden constructed their theologies of time, it demonstrates that time is an important thematic and theological concern, and it reveals that an understanding of these authors' works is incomplete without the consideration of Bergson.

Although connections seem tenuous between the Christian faiths of C. S. Lewis, T. S. Eliot, and W. H. Auden and the Bergsonian philosophy that pervades their literary works, each author's theological articulations on time and Bergson's secular philosophy are inseparably woven. While I will exhaustively explain Bergson's theories in chapter 2, I will here simply gloss Bergsonian duration as the belief that time is a force that works on an individual's inner emotional and spiritual states. Also important to this concept of durative time is the role of intuitive knowing and experience as a way to access duration. In Bergsonian duration, one's consciousness is connected to duration (i.e., time) through intuition, which allows the force of time to dynamically change the individual's inner states, or what Bergson calls *intensities*.

In the case of each author, Bergson's theory of duration served as a catalyst for his respective post-conversion treatment of time, and in the case of each author, ironically, his post-conversion theological writings also retained elements of Bergson's non-Christian theories. Indeed, the post-conversion works of all three writers exemplify Bergsonism and Christianity cooperating in ideological cross-fertilization. Though diverse in literary and personal expressions of their faith, Lewis, Eliot, and Auden are the twentieth-century's paramount examples of prominent English writers operating in and perpetuating a complicated Christian-Bergsonian binary.

Because Lewis, Eliot, and Auden retained Bergsonian ideas about time that might logically be abdicated following conversion to Christianity, each author can fruitfully be seen as a reactionary Christian figure whose post-conversion writings were direct commentaries on a prominent, non-Christian twentieth-century philosophy of time. Spanning slightly over a decade, the conversions of T. S. Eliot in 1927, C. S. Lewis in 1931, and W. H. Auden in 1940 inaugurated an unprecedented creative and critical body of work that joins theological with distinctly secular philosophical writing. For Eliot and Auden, their already prominent literary careers were reanimated by religious conversions, whereas Lewis's conversion fostered the ideas that defined his corpus. Each writer's conversion would create a new phase of heightened poetic intensity and leave indelible marks on his post-conversion body of work by providing him a belief system on which he could expound.

Eliot, the creator of the indelible poem *The Waste Land*, who cried in his pre-conversion state "these fragments I have shored against my ruins"[2] would become known for this prayer in "Ash Wednesday": "Suffer me not to be separated / And let my cry come unto Thee."[3] Auden would turn from his controversial political works like "Spain" to his highly theological Christian works like *The Double Man*—an entire collection devoted to his return to the Anglican Communion. For Lewis, already an aspiring poet and promising academician, conversion to Christianity would

---

2. Eliot, *The Waste Land*, V. line 431.
3. Eliot, "Ash Wednesday," VI. lines 35–36.

produce vastly popular fiction, a prolific body of literary criticism, and the twentieth-century's most significant works of Christian apologetics.

In their post-conversion careers, all three authors were often unable to see literature and literary criticism except through the eyes of faith, and some of the authors' most significant works were theological responses to what they saw as threatening secular philosophies, for example, Lewis's *Abolition of Man*, Eliot's *After Strange Gods*, and Auden's *On Secondary Worlds*. In fact, some of the theological beliefs most seminal to Eliot's verse and literary criticism are congruent to Lewis and Auden's beliefs, as when Eliot says, "Literary criticism should be completed by criticism from a definite ethical and theological standpoint."[4] Eliot's definite theological standpoint of Christianity encompasses the Bergsonian philosophy, which he, Lewis, and Auden employed. It is an important goal of my work to suggest that post-conversion Lewis, Eliot, and Auden as literary figures are far better understood when placed at the crossroads of Christianity and Bergsonian philosophy.

My primary and much narrower goal here, however, is to explore one theme prevalent in the works of twentieth-century writers, Christian and non-Christian alike, as well as being prominent in theologians' writings in the early to mid twentieth century: the theme of time. The rapid acceleration of the first decades of the twentieth century fostered the feeling that time was out of human control. The concept of time and man's seemingly insignificant subjective place in it troubled twentieth-century writers. Novelists departed from strict chronology, made extensive use of flashbacks and foreshadowing, and explored the disjuncture between private and public time. For example, Joseph Conrad's *The Secret Agent* (1907) imagines an anarchist plot to blow up Greenwich Observatory, where standard time was measured, as a symbol of a more general attack on objective standards. In Conrad's novel time itself is out of joint; after recording the explosion, the narrative flashes back without warning to an earlier time frame, leaving the plot's projection of time uncertain.

Another vivid example of twentieth-century anxiety over time occurs in Walter Benjamin's "Theses on the Philosophy of History" (1940). In discussing Paul Klee's painting *Angelus Novus*, Benjamin interprets its central figure as the angel of history.

> Where we perceive a chain of events, the angel sees one single catastrophe that keeps piling wreckage upon wreckage and hurls it in front of his feet. The angel would like to stay, awaken the

---

4. Eliot, "Religion and Literature," 343.

> dead, and make whole what has been smashed. But a storm is blowing from Paradise; it has got caught in his wings with such violence that the angel can no longer close them. This storm irresistibly propels him into the future to which his back is turned, while the pile of debris before him grows skyward. This storm is what we call progress.[5]

Here Benjamin depicts time as a violent, uncontrollable force. In time's wake nothing remains whole, and even notions of the supernatural have been swept by the thrust of rapidly passing time. A virtually inescapable critical conversation about time was created by the influential philosopher Henri Bergson's work on time, reality, and the subjective experience of the individual in time (*Time and Free Will*, 1913); the works by prominent literary figures like Wyndham Lewis that privileged the import of understanding time (*Time and Western Man*, 1927); and monumental literary works like Joyce's *Ulysses* (1922) that completely reconfigured how time could operate in a narrative. In fact, one of the greatest links between Lewis, Eliot, and Auden is that they each entered the conversation about time and meaning with creative theological voices. Lewis, Eliot, and Auden saw time as a problematic divide between a non-Christian approach to literature and a distinctly Christian one.

In fact, each author held the idea of time to be not only a theological tenet but also a fundamental literary theme of a Christian construction of human experience with God. Before moving on to my argument for how time functions theologically in Lewis, Eliot, and Auden, I want to briefly anthologize the problem of time as raised by each author in his own words. In Lewis's apologetic work, *Miracles*, he says about time:

> It is probable that Nature is not really in Time and almost certain that God is not. Time is probably (like perspective) the mode of our perception. There is therefore in reality no question of God's at one point in time (the moment of creation) adapting the material history of this universe in advance to free acts which you or I are to perform at a later point in Time. To Him all the physical events and all the human acts are present in an eternal Now. The liberation of finite wills and the creation of the whole material history of the universe (related to the acts of those wills in all the necessary complexity) is to Him a single operation. In this sense God did not create the universe long ago but creates it at this minute—at every minute.[6]

5. Benjamin, "Theses on the Philosophy of History," 257–58.
6. Lewis, *Miracles*, 176–77.

Introduction

Lewis equates temporal time with human perception, divine creation, and God's presence. According to Lewis, all moments are "eternally Now" to God, therefore any perception of time from a theological standpoint must take into consideration that though humans understand God to work in time, God by His own nature transcends time. Important to Lewis's idea of God occupying all moments as if they were present is the assumption that time *is* the medium through which God is known and made known. In Lewis's thinking, because time is God's medium, it is of the utmost theological importance.

In his fictional *Screwtape Letters*, Lewis says of time, "Humans live in time . . . therefore . . . [they] attend chiefly to two things, to eternity and to . . . the Present. For the Present is the point at which time touches eternity . . . in it alone freedom and actuality are offered."[7] It will be the leitmotif of *The Great Divorce* that the Present is the point at which time touches eternity. According to Lewis, living in time means to experience both eternity and the Present, which in Lewis's work is akin to Eliot's "always present" and Auden's "Kairos" in that the Present represents the moment in time in which God meets man. That moment is not found in the past or in the future, but in the direct experience of time in the Present. Apart from the Present, Lewis imagines no way for temporal man to know God. In *Till We Have Faces*, a retelling of the myth of Cupid and Psyche and arguably his most developed work of fiction, Lewis intimates of the apocalyptic implications of time:

> Lightly men talk of saying what they mean. Often when he was teaching me to write in Greek the Fox would say, "Child, to say the very thing you really mean, the whole of it, nothing more or less or other than what you really mean; that's the whole art and joy of words." A glib saying. When the *time* comes to you at which you will be forced at last to utter the speech which has lain at the centre of your soul for years, which you have, all that time, idiot-like, been saying over and over, you'll not talk about joy of words. I saw well why they gods do not speak to us openly, nor let us answer. Till that word can be dug out of us, why should they hear the babble that we think we mean? How can they meet us face to face till we have faces?[8]

The narrator and protagonist, Orual, recounts the instructions of her pedagogue, the Fox, about saying what one truly means. Here Orual

---

7. Lewis, *Screwtape Letters*, 67–68.
8. Lewis, *Till We Have Faces*, 294.

reflects on the Fox's teaching, wondering if saying what one really means will matter when the time for speaking finally ends. When the time comes and mankind is spiritually ready, when men "have faces," then glib sayings and Job-like audacity to treat with the gods will cease to be. Not only does Lewis see time as the medium through which God meets man, he also sees time as a revealer of divine judgment. *Till We Have Faces* associates time with the ultimate reckoning between the divine and human, as does *The Great Divorce*.

Eliot shares Lewis's concern for the theology and theme of time. In his post-conversion poem "Ash Wednesday," Eliot laments man's temporal condition:

> Because I do not hope to know again
> The infirm glory of the positive hour
> . . . .
> Because I know that time is always time
> And place is always and only place
> And what is actual is only for one time
> And only for one place.[9]

Here Eliot bemoans temporality without divinity. When unoccupied by the eternal, the temporal is vacant of spiritual meaning. To see time as "always and only" being only time is a concession to temporality's limitations and a theologically bereft position. "Ash Wednesday" presents the possibility of experiencing the temporal without the eternal. The possibility of abdicating the eternal and only experiencing the temporal is also a recurring theme in *Four Quartets*. In both "Ash Wednesday" and *Four Quartets* Eliot uses the theme of time in service to a theology of Incarnation, by depicting the temporal present as the means for the Incarnation. Like Lewis, Eliot invests time with a great deal of theological meaning. Indeed, Eliot opens his *Four Quartets* with:

> Time present and time past
> Are both perhaps present in time future
> And time future contained in time past.
> If all time is eternally present
> All time is unredeemable.[10]

I will treat this passage fully in the fourth chapter, but for now it is sufficient to say that time in the *Four Quartets* is concerned with the

---

9. Eliot, "Ash Wednesday," lines 1, 9–10, 16–19.
10. Eliot, *Four Quartets*, lines 1–5.

Introduction

possibility of theological redemption. The speaker sees theological redemption as interconnected with time, so interweaving the two that the poem will imagine no form of redemption outside of time. The speculative possibility that all time is unredeemable if all time is eternally present will run throughout the entirety of the poem, which finally concludes that time is the agent of redemption.

Lewis and Eliot's interest in time is matched by Auden's. In his "Kairos and Logos," a poem partly written in response to *The Interpretation of History* (1936) by German theologian Paul Tillich, Auden also depicts time as the vessel for the Incarnation. In this poem, time is both a theological event and a type of literary trope, as indicated by the first line, "Around them boomed the rhetoric of time." And in "For the Time Being," Auden poetically theologizes the meaning of the birth of Christ in time: "Before the Infinite could manifest Itself in the finite . . . . But here and now the Word which is implicit in the Beginning and in the End is become immediately explicit."[11]

Lewis, Eliot, and Auden considered time to be the sphere in which their Christian faiths and their creative works intensely met, and it is their treatments of time that simultaneously reveal their identities as both Christian thinkers and philosophically Bergsonian writers. It is also in that treatment of time that one sees these authors' complex theological and creative attempts to engage the issue of man's temporal existence—an issue that thinkers like Bergson brought to the philosophical forefront in the first decades of the twentieth century. Furthermore, Lewis, Eliot, and Auden imagined their treatments of time to involve both the ideas posed by Bergson (e.g., man's ability to be transformed through the force of time) as well as their own particular theological articulations. It is somewhat ironic that to fully express what they thought to be the Christian theological answer to the problem of man's existence in time, each author created a theology that retained certain traits of Bergson's non-Christian theory of duration.

The reason for Lewis, Eliot, and Auden's implementation of a prominent secular philosophy is that writing theology in the twentieth century was marked in its demand for a new presentation. Ezra Pound's cry to "make it new" can be applied to the task of writing theology in the twentieth century, as theologians and Christian writers like Lewis, Eliot, and Auden all saw the need for theological writing suitable for the radically reimagined world in which they lived. The philosophy of Henri Bergson

---

11. Auden, *Collected Poems*, 387.

had already made a significant impact on philosophy by the time Lewis, Eliot, and Auden converted to the Christian faith. And it was Bergson's philosophy that gave each author a contemporary, innovative, and effective theory of time that both complemented their Christian beliefs about duration and enabled them to create entirely new depictions of time that conveyed theological belief to a twentieth-century audience.

Theologically poeticizing time was for Lewis, Eliot, and Auden a primary way to address a philosophical concern while espousing a Christian understanding of time that metonymically stood for the entire Christian mythos. By focusing on the theologies of time in the works of these three eminent Christian authors, this book voices a unique argument in the field of theological criticism of twentieth-century literature and can shed yet more light on literary Christianity in the twentieth century.[12] And while I attempt to formulate the theory that Lewis, Eliot, and Auden's Christian theological articulations are inseparably interconnected with and dependent on the secular philosophy of Henri Bergson, I more give equal attention to placing Lewis, Eliot, and Auden in unprecedented direct conversation with one another about theme and theology.

No scholar has linked Lewis, Eliot, and Auden in terms of how all three prominent writers shared aspects of Christian belief that were manifested in the same literary theme of time. And while there is no shortage of works on time in twentieth-century literature, not to mention works on time in Lewis, in Eliot, and in Auden's works, there is a dearth of scholarship on theological time in these authors' writings. For the sake of defining the terms that comprise this conversation, theological time is simply defined as the belief that temporal time operates in conjunction with God's eternality. God's eternal nature is not erased in the temporal; rather, the eternal infuses the temporal with divine will, revelation, and redemptive purpose. In other words, theological time insists that God reveals Himself through time and that man may know God through time.

Despite the importance of theological time in the post-conversion work of the Lewis, Eliot, and Auden, scholarship has been largely silent about how time theologically operates for these three Christian authors.

---

12. For other writers that similarly work at the intersection of theology and literature, see Jasper, *European Literature and Theology in the Twentieth Century*; Jeffrey, *Christianity and Literature*; Ward, *Planet Narnia: The Seven Heavens in the Imagination of C. S. Lewis*; Wood, "The Baptized Imagination: C. S. Lewis's Fictional Apologetics"; *Literature and Theology*; Spurr, "Anglo-Catholic in Religion": T. S. Eliot and Christianity; Kirsch, *Auden and Christianity*; and the more dated but insightful work by Edwards, *Toward a Christian Poetics*.

And I have been unable to locate any critical argument positing that time operates as a theological tenet simultaneously reacting against and adhering to modernist literary conventions. The several strong critical works that examine how time operates in the works of any of these authors do not really engage time's theological significance. Indeed, even while critical publications about Lewis, Eliot, and Auden are so extensive as to defeat any attempt at an exhaustive literature review, they either fail to place these writers in conversation with one another or they neglect the importance of time as a theological and literary topic. The following selected studies have been instrumental in my own thinking about these authors and the theme of time. This project will add to their findings.

On C. S. Lewis, the scholarship is overwhelmingly theological, and some of the most relevant and helpful works for my approach to Lewis privilege Lewis's role as theologian and twentieth-century author. But the majority of critics of Lewis's theology do not privilege the "doctrine" of time that appears so prominently in his fiction. In their collection of essays *C. S. Lewis as Philosopher: Truth, Goodness and Beauty* (2008), David Baggett, Gary Habermas, and Jerry Walls attempt to situate Lewis in the classical philosophical tradition, claiming that "The great classic triumvirate of Truth, Beauty, and Goodness is a particularly apt framework for engaging C. S. Lewis and philosophy."[13] As helpful as the collection is at showing Lewis to be a deeply philosophical thinker, its focus on truth, beauty, and goodness rules out most philosophical considerations of time. The collection also often overlooks any ideological relationship between Lewis and Bergson. The usefulness of this work for my own is in various close readings that identify philosophical ideas deeply woven into Lewis's fiction.

A work on Lewis that swings far in the direction of understanding his relationship to his twentieth-century world is Louis Markos's *Lewis Agonistes: How C. S. Lewis Can Train Us to Wrestle with the Modern and Postmodern World* (2003). According to Markos, "Perhaps no age has so dulled the edge of the Christian *agon* as a time in which modern and postmodern ideologies have proven so monolithic . . . thankfully, though, our age also produced one of Christianity's greatest wrestlers, a man whose vision allowed him to pierce through the modern and postmodern tree to examine the roots that sustain it."[14] However, for all his attention to

---

13. Baggett, Habermas, and Walls, *C. S. Lewis as Philosopher: Truth, Goodness and Beauty*, 17.

14. Markos, *Lewis Agonistes*, x.

Lewis as a cultural critic, Markos does not engage Lewis's dependence on the philosophical climate under his critique. Far from being a theologian living in a cultureless vacuum, Lewis's career began in and flourished by his conversance with secular philosophy. Because approaches to Lewis have been one-sided, overwhelmingly theological in their approach, even heralding him as the greatest literary Christian of the twentieth century, Lewis's identities as a philosopher and writer have been obscured. While my project is theological, it is also thoroughly philosophical and literary. I will show Lewis to be a philosophical writer, whose theological agenda is inseparable from his conversance with and employment of secular philosophy.

An unpublished work that is proving most helpful to my own is the dissertation of Rebecca Radmacher, "'Nothing Said Clearly Can Be Said Truly': Modernism in C. S. Lewis's *Till We Have Faces*." Radmacher's is one of the only works that I have come across that reads Lewis's novel as a twentieth-century theological retelling of myth. The strength of Radmacher's reading of Lewis is her attempt to situate him in his twentieth-century milieu. Radmacher rightly argues for a Lewis in conversation with twentieth-century ideologies and literature. But Radmacher's work narrows Lewis's theological agenda in that she does not see time as a crucial trope in the novel, thereby losing the theological implications of the idea that man's relationship with the gods and knowledge of the divine are all temporal contingencies. *Till We Have Faces* depicts time as the darkened window through which man must look in order to see the hand of the divine on human affairs. Indeed, along with *The Great Divorce*, *Till We Have Faces* demonstrates Lewis to be a creative theologian whose literary work and Christian faith shape one another through the idea and theme of time.

In *The Company They Keep*, Diana Glyer looks at Lewis in the context of his friends in the writing circle—known as the *Inklings*—comprised primarily of C. S. Lewis, J. R. R. Tolkien, Charles Williams, and Owen Barfield. Glyer attempts to discover the implications of community in relation to creativity.[15] For example, in what ways and to what extent did Tolkien and Williams influence Lewis's fiction? Through extensive biographical and textual analysis, Glyer concludes that "Lewis, Tolkien, and the other Inklings all place significant value on continuity as an essential attribute to the creative process."[16] My interest in Glyer revolves around her work on Lewis as a part of a Christian literary community.

15. Glyer, *The Company They Keep*, xix.
16. Ibid., 222.

Introduction

While Lewis, Eliot, and Auden never shared a communal relationship like the Inklings, Glyer's study has helped me formulate my own ideas about the theological and thematic relationship between these three writers. I intend to show a theological and thematic continuity between Lewis, Eliot, and Auden's post-conversion work on time. Donald Williams, in *Mere Humanity: G. K. Chesterton, C. S. Lewis, and J. R. R. Tolkien on the Human Condition* (2006), uses the same biographical approach and comes to some of the same conclusions as Glyer. His strongest move is expanding Lewis's literary community to include G. K. Chesterton, whom Lewis greatly admired. Williams's work is useful to my own in how he connects several prominent literary figures around one common theme, in this case a concern for the human condition shared by each author. I seek to do the same kind of situating as do Glyer and Williams, though in my case it is Lewis, Eliot, and Auden's shared theological treatments of time that join them together rather than personal relationships.

I also want to mention the works of Sanford Schwartz, *C. S. Lewis on the Final Frontier: Science and the Supernatural in the Space Trilogy* (2009), and the much earlier *The Literary Achievement of C. S. Lewis* (1987) by Colin Manlove; both critics build strong arguments about Lewis's agenda through almost line by line close readings, and both have been greatly influential to my work in their diligent readings of Lewis's fiction. My greatest interest in their work lies not in what they discovered about Lewis but the process by which they discovered it: through thematically-focused close readings. These two authors provide a concentrated close reading of Lewis's work, which is their criticism's greatest strength and an area I hope to continue in my work by moving from the texts to a fully formed theology of time. Like Schwartz and Manlove, what most of the critics I mention here produce are careful and scholarly sound treatments of Lewis, Eliot, and Auden. I should note that their arguments do not produce an explanation for how and why Lewis, Eliot, and Auden chose to employ Bergsonism in their theologies of time.

On Eliot, the work of Lois Cuddy is closely akin to mine in topic. Cuddy's "Making a Space in Time: T. S. Eliot, Evolution, and *The Four Quartets*" (1994) sees time as an important poetic and philosophical device, though giving no substantial attention to the theological meaning of time in Eliot. For Cuddy, time is Eliot's way of drawing on an anti-theological tradition in order that the poem might produce a naturalistic experience between man and time. I hope to advance beyond Cuddy's work by showing time to be the province of theology in *Four Quartets*. While also bringing in Eliot's other poems about time, I will argue that *Four Quartets* is Eliot's most concentrated work on theological time.

Barry Spurr's recent work on Eliot, *"Anglo-Catholic in Religion": T. S. Eliot and Christianity* (2010) moves in the same direction as my work, and though his approach is thoroughly biographical with less attention paid to close reading and prevalent themes, it is nevertheless helpful in its focus on the intersection of theology and literature that is so important to my project. Spurr's adeptness at merging the biographical with the literary serves as a model for how I framed aspects of my thinking.

Much in the same way that Glyer and Williams treat Lewis, Lee Oser places Eliot within a literary community of Christian writers in a non-Christian world. In *The Return of Christian Humanism: Chesterton, Eliot, Tolkien, and the Romance of History* (2007), Oser makes the claims: "At the heart of twentieth-century letters was the clash between a dogmatically relativist type of modernism and Christian humanism."[17] Oser goes on to deal with each author individually before positioning them together as Christian humanists against such anti-humanist writers as Samuel Beckett. Oser's work serves as a model for my own in structure, but his approach is more informed by philosophical categories than by text-based analyses. Indeed, his work is so abstract at times that one loses sight of the texts that produce Eliot's theological and literary tension.

Concerning Auden, Arthur Kirsch's *Auden and Christianity* (2005) traces the poet's complicated lifelong struggle with the Christian faith, a faith that Kirsch says, "can thus hardly be exaggerated, but as a subject of study, . . . nonetheless poses difficulties."[18] It is in its treatment of these difficulties that Kirsch's work is most useful to me. Kirsch accurately shows Auden to be a man professing the Christian faith but maintaining unconventional views about his expression of faith, for example, in not making explicit statements about theology in his prose or critical works. Kirsch's work does show the importance of theology for Auden's post-conversion work as well as how Auden implemented theology through theme, diction, and trope. I hope to capture Kirsch's ability to deal with the grey areas between the Christian faith and beliefs contradicting it when I deal with Lewis, Eliot, and Auden's concept of time, which while theologically informed cannot always be said to be entirely orthodox.

Mendelson's important *Later Auden* (1999) does a superb job of detailing the second half of Auden's life. Through a chronological approach,

---

17. Oser, *The Return of Christian Humanism*, ix.
18. Kirsch, *Auden and Christianity*, xiv.

Introduction

Mendelson captures Auden's biography as well as the development of his worldview, setting forth an exhaustive portrait of the poet's life and work. Mendelson also provides remarkable readings of Auden's work, often capturing the essence of a poem before unpacking its literary elements. For example, Mendelson identifies "New Year Letter" as "Auden's *Faust*," before spending some twenty pages interpreting it. Mendelson's contribution to my work will be extensive.[19] From the biographical to the literary, Mendelson's is a thorough way to know Auden the man and writer, though individual categories like time are lost in his report of the constellation of Auden's themes.

Gareth Reeves's "Auden and Religion" (2004) includes a partial conclusion about Auden and time, one nascent in vision and limited in scope. In Auden, Reeves rightly says, "Poetry is time-ridden, it belongs to History and our fallen condition, but it can make us, within its enclosed arenas, its parables, conscious of the timeless."[20] It is this idea of enclosure that I want to overturn in my work on time, for the language of time in Auden (as well as Eliot and Lewis) does not merely serve to raise consciousness of the eternal in the reader's mind. The language of time is meant to open new literary understandings of Christian theology as well as to theologize secular philosophy, namely Bergsonism. Where Reeves sees Auden's language as working to evoke, I see it as working to create.

And while some scholars have placed Lewis in conversation with Eliot, and others have placed Eliot in conversation with Auden, and yet still others have placed Lewis in conversation with Auden, no one has thoroughly examined the literary commonalities among all three. This relationship occupied the same period in time, occurred between three authors who converted to the same faith in just over a decade, and saw each author take up the same literary themes. Because of this relationship, it can be argued that Lewis, Eliot, and Auden comprise a literary group of converts that has been under-investigated by scholars of twentieth-century literature.

As writers bound together by the thematic commonality of theo-poeticized time, Lewis, Eliot, and Auden complicate the lines of demarcation between the secular philosophy of Bergson that existed outside the scope of their personal faiths and the Christianity to which they converted.[21] Perhaps most appealing about the idea of time as taken up by Lewis,

---

19. Mendelson, *Later Auden*, 101.
20. Reeves, "Auden and Religion," 193.
21. Though the conversions of Lewis, Eliot, and Auden gave each author a newly

Eliot, and Auden is how for every disconnection between Bergsonism and Christianity, there seems to be another inseparable connection. Each author came to slightly different conclusions and certainly took different textual paths to reach them, but each saw himself as poeticizing Christian theology to a secular philosophy to which he remained ideologically connected. Thus, I intend to identify and further complicate those connections between Lewis, Eliot, and Auden's Christian faith and the Bergsonism from which they drew to construct theology, in hopes that a richer understanding of their theologies of time will emerge.

Obviously, the work of Henri Bergson is foundational to my argument, Bergson being a philosopher whose ideas about time permeate the post-conversion works of Lewis, Eliot, and Auden. Though Lewis, Eliot, and Auden wrote definitively theological works, their Christian writings did not necessarily need to employ Bergson's secular philosophy. It could have been that each author would have chosen to write theological works on time that possessed no distinctly philosophically secular trait. Indeed, it is surprising that each author did not choose to theologize time from a purely biblical vantage point, e.g., that they did not espouse a Pauline, or Mosaic, or Deuteronomistic notion of time. Yet all three authors were certainly capable of such religious writing.

For example, many of Lewis's apologetic works—*The Problem of Pain* (1940), *The Abolition of Man* (1943), and *Miracles* (1947)—are explicitly directed against certain twentieth-century philosophies and show little sympathy for other philosophical views. Eliot's published lectures at the University of Virginia, *After Strange Gods* (1933, published 1934), or his *Christianity and Culture* (1939) read like anti-modernist religious pamphlets. Auden's later poetry became more and more conservative and reactionary against his earlier radically modernist verse. His last decade of work is remarkably void of all his earlier modernist trademarks of anxiety and social consciousness, and his late writings—poems like "Insignificant

---

directed poetic intensity, I will not look at the actual details of the authors' conversions. In fact, the biographical minutiae involved in these authors' conversions will not factor into my analysis of their Christian poetics. What I am most interested in is the theology—or theologies that—their conversions produced. It is on their theological constructs of time in relation to Bergson's ideas, rather than the particulars of their conversions, that this study will focus. For more on conversion to Christianity, see the chapter "Conversion" in Williams James's definitive work, *The Varieties of Religious Experience*, 171–201. For more on Lewis's conversion, see David Downing's *The Most Reluctant Convert* (2004); on Eliot's, see Lyndall Gordon's *Eliot's New Life* (1989); on Auden's, see Mendelson's *Later Auden* (2000).

Elephants" (1966) and his theoretical *On Secondary Worlds*—mark a distinctly religious turn from his works of high modernism.

What makes Lewis's *The Great Divorce*, Eliot's *Four Quartets*, and Auden's "Kairos and Logos" remarkable conflations of Christian theology and secular philosophy is their use of the ideas of Henri Bergson. Bergson's work is in part a response to the Darwinian science so prevalent in the late nineteenth and early twentieth centuries, in part a reaction to the de-humanizing implications of mechanistic positivism, and in part a post-Einsteinian, metaphysically vitalist approach to human consciousness in time. It stands at the crossroads of some of the most formative ideas of the early twentieth century. And what makes Lewis, Eliot, and Auden's articulations about time remarkable intersections of theology and twentieth-century literature is their adoption of Bergson's non-theological duration.

In order to investigate each author's treatment of time and to unearth the blend of Christian and Bergsonian ideologies implemented by all three, I will focus on those works by each writer that best demonstrate the precarious intersection between their Christian faiths and Bergsonism and also speak to their Christian theologies of time. Specifically, I will look at Lewis's *The Great Divorce*, at Eliot's *Four Quartets*, and at Auden's "Kairos and Logos." Of course, I will also consider the pertinent Christian critical writings and other selected literary works of each author. In chapter 3, I will look at Lewis's *The Great Divorce* in light of Bergson's notions of the force of time as well as Bergson's emphasis on the durative present. To frame Lewis's theological approach, I will compare his way of structuring thought in terms of dualism and dynamism with Bergson's own affinity dualistic and dynamistic themes. In chapter 4, I will closely read Eliot's *Four Quartets* through the Bergonsian lenses of durative force, the splintered self, and the consciousness's experience of time. And in chapter 5, I will reiterate Bergson's sense of dualistic time and experience as I close read Auden's "Kairos and Logos." In each chapter I will emphasize the nuances of each author's theological treatments of time as well as show how their theological articulations cohere with Bergson's ideas. Ultimately, I will produce a synthetic reading of Bergsonian philosophy and the theological articulations of Lewis, Eliot, and Auden, and with that reading, a new framework for understanding how these important authors constructed their theologies.

1

The Task of Theologizing Literature in the Twentieth Century

Christian theology is the schema by which Lewis, Eliot, and Auden conceived and implemented their writings. Their Christian faith subsumed their treatments of those themes most pressing to the twentieth-century mind: epistemology, the human condition, the self's relationship to the *other*, man's experience with the divine, and time, all of which were employed in these authors' writings. Not only did Lewis, Eliot, and Auden look at literary themes through a theological lens, but they also engaged in the act of constructing theology, as will be shown in their works on time. However, though their Christian faith influenced their individual productions of art, Lewis, Eliot, and Auden never collectively formulated a Christian view of art, nor did they conceive of any uniform theological hermeneutic or way of viewing the theological in literature.

Other than their occasional correspondence with one another, Lewis, Eliot, and Auden had no contact that would produce a common theological approach to writing as a whole or a particular literary theme. Because the three authors thus never intended to create among themselves a theory of theological literature, I will look elsewhere for such a theory to describe the nature of theologized literature in the twentieth century. So in this chapter I will look at the work of philosopher Charles Taylor and theological writer Dorothy Sayers, who have both produced seminal works about theologized literature.

A note on my use of the word "theology" is in order. "Theology," the study of God, has referred to a variety of fields in the Christian tradition.

Dogmatic theology, also called systematic theology, refers to a taxonomic study of theological concepts, such as God, eternity, salvation, and the like. The categories and conclusions of dogmatic theology have traditionally been based on either the Bible or the creeds of the ancient Christian church. Examples of dogmatic theology are Louis Berkof's *Systematic Theology* (1932, revised in 1938), and Paul Tillich's *Systematic Theology* (1951–63), from which I will occasionally cite. Besides dogmatic theology, there is also biblical theology, which looks to the pronouncements of scriptures as the primary sources for theological truth. Often works of biblical theology focus solely on the theology of the Old or New Testaments, and examples are Walter Brueggemann's *Old Testament Theology* (2001) and I. Howard Marshall's *New Testament Theology* (2004). In addition to dogmatic and biblical theology, there is also the field of confessional theology, also known as creedal theology. Confessional theology formulates its doctrinal beliefs in accordance with the church's creeds, as articulated and accepted throughout Christian history. Examples of confessional theological works are *The Drama of Doctrine: A Canonical Linguistic Approach to Christian Doctrine* by Kevin Vonhoozer (2005) and Paul Hinlicky's *Divine Complexity: The Rise of Creedal Christianity* (2010).

It should be briefly mentioned that since the time of Lewis, Eliot, and Auden's theological works from the 1930s and 40s, the term "theology" has been extended to include various theologies in the traditions of Friedrich Schleiermacher and Otto Ritschl. Both theologians constructed their theologies on human experience and scientific inquiry rather than any notion of authoritative revelation from Scripture or the creeds of the church. Before engaging pertinent twentieth-century theological thinkers, I will explore the task that Lewis, Eliot, and Auden assumed: encoding both theology and philosophy into their literary works for their twentieth-century audiences.

Composing theologized literature in the first few decades of the twentieth century was a unique task, as social upheaval, political tumult, and major ideological shifts in philosophy and religion shook the world of Lewis, Eliot, and Auden. The Christian thinker writing in the early- to mid-twentieth-century faced the challenging task of effectively conveying theology, a task that Alfred North Whitehead described as "the endeavor to frame a coherent, logical, necessary system of general ideas in terms of which every element of our experience can be interpreted."[1] As will be

---

1. Whitehead, *Adventures of Ideas* 223. See also the discussion in Whitehead's *Process and Reality*, 4–26.

evidenced below, the ability to frame theological truth in such a way that accounts for human experience with the divine was of crucial importance to twentieth-century theological thinkers. Lewis, Eliot and Auden are no exception.

Lewis, Eliot, and Auden each saw the creation of a theology of time as a way to account for man's experience with God. And like many theological thinkers in the first half of the twentieth century, Lewis and company turned to new theological articulations. One such method of articulating the theological was conjoining it with the philosophical. Theological thinkers contemporary to Lewis, Eliot, and Auden were intensely interested in discovering how theology could effectively cooperate with secular philosophy. Scholar of twentieth-century theology George Thomas captures the theological zeitgeist of Lewis, Eliot, and Auden's day, when he asks:

> Can a philosophical reason which has not been fully "converted" by the Christian faith correctly formulate the "structure" and "categories" of Being and raise the deepest "questions" implied in existence? If not, will not the Christian "answers," whose form is determined by the nature of the "questions," be distorted or obscured?[2]

Here Thomas captures a major concern for theological writers in the twentieth century. Thomas implies that a philosophical reason cannot "correctly formulate" a precept or sufficiently address the deepest questions about Being and existence without it first being "converted" by the Christian faith.[3] And if a Christian answer can be given to a philosophical question, then it must reflect that philosophical question by assuming its nature, because articulations of theology are connected to the philosophical questions that prompt them. An example from Christian history of this mutual relationship between theological articulation and philosophical categories would be Thomas Aquinas's *Summa Theologica* (1265–74), which systematically treats theological topics through logic and philosophical allusions ranging from the Aristotelian to Augustinian.

This marriage of theology and secular philosophy defined theological articulation in the early- to mid-twentieth century; Lewis, Eliot, and Auden assumed this task of theologizing with the aid of Bergson's philosophy. As more and more theological writers like Paul Tillich, Karl Barth, and

---

2. Thomas, *Theology of Tillich*, 104.
3. Ibid., 104.

novelist Charles Williams came to see old articulations as inadequate, the growing conviction was that for theology to be effectively communicated it must address twentieth-century concerns.[4] The need for new theological expression was due to radical ideological shifts away from Christianity. Indeed, with the twentieth century came widespread dissolution of religious beliefs, new anxieties about human experience, and a movement away from the theological toward the theme of the "self." These ideological shifts are evidenced by the literature of the early- to mid-twentieth century. A newfound concern with the social world and man's relation to it was a pillar of twentieth-century literature. Several works of modernism explored the theme of discovery of the social world and the haunting realities that characters in their texts must face upon this discovery. Texts like D. H. Lawrence's *Women in Love* (1920), Ernest Hemingway's *A Farewell to Arms* (1929), and E. M. Forster's *A Passage to India* (1924) unveil the disturbing nature of the social and relational that lies behind the façade of conventional society. Emphasis on the socially privileged outer life, man's existential being, and experience became central motifs in twentieth-century literature. As will be seen, Lewis, Eliot, and Auden explore this disturbance between man and his world in heightened fashion by shifting experience to the world of time; experience is no less important in their works, but experience in society is replaced with the more theologically important theme of experience in time—a theologically motivated replacement of no little literary and philosophical importance.

Furthermore, understandings about reality—particularly through Western perceptions—underwent skeptical interpretations that divorced the material world from the world beyond. Because of the predominance of scientific rationality, a type of thinking which Bergson will vehemently address, *meaning* beyond the sensory world yet immanently connected with it had become imperceptible, unknowable, and unattainable to many modernist writers. As a scholar of European Modernism, Richard Sheppard, has argued, though there was a universal sense that trees were not just trees, water not mere water, and houses more than wood and nail, many twentieth writers understood these "meta-worlds" as evidence for a great epistemological breach—even an ontological one.[5] The metaphysical

---

4. I will cite specific titles from Paul Tillich and Charles Williams, but I will not devote significant attention to the works of Barth, though it is worth noting that some of Barth's most influential works include *The Epistle to the Romans* (1919), the political *Barmen Declaration* (1934), and the immense multi-volume works that comprise *Church Dogmatics* (1932–67).

5. Sheppard, *Theorizing Modernism*, 17–18.

The Task of Theologizing Literature in the Twentieth Century

world behind the material world breaks through in violent, uncontrollable, and disturbing fashion; twentieth-century writers, in response to this forceful breach, experimented with literary techniques in attempts to reflect their new epistemology. Eliot's *The Waste Land* with its infusion of spiritualism into the poem's socially bleak scene, Lawrence's "The Rocking Horse Winner" with its haunting eruptions of the metaphysical into the domestic, and Rilke's *Duino Elegies* with its theological characterization of the natural world all demonstrate this breach by the metaphysical.

Sheppard helpfully formulates one particular dimension of the twentieth-century crisis of man living in a material reality. He highlights the breach between man's nineteenth-century understanding of reality and the radical shift that occurred with the catastrophes of the early twentieth century:

> the modernist understanding of the relationship between Man and reality is radically different from that of mainstream nineteenth-century thinkers and writers. By and large, nineteenth-century thinkers and writers posited, or at least sought to posit, a consonance, correspondence or substantial unity between the logical structure of the material world, the structure of the human *logos*, and, if they were believers, between those two dimensions and the divine *Logos* ....[6]

With the twentieth century came a divorce between the material world, human reason ("logos"), and any notion of the divine Logos. Because it is such an important tenet in Christian theology and because it is a central concept in the theologized literature of authors like Eliot and Auden, "logos" should be defined. Though the Greek term's broadest definition is "human reason" or "wisdom," the term took on Christological significance with the composition of John's Gospel in the late first century AD. John 1:1 states "In the beginning was the Word [*logos*], and the Word was with God, and the Word was God." Here the gospel writer identifies the logos as the eternal Christ himself. From its Christian inception, the divine Logos was associated with the concept of the Incarnation. The association of the logos with the Incarnation also originates in John's Gospel, where in John 1:14 the writer says, "and the Word [*logos*] became flesh and dwelt among us." Part of the new task of theological writers in the twentieth-century is to reestablish an ideological connection between the disconnected categories of human reason (logos), the material world, and the divine Logos. The material world in which human experience is lived

---

6. Sheppard, *Theorizing Modernism*, 26.

would be the subject of Bergson's philosophy as well as of that of Christian writers like Lewis, Eliot, and Auden. Bergson's *Time and Free Will* and his *Matter and Memory* are both philosophical investigations of human experience in a material world. In *Time and Free Will*, Bergson is particularly interested in how time is wrongly perceived due to scientific rationality's spatial view of time, which was prominent in the late-nineteenth and the early-twentieth-century, and which, Bergson attests, disconnects time from the deepest spiritual parts of human experience.

Lewis, Eliot, and Auden are also interested in reestablishing a connection between the material world and the divine Logos, i.e., the eternal. Lewis's *The Great Divorce*, which I will closely read in the third chapter, explores the nature of material reality and spiritual reality, intimating that the reality of the former is inferior to the reality of the later. In Eliot's *Four Quartets*, time itself is interpreted as the means by which human experience and the divine Logos meet. Auden paints a similar picture in "Kairos and Logos," when he depicts two kinds of people, those solely interested in the material world and those who look to the world beyond, the world of the divine logos. The material, social, temporal world and the nature of its reality was an ideologically contested area for twentieth-century thinkers. And because of divergent philosophies about material reality, Lewis and Christian modernists Eliot and Auden had to specify exactly how man existed in his material world and what that existence meant, existence which they constructed in the realm of time.

Modernist writers contemporary with Lewis, Eliot, and Auden shared an interest in depicting what it means to exist in the temporal world. Indeed, the world and its traditional boundaries of real/unreal, material/immaterial, physical/metaphysical were erased with modernist doubts about perception and reality. For example, modernist scholar Jean-Michel Rabate says: "the idea of material bodies is superfluous, since bodies, like distances, are only ideas in the mind and can never be logically or experimentally proved to exist in themselves . . . perception has been freed from the constraints imposed upon it by commonsense realism."[7] Twentieth-century notions of the material fostered an ideological splintering, leaving a world beyond and outside of the material, a cosmos of fragmentation that produced philosophical and literary reconceptions of the metaphysical world. Lewis, Eliot, and Auden wrote their post-conversion works on time in the wake of this radical shift in ideology.

---

7. Rabate, *1913*, 19. Rabate is discussing James Joyce's use of immaterialist philosophy, e.g., the philosophy of George Berkeley.

Lewis, Eliot, and Auden's theologies of time were also articulated when perceptions of Christianity were changing: the late nineteenth and early twentieth centuries saw a radical shift in perceptions of the Christian faith that resulted in new waves of skepticism and unbelief. In his *A Secular Age*, philosopher Charles Taylor explores the shift from widespread social acceptance of Christianity to a culture increasingly removed from Christian ideals. Taylor evaluates the change the twentieth century brought in understandings of the human condition, belief systems as lived out in society, and collective religious identities. One particular idea on which Taylor premises his work—and one which helps shed some light on Lewis, Eliot, and Auden's theologies of time—is the notion of "fullness," a desirable "moral/spiritual shape" that brings a sense of peace, contentment, joy, fulfillment to an individual's life.[8] For the Christian, fullness is something received from God, the ultimate being beyond the world of the "self":

> For believers, often or typically, the sense is that fullness comes to them, that it is something they receive; moreover, receive in something like a personal relationship, from another being capable of love and giving; approaching fullness involves among other things, practices of devotion and prayer . . . and [Christians] are aware of being very far from the condition of full devotion and giving; they are aware of being self-enclosed, bound to lesser things and goals, not able to open themselves and receive/give as they would at the place of fullness. So there is the notion of receiving power or fullness in a relation; but the receiver isn't simply empowered in his/her present condition; he/she needs to be opened, transformed, brought out of self.[9]

Taylor's descriptors of *opening up, transforming, receiving an outer power as the self is emptied* are foundational notions for Lewis, Eliot, and Auden's theologies of time; each author's post-conversion works exemplify Taylor's descriptors. For example, Lewis's *The Great Divorce* "opens up" (i.e., transcends) the material world when its characters venture into a theologically charged realm in which time receives divine agency and so fosters redemption. Eliot's *Four Quartets* explores the transformative power of time in an individual's consciousness. And Auden's "Kairos and Logos" juxtaposes the temporal with its self-centricity against the spiritual liberation of the Incarnation's eternal moment. The pre-Christian

8. Taylor, *A Secular Age*, 6–8.
9. Ibid., 8.

literature of Lewis, Eliot, and Auden—works like Lewis's *Spirits in Bondage* (1919), Eliot's *The Waste Land* (1922), and Auden's *Spain* (1937)—can be described as cultural laments that turn back on the lamenter. Each author in his pre-Christian state creates a work in which the self is isolated in a state of spiritual depravity and in a degenerating cultural context. For all its fragmentation and disparate dependence on allusive abstraction, which is arguably a constant reaching out for meaning, many twentieth-century texts are intensely concentrated on the self as central.

One scholar of twentieth-century ideology, James McFarlane, has said about a defining characteristic of modernism, "the Modernist mode is not so much that things fall *apart* but that they fall *together*. . . . In Modernism the centre is seen exerting not a centrifugal but a centripetal force; and the consequence is not disintegration but superintegration."[10] McFarlane is here discussing the common theme in modernism of accumulation of philosophical and mythological fragments. Referring to the third line of Yeats's "The Second Coming" (1920), McFarlane argues that twentieth-century ideology is often marked by absorption, a "falling *together*," of philosophical ideas. Indeed, the twentieth century saw a heightened appropriation, meshing, and reframing of various philosophical systems, which ironically created what McFarlane describes as a "centripetal force," a philosophical entropy.[11] As my example from Taylor's *A Secular Age* insists, this centripetal force often had the self as center. My definition of the self is informed by the work of Charles Taylor, Michael Levenson, and Tzvetan Todorov, all of whom depict the self as isolated from the numinous or theological other.[12] By self, then, I mean that which is defined by a certain set of constitutive issues and questions that preclude a relationship with the divine. Among those issues is an inwardness, a reflexive "I," or a turning of the self back on itself. The self's inward turn translates into a paradigm shift detectable in early- to mid-twentieth-century literature in which ultimate authority is transferred from an "othered" source (i.e., God, the gods, fate, or a divine universal soul) to the self.[13] In his work on Nietzsche, critic Remy de Gourmont captures this self-centered twentieth-century paradigm:

10. McFarlane, "The Mind of Modernism," 92.

11. Ibid.

12. See Taylor's *Sources of the Self*, 49–50, 111–14; Levenson's *A Genealogy of Modernism*, 60–70; Todorov's chapter "Themes of the Self" in *The Fantastic*, 107–23.

13. For more on the move away from Christian ideas to a self-oriented worldview in twentieth-century literature, see Lucas's *The Religious Dimensions of Twentieth-Century British and American Literature*, 65–216.

> We have learnt from Nietzsche to pull down the old metaphysical structures built upon a basis of abstraction. All the ancient corner-stones are crumbled to dust, and the whole house has become a ruin.... No more morality, then, save, aesthetic or social morality: no absolute system of morals but as many separate systems as there are individual intellects. What is truth? Nothing but what appears true to us, what suits our logic. As Stirner said, there is my truth—and yours, my brother.[14]

The movement away from metaphysically derived authority to the authority of the self is expressed here. Morality and Truth are subjected to the authority of the self, as the individual becomes the arbiter of what is moral or true. As de Gourmont here notes, the Nietzschean philosophy that dominated the early decades of the twentieth century developed throughout the nineteenth century, since the time of Max Stirner, one of the first philosophers to advocate the self-oriented philosophy that would permeate the twentieth-century context in which Lewis, Eliot, and Auden wrote. Decades before the turn of the twentieth century, in his *The Ego and Its Own* (1844), Stirner asserts that the only reality was egocentrism. Rejecting all previous philosophies, all theological systems, and all sociopolitical forces, Stirner proclaims,

> I am unique. Hence my wants too are unique, and my deeds; in short, everything about me is unique. And it is only as this unique I that I take everything for my own, as I set myself to work, and develop myself, only as this. I do not develop, nor as man, but, as I, I develop—myself.[15]

Stirner's philosophy is utterly self-reflexive, thoroughly characterized by an enduring inwardness that would extend into twentieth-century thought and literature. In his *Struggle of the Modern*, Stephen Spender underscores the reflexive passivity of the modern "I": "The Voltairean 'I' of Shaw, Wells, and the others, acts upon events. The 'modern' 'I' of Rimbaud, Joyce, Proust, Eliot's Prufrock is acted upon by them."[16] Similarly to McFarlane's analogy of centripetal force, Spender's comment touches upon one of the most important aspects of literary modernism: the modernist self being the sun around which all other literary elements orbit. Indeed, part of Lewis, Eliot, and Auden's theologizing of time involves an attempt to transcend the world of the self. By depicting time as the

---

14. Gourmont, *Selected Writings*, 301.
15. Stirner, *The Ego and Its Own*, 482–83.
16. Spender, *Struggle of the Modern*, 71–72.

medium through which the self can know the divine "other," Lewis, Eliot, and Auden seek to go beyond the inwardness of egoistic ideology. Thus, time, in Lewis, Eliot, and Auden's post-conversion works becomes a way man can transcend the self and know the divine.

This centripetal force and its resulting superintergration create that pervasive role for the centralized self in modernist literature; like the anticipated "other" that never arrives in Beckett's *Waiting for Godot*, the modernist search for meaning beyond the self falls back onto the searcher. As Eliot's poem *The Waste Land* shows, it is the self turned inward, so often emphasized in modernism, that suffers dismally as it deteriorates. Eliot bemoans the modernist citizen's futility in *The Waste Land*'s "The Burial of the Dead":

> Unreal City,
> Under the brown fog of a winter dawn,
> A crowd flowed over London Bridge, so many,
> I had not thought death had undone so many.
> Sighs, short and infrequent, were exhaled,
> And each man fixed his eyes before his feet.[17]

Pre-Christian C. S. Lewis also demonstrates what Taylor calls the "modern identity," a constant centralizing of the self in modern philosophy, art, and literature.[18] In *Spirits in Bondage*, published in 1919 under the pseudonym Clive Hamilton, Lewis's poetic persona rails against Christianity's God and scorns His creation as meaningless. For pre-conversion Lewis, the non-existence of a Creator was proven by his reasoning that the created order was as bleak, violent, and humanely void as post World War I Europe. In the poem "De Profundis," Lewis forcibly poeticizes his atheism:

> Come let us curse our Master ere we die,
> For all our hopes in endless ruin lie.
> The good is dead. Let us curse God most High.
> ....
> Come then and curse the Lord. Over the earth
> Gross darkness falls, and evil was our birth
> And our few happy days of little worth.
> ....
> Thou art not Lord while there are Men on earth.[19]

---

17. Eliot, *The Waste Land*, lines 60–65.

18. Taylor, *Sources of the Self*, 3. For Taylor's full treatment on the modern identity, see *Sources of the Self*, 495–522.

19. Lewis, "De Profundis," lines 1–3, 13–15, 36.

The Task of Theologizing Literature in the Twentieth Century

Another poem in Lewis's *Spirits in Bondage*, "Apology," promotes the very opposite of what Taylor describes as the Christian believer's awareness "of being very far from the condition of full devotion and giving; they are aware of being self-enclosed, bound to lesser things and goals, not able to open themselves and receive/give as they would at the place of fullness." Lewis's speaker declares the dismal awakening of the modern condition:

> The loveliness and wisdom feigned of old.
> But now we wake. The East is pale and cold,
> No hope is in the dawn, and no delight.[20]

There is no reception of spiritual fullness from an outside source in Lewis's verse, only the speaker's self-enclosed voice, whose laments find no comfort. Where the dreamer would feign hope and belief in mythic heroes of days past, the poet reminds the reader that there the modern world, "real hell" (line 4) makes no room for empty hopes. Indeed, pre-Christian Lewis uses myth as a vehicle for disillusionment, unaccompanied by the "fullness" of relation to the divine.

Like Lewis's poetic self, disconnectedly exiled from the divine, Auden's pre-conversion verse also captures the cry of the isolated self. In Auden's "Spain," the speaker discounts relational meaning in traditional outlets and is left an isolated, helpless voice of the age,

> The stars are dead; the animals will not look:
> We are left alone with our day, and
> The time is short and History to the defeated
> May say Alas but cannot help or pardon.[21]

Taylor discusses this trend in modernist literature as a nuanced turn into the self, in which the self is positioned as the writer's chief subject. As in the case of Auden's "Spain," the inward turn is not only a shift to the individual self but a move beyond the self to an experience of fragmentation, "which call our ordinary notions of identity into question."[22] The speaker in "Spain" confesses detachment from naturally inspired meaning while also bemoaning history's refusal of a reprieve from the crises of the modern day.

Contrary to the sense of emptied meaning evidenced in their pre-conversion works, the Christian writings of Lewis, Eliot, and Auden insist that personal, social, and theological meaning have a certain source: the

20. Lewis, "Apology," lines 12–14.
21. Auden, "Spain," lines 104–8.
22. Taylor, *Sources of the Self*, 462.

Judeo-Christian God. Likewise, one could say that each author understands his works to perform one underlying function: to create a textual world in which the self is emptied of itself and in which inwardness is abdicated, while the self is simultaneously and paradoxically filled with the divine presence. These converted authors take up the same themes in their earlier works, and their post-conversion treatment of those themes is at times more concentrated. For instance, Eliot's *Four Quartets* rivals *The Waste Land* in length and is concerned primarily with the theological meaning of time.

In theologizing the theme of time, Lewis, Eliot, and Auden did not abdicate the themes, forms, or even the anxieties that drove their earlier efforts; rather, in their theologies of time, each author "made new" existing twentieth-century anxieties about time and human experience through Christian theology. In their theologies of time, Lewis, Eliot, and Auden sought to reframe questions of human experience in a temporal world and in so doing promote a new theological understanding of God, human experience, and time. The promotion of such a new theology is discussed in Cleanth Brooks's *The Hidden God*: "For the very point about the modern world is that the old landmarks are gone—that we cannot afford to trust stereotypes—that one and the same object changes meaning in being moved from one spiritual context to another."[23] Likewise, Lewis, Eliot, and Auden attempted to change the spiritual landscape of their twentieth-century world by imposing on it their Christian theology, and a superb example of the imposition of theological reimagining on a twentieth-century theme is how these three authors treated time.

How Lewis, Eliot, and Auden conceived and executed the theme of time created a crucial intersection between twentieth-century ideology and Christianity. To negotiate that intersection for these writers of Christian commitment meant not only that their faith had to address the motif of time but also subsume it by infusing it with theological meaning. This theologizing of time amounts to a thematic redemption, an addressing of the theme through a Christian paradigm, of what all three authors knew to be a major concern for twentieth-century thinkers. That is, Lewis, Eliot, and Auden all saw time as a fundamental concern of the twentieth century, and all three treated the theme of time with the assumption that its nature is theological and conducive for divine revelation to man.

This task of theologizing time would mean addressing the problem of fragmentation between the temporal and the eternal. Because two times

---

23. Brooks, *The Hidden God*, 81.

exist, the temporal and the eternal, man's experience of time is fragmented. As will be shown in the next chapter, Bergson's theory of duration is partly built on this concept of fragmentation. Bergson imagines two selves, the superficial self and the fundamental self, each of which experience time differently. The superficial self is that which only recognizes the temporal, thus unable to tap the power of time to transform the consciousness, whereas the fundamental self experiences time as duration and so accesses time's transformative powers.[24] Lewis, Eliot, and Auden will also recognize these different kinds of times and selves. Indeed, each author infused a theological understanding of time with the idea that its bifurcated and subjective nature were due to the split of eternality and temporality. For all three authors, twentieth-century understandings of time like Bergson's continual duration provided a theoretical framework within which Christianity could be articulated in twentieth-century terms. Rather than abolishing modern ideas of time, Lewis, Eliot, and Auden constructed a coherent Christian philosophy that engaged and transformed those ideas in creative, theologized works about the relation of temporal man to an eternal God.

What Lewis, Eliot, and Auden embarked on in their theologies of time were Christian and philosophical articulations fitting for the twentieth century. Each author's theological articulations were mutually founded on the tenets of the Christian faith and on Bergson's secular philosophy. Another way to describe their theological work is to say that the literary theme of time is constructed according to their Christian faiths. What makes the theologies of Lewis, Eliot, and Auden fitting for their twentieth-century audiences is that their treatments of time retain some pre-conversion characteristics, such as the sense of fragmented time depicted by modernist authors like Joyce, Woolf, and Conrad; what makes the theme of time Christian is its ultimate subjugation to the authors' Christian beliefs. In this sense, it is fitting to speak of the conversions of not just the writers but also of their writings, for example, Eliot's "Journey of the Magi," which is in one sense a biographical poem about Eliot's conversion but also a poem about how the theme of conversion itself develops structurally and thematically.

"Journey of the Magi" (1930) is a quintessential example of "converted," yet distinctly twentieth-century literature with its understated theology—there is not one mention of God or Christ—its abstract allusion, its subjective reimagining of myth, and its unsettled moral resolution.

---

24. Bergson, *Time and Free Will*, 97.

Conversion itself is absorbed into the poem's abstraction, leaving both speaker and reader uncertain of the phenomenon:

> were we lead all that way for
> Birth or Death? There was a Birth, certainly,
> We had evidence and no doubt. I have seen birth and death,
> But had thought they were different; this Birth was
> Hard and bitter agony for us, like Death, our death.[25]

The poem's speaker makes no mention of Christ or redemption, but rather depicts conversion as an ambiguous experience associated with both birth and death. Conversion to the Christian faith is veiled by anxiety and uncertainty.

Christianity gave Lewis, Eliot, and Auden a new poetic intensity, as each author devoted a large part of their post-conversion careers to theologized literature. Each author attempted to redact and repackage Christian doctrine through poetic language in an attempt to solve the twentieth-century anxieties, particularly the potential erosion of spiritual meaning through fragmentation and subjectivity. In order for the Christian faith as a "solution" to be fully manifest and conveyed, certain traits of twentieth-century ideologies had to be retained. Indeed, the best way to show how any problem can be solved is to show both the problem and its solution. In this case, the author acknowledge the fragmentation of time and then identify a Christian notion that time is split between eternal and temporal to suggest how the fragmentation can be solved. In their post-conversion creative and critical works, all three authors advanced a literary theory intrinsic to their Christian faith. Moreover, each author, in doing literary criticism, saw himself as doing culturally aware theology. Each operated, through his writings, as a cultural "prophet," diagnosing the problems in his social milieu and prescribing theological answers to those problems through his work.

For example, in his essay "Notes Towards the Definition of Culture," Eliot spoke of the cultural degradation that transpires generationally, concluding that, "It is no longer possible to find consolation in prophetic gloom."[26] Eliot insists that although the ancient edifices of learning were being demolished to make room for the "barbarian nomads of the future," simply indicting culture for its degradation was fruitless criticism. Thus, Eliot dismisses prophetic gloom, but maintains the prophetic function of diagnosing the spiritual state of the modern age. Eliot assumes the role of

25. Eliot, "Journey of the Magi," lines 35–39.
26. Eliot, *Christianity and Culture*, 185.

cultural prophet, as he diagnoses the spiritual deterioration of the modern age, "yet the culture of Europe as deteriorated visibly within the memory of many who are by no means the oldest among us."[27] Eliot's interest in assessing the spiritual state of modern culture can be attributed to his concern for delineating a Christian society from the twentieth-century society in which he lived.[28] One sees that Eliot's roles as poet and critic were integral to his cultural sensitivity in that he often applied his creative and critical prowess to the task of cultural critique.

In *Christianity and Culture*, Eliot is particularly concerned with task of critiquing theological thinkers' questionable attempts to alter the fundamental categories of modern ideology. Eliot accuses twentieth-century theological thinkers of merely advocating a "just State" as opposed to a Christian society. Eliot complains that "The political philosopher of the present time, even when he is a Christian himself, is not usually concerned with the possible structure of a Christian state. He is occupied with the possibility of a just State in general . . . ."[29] Against the ineffectual type of social modification attempted by modern theologians, Eliot advocates a definitive "change in [our] social attitude, such a change only as could bring about anything worthy to be called a Christian society."[30] Had I more time I would detail what a Christian society is according to Eliot. What is relevant to my study is Eliot's belief that the task of the Christian thinker is to influence society according to the Christian faith; Lewis and Auden's theologies of time also both demonstrate this belief, as each author also seeks to address twentieth-century culture from theological perspectives. Each author's treatment of time is a theological effort to address twentieth-century questions, like what it means to exist in a temporal world and what an eternal God has to do with temporal man. As will be shown in subsequent chapters, to accomplish this task each author turned to Bergsonian ideas that were common currency in the first half of the twentieth century. And from Bergson's relevant philosophy, Lewis, Eliot, and Auden theologized the theme of time into their literature.

Lewis, Eliot, and Auden were all invested in a theologized literature that would effectively address twentieth-century ideas. In Eliot's case, for example, while his concerns for culture were firmly fixed in his Christian faith, they were perhaps best articulated through what he deemed to be

27. Eliot, *Christianity and Culture*, 185.
28. Ibid., 6.
29. Ibid., 7.
30. Ibid., 8.

an untouched kind of modernist poetry, one most concerned with God's relationship to man. In a letter to William Force Stead, Eliot's priest and personal friend, Eliot confesses that he is in search of a Christian poetics: "a theory I have nourished for a long time [is] that between the usual subjects of poetry and 'devotional' verse there is a very important field still very unexplored by modern poets—the experience of man in search of God, and trying to explain to himself his intenser human feelings in terms of the divine goal."[31] Eliot thought that modernist poets lacked the topoi of both man's relationship to God and man's emotional state in his journey to reach God. Eliot sought to transcend a common modernist theme, man bereft of meaning in a bleak moral space, by creating verse that reached beyond the social into the theological. Indeed, in a 1933 lecture, Eliot said he wanted to create a poetry "so transparent that in reading it we are intent on what the poetry points at, and not on the poetry."[32] Theological agency, the ability to convey transcendent meaning, and the task of "othering" by eclipsing the work itself with a theological message are all foundational functions of poetry for Eliot.

W. H. Auden, Eliot's peer and in some regards his successor, shared remarkably similar notions of poetry. For Auden, poetry should transcend the primary world of the mundane by constructing a secondary, imaginative, spiritual world. In his post-conversion critical work, *On Secondary Worlds*, Auden says, "Present in every human being are two desires, a desire to know truth about the primary world, the given world outside ourselves in which we are born, live, love, hate and die, and the desire to make new secondary worlds of our own or, if we cannot make them ourselves, to share in the secondary worlds of those who can."[33] This creation of worlds "outside ourselves" is an inherently theological act. The goal of art is partly to mediate this creation or sharing in another's creation. The creation of secondary worlds, then, is both inherently transcendent in that it allows one to escape the primary world and mediatory in that it facilitates participation in another's act of transcendence.

Auden is careful to note that art's aim is to manifest the unseen. Having the skeptical view of empirical science common to many modernist authors, Auden sees poetry as the incarnation of true essence, "The job of the arts is to manifest the personal and the chosen: the study of the impersonal and the necessary is the job of the sciences. Though the object

---

31. Kramer, *Redeeming Time*, 14.
32. Ibid., 18.
33. Auden, *On Secondary Worlds*, 49.

of its concern is necessity, Science is just as gratuitous and personal a human activity as Art. To suppose that the sciences can tell us what things are really like, independent of our minds, is a myth."[34] The role of theology in art is to make known what has been concealed. Auden's skepticism about science in *On Secondary Worlds* is due to its inability to explicate human volition; science makes known impersonal data, but art has access to the essence of the human condition, what things are spiritually "really like." Indeed, science cannot create a secondary, spiritual world from art, but the Christian faith can. It is this conviction that the Christian author must delineate the spiritual that most informs Auden's post-conversion theology. The Christian author must transcend, for both his faith and his art demand it. Auden said that it was the task of the Christian writer to transcend all barriers to understanding, including unbelief. Insisting that it is incorrect to assume that his modern audience is Christian, Auden wrote, "In our age and society [a Christian author] can no longer assume, as his ancestors could, that his audience is, at least officially, Christian. He has therefore to try to write something which will have meaning for others as human beings, whether they are believers or unbelievers."[35] As with Eliot's aim to create something that transcends his verse, Auden also sought to transcend the mere act of writing by attempting to create a communicable theology through verse. It is this attempt to transcend, to go beyond the self yet to fill it with meaning as Taylor describes, that chiefly characterizes the theologies of time in Lewis, Eliot, and Auden.

I have discussed some select exemplary attempts to create a theology for the twentieth century, and I have demonstrated Lewis, Eliot, and Auden's commitment to creating theologically effective literature for their twentieth-century readership. I will now expound on the act of creating theology in the twentieth century; an act that I have argued that Lewis, Eliot, and Auden took up in their post-conversion works on time. In order to understand the ideologies involved in Lewis, Eliot, and Auden it is necessary to gloss some prominent theological trends that formed early twentieth-century religious thinking. It is also necessary to explore what theologized literature entails and the theological implications of the role of language in articulating theological beliefs; this I will do in my brief discussion of Christian writer Dorothy Sayers, who helps to inform the theological assumptions behind the post-conversion work of Lewis, Eliot, and Auden.

---

34. Auden, *On Secondary Worlds*, 132.
35. Kirsch, *Auden and Christianity*, 111–12.

Early in the twentieth century, the emergence of Neo-orthodoxy—also known as "theology of crisis" or "dialectical theology"—re-imagined what were seen as the outworn tenets of nineteenth-century liberal theology by emphasizing such conservative doctrines as existentialism, the transcendence of God, the revelation of God through Scripture, and the Incarnation of Jesus Christ. Neo-orthodox works like Karl Barth's seminal *The Epistle to the Romans* (1922), Dietrich Bonheoffer's popular *The Cost of Discipleship* (1937), and Emil Brunner's *Man in Revolt: A Christian Anthropology* (1937) iterated the importance of theological knowledge for twentieth-century laity.[36] The belief that God has spoke and does speak to modern man through history was assumed and taught by Neo-orthodox theologians.

Neo-orthodoxy also brought with it awareness that theology must be socially relevant, and theological thinkers in the Neo-orthodox vein sought to articulate their beliefs in response to twentieth-century notions of existence, God, and human temporality. Christian existentialist philosopher and theologian Paul Tillich, who was influenced by Neo-orthodoxy's emphasis on revealing God to modern man, describes the task of doing theology in the twentieth century. Tillich believed that "the personal encounter with God and the reunion with him are the heart of all genuine religion."[37] According to Tillich, theological articulation must attempt to establish this reunion with the divine by addressing twentieth-century man's concerns.

One such concern is the nature of human existence, an issue that theology must address if is to be effectual. As Tillich puts it, "Man, like every living being, is concerned about many things, above all about those which condition his very existence. . . . If [a situation or concern] claims ultimacy it demands the total surrender of him who accepts this claim . . . it demands that all other concerns . . . be sacrificed."[38] According to Tillich, God is the answer to the question implied by the finitude of human existence. Moderns must surrender their autonomous selves to God's divine will to experience a reunion with the divine. To help mankind achieve this reunion, God has revealed and does reveal Himself through various mediums, such as history, time, and language. The belief that time reveals God to man is an idea that Lewis, Eliot, and Auden espouse in their

---

36. For more on the influence of Neo-orthodoxy on twentieth-century theological thinking, see Smart's *The Divided Mind of Modern Theology*, 11–22, 100–123, 152–220.

37. Tillich, *Systematic Theology* 2:86.

38. Tillich, *Dynamics of Faith*, 1–2.

theologies of time. As will be demonstrated in my chapters on Lewis, Eliot, and Auden, each author viewed time as the medium through which the eternal can be met. Tillich believed that God's divine revelation, the "logos" (the Word of God), could occur through existential mediums, such as time. According to Tillich, to limit God's revelation only to that which is spoken (preaching) or written (Scripture) is "the Protestant pitfall."[39] Because of the works by theological thinkers like Tillich and Neo-orthodox writers like Barth, reunion with the divine through the revelation of extracanonical modes, such as time, became a central theological concern in the twentieth century.

This task of conveying the theological through extracanonical mediums would preoccupy Lewis, Eliot, and Auden's post-conversion writing. What Lewis, Eliot, and Auden sought to effect in their theologies of time was a belief in God's ability to reveal Himself to temporal man, and, in turn, for man to know God salvifically. And each author composed a theology of time that was philosophically relevant. In order to more fully consider these authors' adoption of Christianity to inform their creative theories and to further inform their theological projects, I want to focus on one Christian theorist important to my work: theological writer Dorothy Sayers. Her formulation of theological notions about writing helps influence my own definition of the theological articulations in Lewis, Eliot, and Auden. One work of Sayers, *The Mind of the Maker*, identifies a theologically informed philosophical paradigm for the kind of writing that I see Lewis, Eliot, and Auden doing.

Sayers's *The Mind of the Maker* is the most explicit modern monograph on the relationship between the Christian faith and the practice of writing. In this seminal work, Sayers expounds on the task of the theologizing author and what it means for the author to effectively convey his or her beliefs to a twentieth-century audience. Sayers—Christian, mystery writer, poet, translator of Dante's *The Divine Comedy*, playwright, and fellow member of the "Inklings"—touches upon the vitally important role of the Christian artist as communicator of spiritual matters to the common man. Sayers, who is writing at the same time as the authors studied here, argues that there is a "widening cleavage between the Church and the Arts on the one hand and between the State and the Arts on the other" that "leaves the common man with the impression that the artist is something of little account, either in this world or the next."[40] Sayers attempts to

---

39. Tillich, *Systematic Theology*, 157.
40. Sayers, *The Mind of the Maker*, 214.

correct this pejorative twentieth-century view of the Christian artist by associating the creative act of writing with the divine act of creation. According to Sayers, the writer is the one person in society who can bridge the gap between the church and the arts, and, because of the theological task he undertakes, so prove his craft to be valuable both in this world and the next.

It is precisely the task of bridging the gap between the church and literary expression that so interests Lewis, Eliot, and Auden. All three authors believed that the role of the Christian writer was one of theological mediation, an articulation that would bring the theological to bear on human experience. In their theologies of time, one finds the marriage of Christian thought and literary creation, and it is the Christian writers who enact this union. The artist, Sayers claims, "remains the person who can throw most light on that 'creative attitude to life' to which bewildered leaders of thought are now belatedly exhorting a no less bewildered humanity."[41] Sayers believes the Christian writer is uniquely qualified to theologically enlighten the common man through his or her creative work. And above all, according to Sayers, the Christian writer is to impart ideas of the divine to humanity, for that is the whole theological aim of the imaginative act of writing.[42]

Sayers believes that the imaginative act (i.e., the creation of a literary work) is the primary means of the artist's formation of theology. The artist's creation is the expression—Sayer's calls the actual written expression the "Creative Energy"[43]—"of his own nature in accordance with the law of his being."[44] Sayers's notion of creating in accordance with the "law of his being" is tied to the belief that each individual person, and therefore each artist, bears the image of *the* Creator. The Christian writer is an active reflection of the *Imago Dei* and as such must consider the act of writing to be a theological act. So theological is Sayers's notion of the act of writing that she underpins her theory of the creative act with a trinitarian formulation in which writing is composed of the Creative Idea (corresponding with the Father), the Creative Energy (the Son), and the Creative Power (the Holy Spirit).[45] Quoting her own theological play *The Zeal of Thy House* (1937) to explain this triune theory, Sayers says:

41. Sayers, *The Mind of the Maker*, 214.
42. Ibid., 215.
43. Ibid., 37.
44. Ibid., 42.
45. Ibid., 37.

every work [*or act*] of creation is threefold, an earthly trinity to match the heavenly. First, [*not in time, but merely in order of enumeration*] there is the Creative Idea, passionless, timeless, beholding the whole work complete at once, the end in the beginning: and this is the image of the Father. Second, there is the Creative Energy [*or Activity*] begotten of that idea, working in time from the beginning to the end, with sweat and passion, being incarnate in the bonds of matter: and this is the image of the Word. Third, there is the Creative Power, the meaning of the work and its response in the lively soul: and this is the image of the indwelling Spirit. And these three are one, each equally in itself the whole work, whereof none can exist without other: and this is the image of the Trinity.[46]

Sayers's beliefs about literature comprise a theological understanding of the writing process. The themes created by the theological author (for example, time) and the writerly act of creating them are theological, substantive, and performative, and both the act of creation and the thing created mirror the divine Triune being. As the Triune Godhead, the three-in-one, first manifests itself as an agent of creation (e.g., in Christian readings of the creation accounts in Genesis 1 and 2), the writer further manifests the divine image in the act of writing. Likewise, as man is the image of his Creator, so the written creation is an image of its writer. Sayers's belief that the creative act is a matter of image bearing is founded on her view of the Incarnation, and herein lies the primary reason why Sayers's ideas are relevant to this present study.

Sayers privileges the theological nature of writing by presenting a notion of heightened theological immediacy, a theory of writing that puts as much emphasis on theology as it does on composition. According to Sayers, the chief element of the theological nature of composition is the Incarnate. Sayers insists, "the mind of the maker is generally revealed, and in a manner *incarnate*, in all its creation. The works, severally and jointly, are manifestations within space-time of the Energy and instinct with the Power of the Idea."[47] The literary work is a manifestation of divine "Energy," which Sayers associates with Christ, the "Logos." The Christian writer—like Lewis, Eliot, and Auden—reveals the divine Logos through theological tropes, themes, and the very creative act of writing, which Sayers views as inherently theological. The Logos, which is made Incarnate through the created work, operates in conjunction with the Power (the Holy Spirit) of

---

46. Ibid., 37–38.
47. Ibid., 87.

the divine Idea (God the Father). As previously mentioned, the concept of the Incarnation is vitally important for Eliot's *Four Quartets* and Auden's "Kairos and Logos." In their theologies of time, Eliot and Auden depict the temporal as the medium through which the eternal is made manifest (i.e., incarnated). And while the thematic presence of Incarnation is especially prominent in Eliot and Auden, the notion of Incarnation underpins Lewis, Eliot, and Auden's theological beliefs about literature. The importance of the Incarnation for each author will be discussed in more detail chapters 3, 4, and 5.

The value of Sayers's theory of Christian poetics for my study is in its privileging of the function of theology in literature and, conversely, of the function of literature in theology. According to Sayers, the act of writing is the *doing* of theology, and literature exists as a theological medium. Sayers's thinking elucidates the task of the Christian writers Lewis, Eliot, and Auden in their post-conversion works, which task is to infuse language with the theological and to recreate the theological through the literary. What is particularly relevant to my study is the way Sayers imagines this infusion, or Incarnation, to operate. In her chapter, "The Energy Revealed in Creation," Sayers discusses the scope a Christian writer must allow to the "Energy" (Logos) in order for it to manifest through the creative act. An example of the scope Sayers discusses is the creation of several diverse characters. The theological writer must not only create characters of diverse worldviews, actions, and dialogue, but the writer must also create diversity *within* each character. This internal diversity usually shows itself in the character's mind as paradoxical, complex, or contradictory desires. Without the presence of diversity, the Energy is hindered by the writer's one-dimensionality.

Against this threatened one-dimensionality in the creative act, Sayers asserts that "the vital power of an imaginative work demands a diversity within its unity; and the stronger the diversity, the more massive the unity."[48] By *diversity*, Sayers means the accumulation of various elements that compose a theological work. The truly coherent theological work is exemplified by its massive unity or sources despite various philosophical positions. Sayers insists that the theological integrity of creativity is at stake in this diversity. What ultimately defines theologized literature is not only its Incarnate function but also its ability to encompass diverse and even antithetical ideas so that a cosmos can be created from chaos. This concept of incorporating diverse elements and deploying them in service

---

48. Ibid., 53.

to theology is vital for understanding the post-conversion works of Lewis, Eliot, and Auden, each of whom demonstrates an exercise of Sayers's theory of diversity and unity in their appropriation of Bergsonan philosophy. In merging their Christian theology with Bergson's secular philosophy, Lewis, Eliot, and Auden demonstrate that what defines twentieth-century theological articulation is, in part, an ability to "convert" non-Christian ideas into creative Christian expression. Lewis's *The Great Divorce*, Eliot's *Four Quartets*, and Auden's "Kairos and Logos" are essentially theological incarnations of Bergson's twentieth-century conceptions of time, articulated through fictional and poetic language, and each work strives for the coherence required by Sayers's idea of unity in its theological treatment of time from the composite of theology and Bergsonian philosophy, required by Sayer's idea of diversity.

Lewis's, Eliot's, and Auden's constructions of time directly relate to what they believed to be the larger theological activity of God's eternal interjection into man's temporal existence. Works like *The Great Divorce*, *Four Quartets*, and Auden's "Kairos and Logos" treat the twentieth-century *topos* of man's temporal state with a theological paradigm of divine eternality. From my discussion of Taylor and Sayers, I argue that a twentieth-century theology of time is a cooperation of thematically non-Christian ideas with theological tenets of the Christian faith. It is that which assumes that the theme is incomplete without being theologized, and it is that which seeks to redemptively recreate the theme so that through the literary a higher theological meaning might be reached. The Christian nature of Lewis's, Eliot's, and Auden's theories of time is found in each author's commitment to literarily filling the empty theme of the temporal with the eternal, to transfigure twentieth century—and distinctly Bergsonian—ideas about time by incorporating a theology of Incarnation, and, in so doing, to create a theological world in which time transforms man's inner spiritual states and through which God makes himself known to man.

2

Bergsonian Conceptions of Time

Duration, Dualism, and Intuition

I must begin this chapter with a disclaimer that my treatment of time is neither meant to be exhaustive nor to contribute to any scientific field. Rather, I am discussing a part of twentieth-century conceptions of time by which Lewis, Eliot, and Auden would create their works. The number of works influenced by twentieth-century theories of time is staggering, as is the size of the body of criticism on time in twentieth-century literature.[1] The question could thus be asked, why focus solely on the works of Bergson and not include works by other monumental figures, such as Samuel Alexander's published lectures *Space, Time, and Deity* (1916–18); Wyndham Lewis's critique of the metaphysical in writers Joyce and Pound as well as a refutation of Bergson in *Time and Western Man* (1927); and, arguably the most significant early twentieth-century work in the development of European philosophy, Martin Heidegger's *Being and Time* (1927)? The answer is that to deal with other philosophers as well as authors so important as Lewis or Eliot or Auden is simply beyond the scope of this work.

---

1. E.g., Fabian, *Time and the Other* (1983); the theological look at time by Craig in *Time and Eternity* (2001); see also the helpful Hawking, *A Brief History of Time* (1988); Healey, ed., *Reduction, Time and Reality* (1981); McClure, ed., *The Philosophy of Time* (2005); Bazarnik, *James Joyce and After: Writer and Time* (2010); Whitworth, *Einstein's Wake: Relativity, Metaphor, and Modernist Literature* (2002).

Bergsonian Conceptions of Time

Moreover, Bergson's subjectivizing of time to the level of conscious experience, his theory of dualistic selves operating in two types of time, and his notion of time as a force are explicitly put to use by the theological constructions of Lewis, Eliot, and Auden. Each Christian author appropriates Bergsonian philosophy to effectively articulate a theology of human experience in time that is both true to their Christian faiths and ideologically relevant to their audiences. As I have previously mentioned, it is not insignificant that Lewis, Eliot, and Auden chose to write theologies of time framed by Bergsonian concepts. One underlying contention of my project is that Lewis, Eliot, and Auden tailored their theological treatments of time according to the common currency of Bergonism because of the radical shift in religious ideology, the shift to more philosophically oriented theological orientation, and the emphasis on theological tenets like God's revelation to man through extracanonical mediums (e.g., time). In other words, Bergson provided Lewis, Eliot, and Auden a relevant philosophical framework through which they could most effectively articulate their Christian theologies of time to a twentieth-century readership.

Thus, I am not trying to propose any new theories about conceptions of time in the early to middle twentieth century. Nor am I attempting to shed new light on Bergson; rather, my objective is to demonstrate how Bergson's theory of duration influenced Lewis, Eliot, and Auden. So much of Bergson's theory of time is about the inner states of the perceiver that the jump from Bergson to a Christian poetics—a jump based on inner spiritual experiences—is not a radical one. The relative subjectivity that Bergson championed in his philosophical treatments of time was absorbed, or even *converted*, through its theological appropriation by Lewis, Eliot, and Auden, who are ideologically indebted to Bergson. Their work bears signs of that debt through an acute awareness of and unique engagement with subjective time. In *The Great Divorce*, Lewis will create a multi-verse where time exists dualistically and moves in conjunction with characters' spiritual development. Eliot's *Four Quartets* will disturb notions of any objective correlation between the temporal and the eternal by inserting spiritual meaning into the experience of a moment, creating a dynamic force of time through which the Incarnation is made manifest. In "Kairos and Logos," Auden will subjectivize time by dichotomizing the experiences of two types of selves: the unbelieving self that experiences time as being purely historical and the redeemed self that perceives time as theologically meaningful. Indeed, to convert the Bergsonian ideas of their age into theology, all three writers had to engage those ideas, and their works call attention back to the philosophical trends of their twentieth-century world.

Twentieth-Century Time and the Philosophy of Bergson

The turn of the twentieth century saw revolutionary changes in scientific and philosophical understandings of time. By the time that C. S. Lewis, T. S. Eliot, and W. H. Auden wrote their most significant Christian works, the metaphysical question of time had already been pressing upon the minds of the most prominent thinkers of the early twentieth century. As Paul Valery wrote in 1919, "the time has passed when time doesn't count."[2] From philosophy to the hard sciences, time was at the forefront of discussions about the nature of reality, about the perception of that reality, and about human existence itself.

The most influential scientific thinker of the early twentieth century, Albert Einstein, drastically shook the common, monolithic conceptions of time with his theories of Special Relativity (regarding the measurement of the speed of light in reference to various inertial frames) and General Relativity (generalizing special relativity by providing a unified definition of gravity as the province of space and time). In 1905, Einstein published his paper "On the Electrodynamic of Moving Bodies" that unfolded the principles of the Special Theory of Relativity, the one more immediately relevant to this study, a theory that proposes that two objects can exist and move in the universe in their own time in distinction from one another and also thus a theory that shifted emphasis to the relative position of the observer. When an event (e.g., a car crash) happens in one place, observers of that event would likely agree on the time that the event occurs. But when two events are separated by space (e.g., two different car crashes in the two cities of London and Memphis), the notion of a simultaneous point of impact is relative.[3] Depending on the position of the observer—known as the frame of reference—the car crash in London might occur first, but in another frame of reference (i.e., in a different position of another observer) the car crash in Memphis may occur first. What happens at a certain time of day in London happens at a different time in Memphis because of the spatial position of those perceiving the event. The relativ-

---

2. Valery, *Complete Works* 1.1045.
3. See Einstein's chapter "The Relativity of Simultaneity" in *Relativity*, 22–24.

ity of the time of these occurring events negates any solidarity perceivers might have understanding the event.

To articulate his Special Theory of Relativity, Einstein uses an analogy of two strokes of lightning being witnessed by observers on a moving train and by witnesses on the embankment. Einstein considers the relativity of an event occurring simultaneously to more than one observer, asking, "Are two events (e.g., the two strokes of lightning A and B), which are simultaneous with reference to the railway embankment, also simultaneous relative to the train? We shall show directly that the answer must be negative."[4] Einstein then claims, "Events which are simultaneous with reference to the embankment are not simultaneous with respect to the train, and vice versa (relativity of simultaneity). Every reference-body (coordinate system) has its own particular time . . . ."[5] This notion of each reference-body's own particular time is the heart of Einsteinian relativity: that each object operates in the time relative to the perceiver in that perceiver's particular vantage point, which may be different from the vantage point of a different perceiver.

In Bergson's later theory of duration—i.e., of a subjective, conscious experience of time—he would develop what could be called a philosophical counterpart to Einstein's relativity. Bergson's entire conception of duration is built upon the premise that time exists, operates, and is experienced in ways as variously subjective as the human consciousness. For both Einstein and Bergson, the perception of time—i.e., one's experience with time—defines time's very nature. According to Einstein's theory, time is far from absolute, monolithic, or independent from perception. Rather, time is only as verifiable, as capable of enumeration, and as uniform as those individuals experiencing it. Time was no longer only a scientific subject; it was a matter of experience and perception.[6]

Whereas before Einstein space and time were understood as immutable absolutes under the dominant Newtonian model,[7] after Einstein time was understood in relation to the perceiver. Describing absolute time, Newton posited that,

---

4. Einstein, *Relativity*, 22.

5. Ibid., 23.

6. For an exhaustive look at the development of Absolute Time, see two chapters in Wilcox, *The Measure of Time Past*: chapter 1, "The Rise and Fall of Absolute Time," 16–49, and chapter 7, "The Dating of Absolute Time," 187–220.

7. For more on Newton's absolute space and time, see Hugget and Hoefer's entry in the Stanford Encyclopedia of Philosophy: http://plato.stanford.edu/entries/spacetime-theories/#9.3; Hoefer, "Absolute Versus Relational Spacetime"; and Dieks, "Space-Time Relationism in Newtonian and Relativistic Physics."

> Absolute, true and mathematical time, of itself, and from its own nature flows equably without regard to anything external, and by another name is called duration: relative, apparent and common time, is some sensible and external (whether accurate or unequable) measure of duration by the means of motion, which is commonly used instead of true time; such as an hour, a day, a month, a year....[8]

Newton is careful to distinguish between two types of time, the absolute and the relative. It should be noted that Bergson will make the same type of dualistic move in his articulation of time, even using the same term "duration," though Bergson's ideas and Newton's are quite different. Newton's notion of absolute time is mathematical, objective, and, in comparison to relative time, "true." Relative time, on the other hand, is a socially constructed measuring stick—a way of speaking about the absolute. Absolute time pays no attention to anything "external," and the relationship of external perception to time is inconsequential, in that perception does nothing to define absolute time.

But through the lens of twentieth-century relativity, time is defined by the perception of time rather than the ontology of time, by the perceiver's frame of reference rather than the reality of the hour, and by the relationship of one's point of view with another's within the temporal rather than temporal itself. Einstein's theory of relativity marked a permanent change in how both time and space were understood. In the first decades of the twentieth century, the idea of time had radically changed; in terms of anyone's understanding of time, the subjective perception joined the conceptual paradigm, displacing the original primacy of the mere event itself. Einstein made acceptable the notion of multiple coexistent spheres of time, establishing the concept of relative, subjective, impressionable time for the rest of the twentieth century. Indeed, Einstein built the conceptual house in which the thinking of Lewis, Eliot, Auden and the philosopher Henri Bergson would take up residence. An understanding of Bergson's work on time is necessary for understanding how time was viewed in the early to middle twentieth century, and it is also necessary for an understanding of the ideologies of time with which Lewis, Eliot, and Auden's worked. What Einstein meant for the science of time, Bergson meant for the philosophy of time.

Henri Bergson (1859–1941) was a French philosopher, chair of Greek and Latin Philosophy at the Collège de France, and the recipient

---

8. Newton, *Mathematic Principles of Natural Philosophy*, 6.

of the Nobel Prize in literature in 1927. Born in 1859, the same year that saw Darwin's *Origin of Species*, Bergson would challenge Darwinism by promoting a philosophy of dynamism—a theoretical approach that emphasizes flux, movement, and immeasurable human experience—in opposition to the nineteenth-century science of mechanical determinism that Darwin helped solidify. Bergson's popularity in the years leading up to Lewis, Eliot, and Auden's conversions was immense. Bergson scholar Marguerite Bistis argues that Bergson "belonged to a particular type of French academic whom Terry Clark has aptly named 'the mondain' and whose defining characteristic is a profound rapport with the educated public."[9] Bistis describes the *mondain* as individuals who act as

> "arbiters of the gout public" shaping the intellectual outlook and sensibility of their times. They tend to produce academic bestsellers which make them into celebrities on a par with politicians, writers, and actors. Like the institution with which they are usually but not always affiliated, they occupy the liminal space between the professional world of academe and the non-professional world of general culture.[10]

Bergson was such a thinker, one who not only stood between the academy and culture but one whose ideas breached other intellectual disciplines. Bergson was, indeed, a "mondain," whose works like *Time and Free Will*, *Matter and Memory*, and *Creative Evolution* were widely popular through Europe, even pervading the intellectual discourses of Lewis, Eliot, and Auden's England. When Bergson's theories emerged at the onset of the twentieth century, one factor that led to his popularity was that his philosophy did what philosophical systems were not supposed to do. It questioned the supremacy of human reason.

It will be made clear in this chapter that what Bergson valued most was an intuitive, even spiritual, experience with time that is not informed by empiricism or scientific rationality. The focus of this chapter will largely be on *Time and Free Will* (1889; English edition, 1910), a text that mounts an attack on atomistic views of mental states and time and supports an metaphysical understanding of time working in synthesis with an intuitive view of mental states, which Bergson call *intensities*. What Bergson will offer twentieth-century thought is a new way of understanding the

---

9. Bistis, "Managing Bergson's Crowd: Professionalism and the Mondain at the College de France," 391.

10. Ibid.

intensities of the human condition and how they are manifested through time and acted on by it.

Time, Bergson argues, has been misunderstood by the scientific rationality so prominent to the late-nineteenth and early-twentieth century:

> Time could be enormously and even infinitely accelerated; nothing would be changed for the mathematician, for the physicist or for the astronomer. And yet the difference with regard to consciousness would be profound . . . for consciousness, the weariness of waiting, from one day to the next, from one hour to another, would no longer be the same.[11]

Bergson's point is that nothing would change in scientific rationality if the value of time were changed. If time were accelerated or halted, it would merely be a matter of notation to the scientific mind. However, to the consciousness, time is felt.

Time molds the conscious mind, acting on it and transforming into another state of consciousness through what Bergson will describe as the "force" of time. Bergson will even go so far in his philosophy of time to ascribe the force behind duration (time) and one's life in duration as "an eternity of life."[12] Bergson claims to believe in an eternity of life that transcends both time and temporal experience, but which can be accessed through an intuitive knowledge of duration. It is this reach past the scientific toward the metaphysical that makes Bergson so employable by Lewis, Eliot, and Auden. While Bergson never goes so far as to espouse a Christian view of time such as articulated by Lewis, Eliot, and Auden, his theories are a middle ground between non-Christian philosophies (e.g., positivism or scientific mechanism) and Christian theology. More so than the thinking of any other twentieth-century thinker on time, Bergson's philosophies provide a sort of metaphysical via media between twentieth-century philosophy and the Christian theologies of Lewis, Eliot, and Auden.

One element important in Bergson's influence on twentieth-century conceptions of time was his philosophical continuation of Einsteinian relativity. Bergson furthered Einstein's principle of relativity and pushed for dynamic, innumerable understandings of how an event occurred in time.

---

11. Bergson, *The Creative Mind*, 3.
12. Ibid., 176.

> When you raise your arms, you accomplish a movement of which you have, from within, a simple perception; but for me, watching it from the outside, your arm passes through one point, then through another, and between these two there will still be other points; so that if you begin to count, the operation would go on for ever. Viewed from the inside, then, an absolute is a simple thing; but looked at from the outside it is [subject to] an inexhaustible enumeration.[13]

Bergson's argument that being outside an event produces innumerable understandings derives from Einstein's analogy of a flash of light being seen by numerous viewers in various frames of reference. By focusing on the infinite understandings inherent in perception, Bergson's theories would expand philosophical understandings of the perception of an event in relation to the actual event perceived. In terms of time, Bergson would seek to expand the very notion of successive moments and of human perception of those moments, as well as of the concept of knowing *in* time. In doing so, he would apply an epistemological paradigm with Einstein's faint fingerprints on it. Like Einstein's theory of special relativity, Bergson's theory of time approaches the phenomenon of an experienced moment from the perceiver's perspective and so expands the definition of time to include multi-dimensional understandings, all relative to the observer. Unlike the ideas of his scientific forebear Einstein, Bergson's claims were explicitly philosophical and always supported by the "inexhaustible enumeration" of a theory rather than by mechanistic, empirical evidence. But, just as Einstein proposed his theory of relativity against the antithetical backdrop of Newtonian concepts of time, so Bergson proposed his vitalistic theories of duration (time) and intuition (consciousness in time) against an inimical philosophical milieu dominated by the influences of determinist positivism.

As a worldview, positivism held sway over the areas of philosophy, science, and psychology in the late nineteenth and early twentieth centuries. Positivism was an extension of Darwinian determinism that swept the fields of science, psychology, and philosophy in the late nineteenth and early twentieth centuries. Positivism sought to explain every facet of human existence through the mechanical language of science. According to this school of thought, all phenomena pertaining to human life and nature occur prescriptively by the determined conditions of the cosmos, and all phenomena are adequately accounted for by scientific method. Auguste

---

13. Bergson, *An Introduction to Metaphysics*, 5–6.

Comte, founder of the philosophy of positivism, declared all areas of human life under the domain of natural science:

> Now that man's history has been for the first time systematically considered as a whole, and has been found to be, like all other phenomena, subject to invariable laws, the preparatory labours of modern Science are ended. All knowledge is now brought within the sphere of Natural Philosophy. . . . A firm objective basis is laid down for that complete co-ordination of human existence towards which all sound Philosophy has ever tended.[14]

Comte's assumption that all facets of the human experience were thoroughly accounted for by modern science saturated the latter half of the nineteenth century. Comte's pronouncements were extended by Hippolyte Taine, literary critic and advocate of social positivism, who extended scientific processes to the subject of psychology. Taine declares that science has conquered nature and now accounts for the human condition:

> Science approaches at last and approaches man; it has gone beyond the visible and palpable world of stars, stones, and plants, to which it had been contemptuously confined—it now *challenges the soul,* armed with exact and piercing instruments whose precision and whose reach have proved themselves over three hundred years of experience.[15]

Taine's presumption about the ability of science to assimilate human nature through its "piercing instruments" speaks to the spirit of the age, an age that sought "to push science to its ultimate limits," as wrote French philosopher, theologian, and famed nineteenth-century progressive thinker Ernest Renan in *The Future of Science*.[16] Like the physical sciences of the era, late nineteenth-century psychology saw the human soul as the province of science and so held it to be quantifiable.

In the realm of biological science, Herbert Spencer likewise championed the positivist doctrine of mechanical evolution. Even before Darwin's *Origin of Species*, Spencer's essay "Progress: Its Law and Cause" (1857) promoted an adaptive form of evolution through which the human race has steadily progressed to a type of epistemological teleology, an ultimate state of knowing. This evolutionary concept of epistemology was further promoted in the essay's fuller version *First Principles of a New System*

---

14. Comte, *General View of Positivism*, 35, 37–38.
15. Pilkington, *Bergson and His Influence*, 219.
16. Renan, *The Future of Science*, 31.

of Philosophy (1862). Spencer held science to be "an organized body of truths, ever growing, and ever being purified of errors."[17] Spencer's notion of science's "ever growing" progressive nature reveals an utter faith in the empirical processes of science. In fact, Spencer went so far as to foretell that the "veritable revelation" of science would continually disclose the "established order of the Universe."[18] Spencer saw the rationalist state of the nineteenth century as the culmination of the human epistemological journey: "mechanistic science of the last century represents the last stage of the adaptive process by which the human mind gradually adjusts itself to the structure of reality."[19] It was on this "last stage" that Bergson would emerge to counter the Darwinian philosophies of Comte, Taine, and Spencer.

The denunciation of Darwinian science along with its promotion of philosophies of mechanistic determinism constituted the core of Bergson's philosophical agenda. According to Bergson, the biggest problem with Darwinian thinking was its incapability to account for the dynamic, the "becoming" nature of life:

> Science has nothing to change in what it tells us, we must conclude that, in what it tells us, it takes account neither of succession in what of it is specific nor of time in what there is in it that is fluent. It has no sign to express what strikes our consciousness in succession and duration. It no more applies to becoming, so far as that is moving, than the bridges thrown here and there across the stream follow the water that flows under their arches.[20]

This accusation of science's inability to account for the processes of life is important for Bergson's own thinking. According to Bergson, no system of thought is adequate if it cannot explain dynamic natural change. Science cannot explain time, evolution, or the human condition because the mechanistic philosophy on which nineteenth-century and early-twentieth-century scientific inquiry is built will not allow for life's volatile nature. To use a Bergsonesque metaphor, the dams of science stop the flowing waters of life. Bergson's critique of science's inability to express "duration"—the name Bergson gave to his theory of time—is particularly important for this present work and will be the focus of the second half of

17. Spencer, *First Principles*, 17.
18. Ibid.
19. Capek, *Bergson and Modern Physics*, 10.
20. Bergson, *Creative Evolution*, 169.

this chapter. It could be said that Bergson's entire philosophical trajectory can be traced along the reactionary lines against Darwinian influenced philosophies.[21]

Bergson's body of work is replete with indictments against any system of thought that promotes mechanistic finalism. Important to understand in Bergson's criticism is his rejection of the determinist philosophy in Darwinian mechanistic science. And, indeed, when the ideas inherent in Darwinian evolution bleed into other disciplines, as they do in Taine's psychology, Bergson has much to say: "The error of radical finalism, as also that of radical mechanism, is to extend too far the application of certain concepts that are natural to our intellect";[22] "Bound, like the physics of the moderns and the metaphysics of the ancients, to the cinematographical method, it ended with the conclusion, implicitly admitted at the start and immanent in the method itself: All is given";[23] "Never could the finalistic interpretation, such as we shall propose it, be taken for an anticipation of the future. It is a particular mode of viewing the past in the light of the present. In short, the classic conception of finality postulates at once too much and too little: it is both too wide and too narrow. In explaining life by intellect, it limits too much meaning of life."[24] Each of these passages share a common critique of science's finalistic assumption that life can be blueprinted down to its ultimate end. In Bergson's dynamism, no such assumption made, and in his theory of duration, all is not given. Yet in all of his engagements with scientific discourse, Bergson wrote with refreshingly anti-empirical illustration, often drawing on the most metaphysical, emotional, and even spiritual analogies to reconceptualize time and promote a dynamic theory of life.

To have a fuller understanding of Bergson, one must appreciate that he wrote in the late nineteenth and early twentieth centuries, when the scientific as well as philosophical discussion of vitalism was a major point of contention.[25] Vitalism is a philosophy that holds that the functions of

---

21. For more on Bergson's response to mechanical determinism and the twentieth-century's move to more indeterminist philosophies, see Guerlac's helpful chapter, "From the Certainties of Mechanism to the Anxieties of Indeterminism" in *Thinking in Time*, 14–41.

22. Bergson, *Creative Evolution*, 30.

23. Ibid., 172.

24. Ibid., 34.

25. For more on Bergson and vitalism, see Schwartz's "Bergson and the Politics of Vitalism," 277–305.

an organism are caused by a vital principle—or as Bergson put it, an *élan vital*, or a "vital impulse"—separate from biochemical catalysts. Vitalism proposes that because life is organic and ever flourishing it cannot be reduced to governing mechanistic laws. Vitalism also insists that neither physics nor any other physical science can account for the processes of life. Vitalism posited that human experiences and actions cannot be explained in mechanistic terms, though the scientific tendency to explain life in automated, ironically lifeless terms had bled over into the realm of philosophy. Philosophical vitalism—often called *Lebensphilosophie* ("philosophy of life")—emerged in response to positivism and its application of scientifically physical language to describe human experience.[26] Opposed to the static scientific diagnosis of positivism, the essential tenet of vitalism is its emphasis on progressive dynamism. Fixity is antithetical to life, according to vitalistic principles, and becoming is superior to being. As Schwartz points out, it is precisely vitalism's emphasis on dynamic change, multiplicity, and becoming that made it an appealing alternative to religion for secularists, who could not reduce life to the mechanical projections of positivism.[27] It is at the point of divorce between the determinist leanings of positivism and vitalism's promotion of the dynamic that Bergson would insert his theories of creative evolution and time duration. Bergson, who viewed life as a constant process of growth and change that perpetually produces new forms, would be one of vitalism's greatest proponents and positivism's greatest opponents.

Indeed, life was for Bergson "a constant state of becoming"—a concept he coined as "creative evolution." From the most subjective human experience to the overall order of the cosmos, every facet of natural life is in dynamic flux. Inherent in existence is change, "Organic creation ... the evolutionary phenomena which properly constitute life, we cannot in any way subject to a mathematical treatment."[28] Contrary to Darwin's mechanistic evolution, Bergson's position is that the process of evolution moves along according to a vital impetus (*élan vital*), and that all life develops dynamically and leads to a dynamically open end, as opposed to a mechanistic teleology in which "all is given."[29]

---

26. See Schwartz, "Paradise Reframed," 571–73.
27. Ibid., 573.
28. Bergson, *Creative Evolution*, 19.
29. Ibid., 34. For more on Bergson's treatment of mechanistic scientific systems, see ibid., 10–55.

> The truth is we change without ceasing. . . . [T]here is no essential difference between passing from one state to another and persisting in the same state. If the state which "remains the same" is more varied than we think, [then] on the other hand the passing of one state to another resembles—more than we imagine—a single state being prolonged: the transition is continuous. Just because we close our eyes to the unceasing variation of every physical state, we are obliged when the change has become so formidable as to force itself on our attention, to speak as if a new state were placed alongside the previous one. Of this new state we assume that it remains unvarying in its turn and so on endlessly.[30]

Bergson's diction ("change without ceasing, passing, transition is continuous, unceasing variation, force, endlessly") captures his overall philosophy of the nature of life: to live is change. Existence itself is more aptly described as becoming rather than being. Existence is dynamic change, an ever becoming and never static process. Bergson says of human existence, "We are seeking only the precise meaning that our consciousness gives to this word "exist" and we find that, for a conscious being, to exist is to change, to change is to mature, to mature is to go on creating oneself endlessly."[31] Bergson developed a philosophical system in which an endless natural dynamism is the foundation for understanding the human condition. This vital philosophy of life is important for Lewis's fiction and for the poetry of Eliot and Auden, as each author creates worlds of progressive morality and dynamic being. All three writers resist existential fixity (e.g., Lewis's moral dynamism and the theme of transformative time in Eliot and Auden's verse) and, by relying on Bergsonian thought, construct theological worlds in which both man and time interrelate. This ever-changing existence in which the orders of nature, of human experiences, and of human knowledge adhere to unpredictable processes of change is a central tenet to Bergson's thinking. Both life and even man's knowledge of life are subject to the experiences inherent in a dynamic, evolving world.

---

30. Bergson, *The Creative Mind*, 165.
31. Bergson, *Creative Evolution*, 13.

Bergsonian Intuition

In the Bergsonian system, even epistemology conforms to principles of existential dynamism as man *knows through*, which, for Bergson, is a knowing gained through experience—an *entering into* something rather than learning about it through analysis.[32] It is intuition, not intellect, that allows the individual to connect with ultimate reality, and it is intuition that leads to Bergson's theory of time, called duration. Bergsonian intuition is antithetical to empirical perception, with its emphasis on accumulation of facts, analysis, and synthesizing of various facts. Bergson calls an epistemology of perception "pure knowledge,"[33] and like the scientific process, this type of empirically based perception means "above all to know."[34] However, knowing only accumulates facts about a thing, rather than allowing the knower to actually experience the thing. The inability of empirical perception to truly know a thing is due to perception's location in the brain, and because the brain is a material object, its epistemological relationship to the outside world is one of "action" rather than knowing.

Bergsonian action is the result of the brain's reception of images and resultant physical stimuli and is described as "movement,"[35] a term connoting material dynamism or the actions of a corporeal object. Because perception is reduced to action, and action is the working of a material object, Bergson describes the brain's limitations on knowing in mechanistic terms. As Guerlac notes, for Bergson, "perception serves action, not knowledge."[36] Because the material brain is not where true knowing occurs, Bergson minimizes the brain's role in knowing *a thing in itself* (a phrase that connotes an experiencing of something's essence, its truest nature) and negates the brain's inability to understand a thing's true essence by describing it mechanistically:

> The brain is nothing but a kind of central telephone switchboard. Its role is to connect communications or put them on hold. It adds nothing to what it receives. . . . In other words, the brain appears to us to be an instrument of analysis with respect selection in relation to movements . . . performed. But in the one

---

32. See *Matter and Memory*, 184–85; *The Creative Mind*, 159–85.
33. Bergson, *Matter and Memory*, 17.
34. Ibid.
35. Ibid., 26–27.
36. Guerlac, *Thinking in Time*, 111.

case as in the other, its role is limited to that of transmitting and dividing movement.³⁷

Bergson's criticism of the brain's inability to truly *know* something sounds remarkably close to his aforementioned critiques of nineteenth-century positivism. An epistemology based on philosophical positivism and on the mechanical aptitude of the material brain privileges the empirical over the intuitive, assumes man's ability to truly know something through rational acuity, and mistakenly conflates knowledge of the material world with the true understanding of a thing. As he did in his critique of late nineteenth- and early twentieth-century mechanistic paradigms, Bergson held empirical epistemology to be incapable of knowing a thing in itself, as the knower relies on the brain's telephone switchboard, which only serves to transmit information. Bergsonian intuition rejects this type of epistemology and, instead, hinges on what Bergson calls the "turn of experience," an entering into something through an act of "sympathy," as Bergson phrases it.³⁸

Sympathetic intuition is an epistemology of existential engagement, a knowing through experience. Like "sympathy," which seeks to put one in the place of another in order to know an experience, Bergsonian intuition is an entering into something to know it rather than approaching it analytically from the outside. Bergsonian intuition thus meets duration at the intersection of man's experience and time. Because intuition is both an experiential act of *entering into* and an immeasurable, anti-empirical way of knowing, it is not accessible to reason, science, or analysis. True intuition *is* consciousness and exists in the occurrences of perception and of memory in duration (time), which, for Bergson, is not a measurable chronological period or an element of space.³⁹ Rather, duration is the mode of existence intimately experienced by an intuitive consciousness—a concept Bergson calls "immediate consciousness." As opposed to a conceptual knowledge, immediate consciousness is a knowing from one's inner states, from pure experience without the application of an imposed rational process.

Lewis, Eliot, and Auden's post-conversion works include some version of Bergson's immediate consciousness in duration. The Christian theology of each author's treatment of time promotes an epistemology of intuitive knowing, a realization that comes from the deepest parts of

---

37. Bergson, *Matter and Memory*, 26–27.
38. Bergson, *The Creative Mind*, 175.
39. For more on how tuition works as an epistemology, see Deleuze's chapter "Intuition as Method" in *Bergsonism*, 13–36.

human consciousness. Indeed, the preeminence of inner states is vital to each author's depiction of Christian existence. Lewis's *The Great Divorce* opposes the rationalist epistemologies that foster spiritual skepticism, in turn promoting a deeper kind of knowing that fosters spiritual intuition. Likewise, Eliot's *Four Quartets* warns against a knowing void of inner spiritual meaning, instead espousing an epistemology of immediate experience. Auden's "Kairos and Logos" dichotomizes knowing between empty rational understanding and a deeper theological way of knowing. All three authors hold to a theology of immediate knowing in time connected to a deep sense of intuitive consciousness as the key to this kind of knowing.

Bergson's *Time and Free Will*, originally entitled "Essay on the Immediate Data of Consciousness," is devoted to this concept of immediate consciousness. In it, Bergson argues for a distinction between *immediate consciousness*, which is how something feels to an individual directly without any cognitive process or attempt at representation through language, and *reflective consciousness*, which requires thinking and implies through logic, language, science, or some other form of representation.[40] Inherent in the distinction between types of consciousness are two distinct conceptions of time. As Bergson's analogies will demonstrate, reflective consciousness thinks of time in terms of space and takes no account of duration, because that duration is accessed through intuitive experience. This mistaken notion of thinking of time in terms of space is Bergson's major critique in *Time and Free Will*, i.e., that mechanistic, empirical thinking has mistakenly overreached in trying to analyze human experience and that science has wrongly conflated duration with space and thus wrongly conflated man's experience in duration with his perception of space. Here again we find Bergson taking his stand against scientific bias by promoting a doctrine of subjective dynamism at the same time as immediate consciousness is rooted in the relative experience of the individual and not explicable through scientific theory.

To articulate his theory of duration and to attack the wrongful conflation of consciousness in space and time, Bergson employs his concept of multiplicity, a distinct way of thinking in spatial terms. According to Bergson, multiplicity is only applicable to external actions, measurable phenomena, and material objects. While Bergson will go on to discuss two types of multiplicity in *Time and Free Will*, the type of multiplicity currently being discussed here is one of quantity, not quality—a distinction

---

40. For Bergson's full treatment of immediate and reflective consciousnesses, see *Time and Free Will*, 1–74.

that Bergson promotes. According to Bergson, quantity is a verifiable idea that connotes knowing in space. Bergson will use the analogy of counting to explain multiplicity. When one counts objects one does so spatially, moving successively from one item to the next; thus, a spatial knowing takes place. I will return to Bergson's analogy of counting in a moment.

Bergson will argue that this type of quantitative knowing cannot be applied to qualitative human states or time. As noted by Gilles Deleuze—the late twentieth- to early twenty-first-century philosopher most associated with extending Bergsonian philosophy—to qualitatively know in time, rather than quantitatively know than space "is the Bergsonian leitmotif: People have seen only differences in degree where there are differences in kind."[41] Bergson constructs his theory of multiplicity to dislodge spatial thinking's emphasis on successive degree and to promote a thinking oriented in kind. To explain multiplicity, Bergson uses the analogy of counting sheep. When a shepherd counts sheep, he ignores the individual characteristics of each sheep and equates the living animals into equivalent units. The shepherd counts these units in a space; moving from sheep to sheep is a spatial movement that positions each object in relation to the next. Bergson's conclusion is that multiplicity (which in this analogy means counting or spatial knowing) is a spatial phenomenon, not one of duration. To count, one has to process objects successively, keeping the previous image in mind as the next one is counted in spatial succession. Multiplicity of quantity accounts for measurable degree, tallies the countable, and seeks to empirically assess the external.

As with the analogy of counting sheep, each image lies in juxtaposition to the next, and because juxtaposition is a form of spatial perception, understanding is subjected to multiplicity: "it is in space that such a juxtaposition takes place and not in pure duration. In fact, it will be easily granted that counting material objects means thinking all these objects together, thereby leaving them in space."[42] Juxtaposition implies simultaneity, and, according to Bergson, perception of juxtaposition and simultaneity presupposes space. Bergson's theory of duration, antithetical to the application of spatial thinking to conceptions of time, precludes spatial perception and reflective consciousness by asserting that human experience, human feeling, and immediate consciousness are manifested in duration.

---

41. Deleuze, *Bergsonism*, 23.
42. Bergson, *Time and Free Will*, 59–60.

The assertion that time is the medium for the manifestation of human experience, feeling, and immediate consciousness is at the heart of Lewis, Eliot, and Auden's theologies of time. In *The Great Divorce*, duration is where the divine meets the temporal. But, beyond duration being "when the eternal can be met," time also reveals the nature of one's dynamic spiritual growth. In Lewis's novel, one's spiritual state, whether redeemed or unredeemed, manifests itself progressively *and* retroactively through time. Hence, "heaven" and "hell" in the novel are said to work through time to either redeem or damn: "not knowing that Heaven, once attained, *will work backwards and turn* even that agony into a glory . . . little dreaming *how damnation will spread back and back* into their past and contaminate the pleasure of sin. *Both processes begin* even before death."[43] Likewise, the process of one's immediate consciousness working in time operates in conjunction with this spiritual dynamism. The development of consciousness in time is played out by how characters in *The Great Divorce* react to the novel's theological theme of salvation, resulting in a conflation between immediate consciousness and spiritual inclination. Thus, the growth or regression of characters' immediate consciousness in time is inseparable from their spiritual growth through time.

In *Four Quartets*, Eliot also employs a Bergsonian model of epistemology in which knowing is divided between superficial perception and deeper spiritual perception. Purely experiential knowledge unaccompanied by spiritual enlightenment is partial knowing. Like Bergson's theory of the superficial self succumbing to social constructions of epistemology (explained later in this chapter) or his view of the misguided epistemology of distinct multiplicity, Eliot's experiential knowledge has, "at best, only a limited value."[44] The poem devalues this kind of learning because it applies a false pattern, a type of epistemological fixity, which runs counter to the dynamic reality of moments in duration:

> In the knowledge derived from experience.
> The knowledge imposes a pattern, and falsifies,
> For the pattern is new in every moment
> And every moment is new and shocking
> Valuation of all we have been.[45]

Experiential knowledge imposes a false pattern that takes on the newness of each moment but remains unable to impart meaningful

43. Lewis, *The Great Divorce*, 69.
44. Eliot, "Four Quartets," line 83.
45. Ibid., lines 84–88.

knowledge. The deeper knowledge that the poem's theology advocates entails both an experience of time and perception of that experience's meaning. This stanza ends with a proclamation that the only wisdom that one can hope for is that which leads to humility, and "humility is endless." Here Eliot couples epistemology with chronology in quintessentially Bergsonian manner. As the culmination of a deeper knowledge (immediate consciousness) dynamically experienced in time, humility takes on a durative nature, which for both Eliot and Bergson is "endless." If time manifests immediate consciousness, then it also takes part in shaping consciousness. In both Bergson and Eliot's work, duration contains the eternal; therefore, immediate consciousness partakes in that eternality. More will be said in chapter 4 about how Bergsonian duration develops in *Four Quartets*.

Like Lewis and Eliot, Auden promotes a theological form of immediate consciousness. Indeed, "Kairos and Logos" advances this correlation between consciousness and the Christian faith: if immediate consciousness is a true knowing from one's inner states, then from the vantage point of the Christian faith that knowing must come from one's inner redeemed spiritual state. "Kairos and Logos" begins with a condemnation of those who only attend to the "smells and furniture of the known world / Where conscience worshipped an aesthetic order."[46] Those fixed solely on the external are time-obsessed unbelievers condemned to death in time. On the other hand, there are others that experienced a "condescension of eternal order,"[47] when "predestined love fell like a daring meteor into time."[48] This latter group is Christians. Each group promotes an epistemology, the unbelievers a material, social knowing (akin to Bergson's distinct multiplicity) and the Christians a theological, perceptive knowing (akin to immediate consciousness). The poem moves from the epistemologies held by each group to their theological conclusion. The external thinking of the unredeemed results in echoes of "cold and absence" that say "we are your conscience of your own confusion."[49] The deeper thinking of the redeemed sees beyond the external to the spiritual workings of God in time. While the unredeemed have missed the meaning of the theological in time, the redeemed see potential for spiritual ascent in time. The redeemed proclaim their spirituality in time: "we are not lost."[50]

46. Auden, "Kairos and Logos," lines 2–3.
47. Ibid., lines 30.
48. Ibid., lines 28–29.
49. Ibid., lines 137–38.
50. Ibid., lines 145.

Bergson asserts immediate consciousness as a necessary fissure to distinct multiplicity, a way of breaking one's mistaken tendency to think about human nature scientifically. While an epistemology of "distinct multiplicity" (thinking in terms of space) can assess external phenomenon, it is precluded from measuring the inner states of immediate consciousness. Duration is where immediate consciousness is experienced. The problem that the scientific and philosophical model of the late nineteenth and early twentieth centuries created was to think about time the way one would think about space, through objective quantitative assessment.

It is the habitual way of spatial thinking that Bergson sought to dislodge: "let us note that when we speak of time, more often that not we think of a homogenous milieu where the events or facts of consciousness line themselves up, juxtaposing themselves as if in space, and succeed in forming a distinct multiplicity."[51] Here Bergson says that people are ingrained with spatial thinking, even in thinking about time. Thus, distinct multiplicity has encroached into human perceptions of time and so distorted the consciousness's relationship to duration. Besides reflective and immediate consciousness, intuition and analytical thinking, space and time, Bergson constructs another dualistic binary in *Time and Free Will*: homogeneity and heterogeneity. Bergson's mention of "homogeneous milieu" in the passage above was earlier analogized in the counting of sheep, where spatial thinking overlooks individuality and heterogeneity and one image is lined up in orderly juxtaposition to another. However, one cannot think of time in this way, as duration is only known through lived experience, and experience is thoroughly heterogeneous.

Indeed, the problem of applying spatial thinking to time is that no human's experience of time operates in homogeneous succession. Rather, human experience presupposes heterogeneity. For Bergson, the force of life is always in mind, and life itself always reveals heterogeneities: "In fact, qualitative differences are everywhere in nature . . . heterogeneity . . . constitutes the very foundation of our experience."[52] Human experience, reality itself, and their manifestations in duration are heterogeneously dynamic. No one perceives the same thing in the same way twice, and no experience is the same once repeated. Bergson critiques homogenized conceptions of space and the traditional mechanistic view of time in spatial terms as a "kind of reaction against this heterogeneity that constitutes

---

51. Bergson, *Time and Free Will*, 67.
52. Ibid., 67.

the very foundation of our experience."[53] Experiences, which stem from unfiltered inner states, have no boundaries and by sheer force of their dynamic nature undo the spatial conceptions that Bergson argues has overtaken philosophical understandings of time.

Western philosophy has privileged spatial thinking, which Bergson argues has intruded into man's thinking of time. The spatial thinking that prevailed in the late nineteenth and early twentieth century had created a "bastard concept" of time by which time itself is reduced to an annex of space. This dichotomy between space and time will be important for the theologies of time in Lewis, Eliot, and Auden. Each author shares Bergson's affinity for durative thinking, and each chooses time over space as the vehicle for themes of the eternal, salvation, and the development of spiritual consciousness. Indeed, Lewis, Eliot, and Auden will each endorse Bergson's idea that duration, not space, must subvert, even replace, the "phantom of that space which obsesses . . . consciousness."[54] Inner states move dynamically, interpenetrate one another, and organically succeed each in overlap and unpredictability. But, when reduced to spatial thinking, inner states take on a homogeneous nature, and are thus stripped of their inherent dynamism.

The very definition of Bergsonian "pure duration" is inseparably tied to its resistance to spatial homogenization. Bergson defines pure duration as "the form taken by the succession of our inner states of consciousness when our self lets itself live, when it abstains from establishing a separation between the present state and anterior states."[55] In other words, pure duration is the unhindered expression of the consciousness's inner states with no bifurcating notions of past, present, and future. What is particularly important here is Bergson's notion that true duration is contingent on abstaining from making a separation between present from past. Science compartmentalizes, categorizes, and catalogues anything under its jurisdiction. When applied to consciousness's inner states made manifest in time, the scientific approach objectifies the experience in attempts to classify it. An attempt to classify a past from a present from a future enacts this objectification. This approach, for Bergson, is not fitting for the subject of life. Life's dynamism works with time and time with life because by nature both are incalculably vitalistic. Therefore, past, present, and future flow seamlessly into one another as one durative state. Likewise,

53. Ibid., 72.
54. Ibid., 74.
55. Ibid., 74–75.

consciousness works in time, and neither time nor consciousness should be subjected to the non-intuitive thinking of science. Bergson's insistence that present and past must not be systematically separated coheres with his overall resistance to the scientific absorption of human experience. In his *Creative Evolution*, Bergson laments traditional scientific thinking's failure to capture the complex essence of duration,

> in time [scientific, mechanistic time] thus conceived, how could evolution, which is the very essence of life, ever take place? Evolution implies a real persistence of the past in the present, a duration, which is, as it were, a hyphen, a connecting link. In other words, to know a living being or natural system is to get at the interval of duration, while the knowledge of an artificial or mathematical system applies only to the extremity.[56]

Duration, as an extension of dynamic evolution, is the means of knowing the "interval of duration," that is, the present moment as a part of the larger process of evolution. The durative is the present, and the present only exists in the durative. The persistent force of time—a nuance of Bergson's theory that will be particularly important to Lewis, Eliot, and Auden's view of time as a theological conduit—makes the present moment a "hyphen" in the ever-evolving nature of life itself. To know the durative present is to practice intuition. Indeed, as will be further explored, to know the present is to know the essence of human life as it has been carried from the past. Bergson posits that scientific systems apply only to "extremity," the measurable material, and have nothing to say to an erasure of past and present. Duration is past, present, and future collapsed and experienced at once.

To explain the erasure of past and present and future in duration, Bergson gives the analogies of a melody and a shooting star. Melody he uses as a representation of duration. Melody presupposes an organization that, when heard, requires a perception that collapses any division into of past, present, and future. Melody collects past musical notes with present to produce a singular sensation. Interrogating one's perception of the succession of those notes, Bergson asks: "Could we not say that, if these notes succeed one another, we still perceive them as if they were inside one another and their ensemble were like a *living being* whose parts, though distinct, interpenetrate through the very effect of their solidarity?"[57] Though

---

56. Bergson, *Creative Evolution*, 20.
57. Bergson, *Time and Free Will*, 75.

the melody's notes are individual and successive, Bergson claims that each part comprises a single entity.

The experience of a melody is qualitatively holistic, not quantitatively distinct. Bergson builds on his analogy by saying the proof that a melody is like a singular living being is found when someone holds a note too long. In which case, attention is paid to the musical miscue not because someone broke the note's successive place in the tune, but because the long note shapes the entire tune's quality: "It is not its exaggerated length as such that will avert us to our mistake, but rather the qualitative change brought to the musical phrase as a whole."[58] When considering the entire melody as a whole qualitative entity, Bergson notes that "one could thus conceive succession without distinction as a mutual penetration, a solidarity, an intimate organization of elements of which would be representative of the whole, indistinguishable from it, and would not isolate itself from the whole except for abstract thought."[59]

As a symbol of duration, melody promotes a "succession without distinction," a blend of nuanced feelings and musical qualities experienced as a singularity. Trying to make distinction between the notes of a melody is qualitatively impossible; melody resists understanding in terms of spatial succession, thus exemplifying the heterogeneity of overlapping elements that constitute duration. Experiencing melody requires a synthesis of past, present, and future as the succession of each note collapses to one singular experience.

As Suzanne Guerlac describes in her explanation of the melody metaphor, "the musical phrase conveys the notion of ensemble that attaches to the experience of duration, and to the idea of the heterogeneous multiplicity—a multiplicity without homogeneity, in which states or feelings overlap or interpenetrate one another, instead of being organized into a distinct succession."[60] Time, or duration, hosts the dynamic interpenetrative nuances of experience. The melody proves a picture of how one can experience durative succession without distinction, and it is duration's nature that appeals so greatly to the Christian writers studied here. Lewis, Eliot, and Auden all found a theological conduit that can capture man's experience with God, and all find that conduit in a type of time that accounts for existential complexity and the force of time. As a theological conduit,

---

58. Ibid., 75.
59. Ibid., 75.
60. Guerlac, *Thinking in Time*, 67.

it is Bergsonian time that each author finds most fitting, and each injects Bergsonian duration with themes of divinity.

To further explain the nature of duration, Bergson uses the analogy of the shooting star. Bergson poses the question: what does it mean to talk about a type of movement that does not occur in space? Bergson's answer is what he calls "real movement" or "mobility,"[61] which are movements of quality or intensity, unexplainable in spatial terms. Bergson investigates what happens when one sees a shooting star:

> A rapid gesture, made with one's eyes shut, will assume for consciousness the form of a purely qualitative sensation as long as there is no thought of the space traversed. In a word, there are two elements to be distinguished in motion, the space traversed and the act by which we traverse it, the successive positions and the synthesis of these positions. The first of these elements is a homogeneous quantity: the second has no reality except in a consciousness: it is a quality or an intensity . . . .[62]

Bergson emphasizes that perceiving a shooting star is so instantaneous due to the speed of the star's movement through space that all sense of mobility is felt as "intensity," or as an act of conscious awareness. Though it is possible to chart the points in space through which the shooting star passes, the experience of witnessing the star's mobility requires an singular act of synthesis in which all points are perceived as one action. Bergson goes on to explain one perceives the shooting star as an *act*, not as a spatial movement:

> we attribute to the motion the divisibility of the space which it traverses, forgetting that it is quite possible to divide an object, but not an act: and on the other hand we accustom ourselves to projecting this act itself into space, to applying it to the whole of the line which the moving body traverses, in a word, to solidifying it: as if this localizing of a progress in space did not amount to asserting that, even outside consciousness, the past co-exists along with the present![63]

As a symbol of duration, the *act* of the shooting star cannot be counted, spatially measured, or divided into smaller units. Rather the star's movement from one point in space at one moment in time to another point in space at a successive moment requires temporal synthesis. Like

61. Bergson, *Time and Free Will*, 83.
62. Ibid., 83.
63. Ibid., 78.

intuition working in time, the singular experience of perceiving the star requires that the perceiver collapse notions of past, present, and future. Unlike science, which seeks to cut time and movement into successive moments, duration is concerned with qualitative elements of experience, which cannot be divided and scientifically processed. The shooting star *is* intuition in duration, an experiential perception in time that removes the temporal elements of time past, present, and future.

The Fragmented Self in Two Realms of Time

While duration is Bergson's theory of time as naturally, immediately experienced by consciousness, Bergson reveals that *time* itself is not duration. Rather, "time" is the symbolic representation of pure duration. Here Bergson begins to unfold the multi-dimensionality of his theory of duration. Bergson holds "time" to be the system through which we consciously experience duration, but as a system of representation it always hinders true immediacy. Duration is the consciousness's most immediate contact with time, but *time* is the symbol of duration as one conceptualizes it, speaks of it, and tries to represent it in some way. Duration is the thing itself, while time is its episteme. In differentiating duration from the episteme of time, Bergson embarks on a critique of language as a system of representation. Language, while necessary, is ultimately a system of representation that prevents one from true intuitive knowledge of real duration. Bergson explains, "Our external . . . social life has more practical importance for us than our individual, inner experience. We instinctively tend to solidify our impressions in order to express them in language . . . this reason that we confuse the feeling itself, which is in a perpetual mode of becoming, with its external object, which is permanent."[64] Bergson's critique of language is really one of daily human practice. People invest more in their social lives than in their interior ones, and when inner feelings are expressed they are done so in the language of the external. Whereas feelings always change and evolve, like the change in Bergson's *élan vital* and dynamic intuition, language is permanently fixed to external antecedents.

Thus, language simplifies, reduces, and distorts inner states. Bergson claims "above all we confuse [feeling] with the word that expresses this object. Just as the fleeting duration of our inner self fixes itself by projecting itself into homogenous space, so our impressions are constantly changing,

---

64. Ibid., 97.

wrapping themselves around the external object . . . adopting its precise contours and its immobility."[65] Intuition in duration is a knowing in time through immediate consciousness. However, language constantly calls the consciousness out of intuition into the external world, where any expression of inner states is reduced by the external's precise and immobile parameters. An example would be when someone confesses some personal pain by saying, "my heart broke in two." For Bergson that language could never convey the reality of the emotion. Even as the words are uttered the truest meaning of the expression is reduced to metaphor of quantity, physicality, and distinct multiplicity. Thus, the deepest experience of the one whose heart is broken is simplified through the language used to express its brokenness.

Because language obscures immediate consciousness *in duration* through symbolic representation that simplifies inner experience, Bergson builds into his theory of duration yet another layer of duality to account for modes of subjective experience in both types of multiplicity. As already noted, distinct multiplicity is quantitative thinking in spatial terms, and confused multiplicity is qualitative thinking in time (a knowing in duration). Because, as noted previously, Bergson holds that people are more interested in the practical issues of their social lives; because the dominant mode of thinking is scientific and spatial; and because language distorts inner states, he constructed a theory of two selves. Essentially, the two types of multiplicity (distinct and confused) and the two concepts of duration (real duration and its representation, "time") correspond to two types of experience, the socially conventional and the heterogeneously real. This observation leads Bergson to propose a superficial self and a fundamental self.

Whereas the superficial self conforms to the restraints of socially prescribed conventions and the restraints of language, the fundamental self connects with the humans passions and the heterogeneously real. According to Bergson, "the self only touches the external world by its surface" and "that is why our superficial psychological life unfolds in a homogenous milieu, without this mode of representation costing us much effort."[66] Because of its failure as a representative system due to spatial and reductive thinking, the external world easily enables the fundamental self, with its deeper inner passions, to be reduced into a state of homogeneity. Bergson notes that a way one can tell that duration has so easily been

---

65. Ibid., 97.
66. Ibid., 93–94.

imposed upon by spatial, quantitative thinking is because one only needs to "remove from the self the faculty of perceiving homogenous time" and to "detach this superficial layer [of homogenous time] from the psychic events [of superficial perception] that it uses to regulate itself."[67] Bergson here introduces dreams as a way of exemplifying how the fundamental self can create such a break superficial knowing from homogeneity.

As an example of the kind of intuitive knowing that connects the knower to duration, dreams remove the filters of representative systems and allow for immediate consciousness of duration. Bergson claims "Dream places us precisely in [the break from the homogeneous and connection with the heterogeneous real]. For sleep, by slowing down the play or our organic functions, mainly modifies the surface of communication between the self and external things."[68] In this state of modification via dreams, "we no longer measure duration, we feel it."[69] Again emerges Bergson's motif of an existential knowing without measurability. In terms of the preceding discussion of the dynamic nature of human interiority expressed in Bergson's *élan vital* ("vital impulse"), dreams demonstrate the qualitative state of duration that Bergson for which strongly advocates. It is true to the vital impulse of human interiority to experience time without the *confused instinct* of scientifically quantifying time in measurable units.

What dreams demonstrate for Bergson is the ability for the self to experience duration intuitively. Dreams also exhibit a splitting of the self and the self's inclination for superficiality at the expense of intuitive interiority. Dreams highlight the two selves' representation (superficial and fundamental) of two conceptions of time (mistakenly understood quantitative "time" and real duration) and reiterate the importance of consciously experiencing duration. For it is the "attentive psychology" (i.e., the intuitive knower) that discerns "a duration whose heterogeneous moments interpenetrate . . . beneath homogeneous duration."[70] According to Bergson, the challenge is to delve "beneath the numerical multiplicity of conscious state" to find a "qualitative multiplicity," but, as Bergson complains "we usually content ourselves with the . . . shadow of the self, projected into homogeneous space."[71] Bergson divides the superficial self from the fundamental self on the basis of which duration one seeks to

---

67. Ibid., 93.
68. Ibid., 94.
69. Ibid.
70. Ibid., 95.
71. Ibid..

know. Bergson lauds the fundamental self as that which breaks beyond the socially conditioned concept of time, while he criticizes the superficial self for its contentment with a homogenized construction of duration, rather than of real duration.

This critique of the dichotomized self's tendency to shift to the superficial is important for understanding what Lewis, Eliot, and Auden do with the Bergsonian system. In the "Dry Salvages," Eliot will cry, "we had the experience but missed the meaning. / And approach to the meaning restores the experience in a different form." As will be further demonstrated in chapter 4's look at *Four Quartets*, Eliot depicts a Bergsonesque bifurcation between superficial experience and deeper spiritual meaning. In so doing, Eliot splinters the existential self into two types, the self that merely has the experience and the self that restores the meaning through experience. Theologically, Eliot's dualistic differentiation of experience and meaning, the mere "experiencer" and the restorer of meaning, will be shared in Lewis's narrative in *The Great Divorce* and in Auden's rhetoric in "Kairos and Logos." Like Eliot, Lewis and Auden employ a Bergsonian multi-dimensionality through which both authors complicate concepts like experience, perception, spiritual states, and, of course, time. Chapter 3 on *The Great Divorce* will show that Lewis builds upon a Bergsonian dualism, founded upon two types of "self," two modes of experience, and two kinds of time. Auden's very title, "Kairos and Logos," sets up a dualism of chronology and theology. The poem will unfold a Christian view of history that oscillates between the temporal and the eternal that interrupts it. Caught in that oscillation are those whose perceptions of time determine their experience, and whose experiences help form what self they are, whether redeemed or not.

Lewis, Eliot, and Auden all share Bergson's interest in the world beyond the superficial and in the self that relates to that world. Lewis's *The Great Divorce* will especially explore Bergson's concept of the shadowed self that has mistakenly taken the superficial for the real. Perhaps there is no starker an image in Lewis's work than when a bus full of "people" find themselves to be ghosts once in the presence of ultimate spiritual reality. Eliot's *Four Quartets* will also approach Bergson's paradigm of the fundamental self with what has been described as the poem's "plea for the inner life."[72] Auden will poetize the Incarnation as the moment in time when the atemporal interrupts the temporal "ego-centric world" of shallow

---

72. Carpenter, *Brideshead*, 92–93.

selfhood.⁷³ In that divine, incarnate act a deeper sense of time and self can emerge, if the "unconditioned" eternal is sought.

Like Bergson, the three authors I am investigating see an inexorable connection between the experiences of the deeper self and its manifestations in time. The manifestation of the fundamental self's inner states must break through superficial self, which "substitutes the symbol for the reality, or only perceives the reality through the symbol."⁷⁴ Because the superficial self substitutes the real with the symbolic so perpetually it remains in a "refracted and subdivided" that "lends itself much better to the demands of social life in general and of language in particular."⁷⁵ Bergson holds that the regression of the self results in losing sight of the fundamental self with its inner states, which ultimately leads to an inability to intuitively know duration. Once the self has succumbed to superficiality, it hinders experience of the durative. Bergson's concern for the removal of superficial symbols is an attempt at a new way of knowing and, by extension, living. Indeed, to remove the superficial representations that entrap the self is to return to the transformative task of intuition through which the self can truly know and experientially act in the durative.

THE FORCE OF TIME

Because of a number of hindrances, the spatially dominated way of thinking that characterized Western consciousness, language's reductive nature, and the self's tendency to succumb to the problems of the aforementioned, most people do not experience intuition. Of all the aforementioned hindrances to an intuition unto duration, Bergson highlights the problem of language in *Time and Free Will*, positing it as the most common obstacle to intuition. Beyond the previously discussed problem of language's inability to express inner states due to its reductive nature, language also imposes an artificial repetition by the act of naming. No two inner states or experiences in time are the same, but language's limitations in labeling an experience forces an over-simplifying repetition on the experience. An example of Bergson's complaint with language's repetitive nature is how one describes the feeling of falling in love—an example that Bergson will himself use to demonstrate the force of time on consciousness. At thirteen

---

73. Pandey, *The Religious Poetry of W. H. Auden*, 73–74.
74. Bergson, *Time and Free Will*, 96.
75 Ibid.

year's old the feeling is excited, jovial, and maybe wildly irrational. At fifty-three years old, the feeling of being in love might be better expressed as an assured calm, a peace, or a sense of emotional security. Though the feelings between the two individuals are vastly different, the language used to describe both would be identically expressed as, "being in love." Clearly language is not sufficient to capture an experience.

Bergson uses the experience of a sensation to indict language's restrictions. He complains, "A particular taste, a particular scent, pleased me when I was a child and repels me today. Nevertheless, I give the same name to the sensation, and I speak as if the scent and the taste had remained identical, and as if it were just my tastes that had changed."[76] This naming the qualitatively different is a false solidifying of sensation, which leads to an objectifying of experience: "For sensations and tastes appear to me as things as soon as I isolate them and name them."[77] The heart of Bergson's critique is a return to the vital impulse of both human nature and time. Both life and time ever progress, constituting a greater nature than the language that seeks to translate them: "for in the human soul there is hardly anything but progressions."[78] All sensations, all experiences, and all inner states "are modified through repetition" and if one perceives life as unchanging, then that is because it has been perceived "through the object that was its cause, or through the word that translates it."[79] One might wonder what relevance Bergson's critique of language has for his understanding of time, but within this critique he makes his strongest argument for the connection between inner states and time: that the force of time ensures that one never experiences the same feeling twice.

Despite language's influence on conforming every experience to its reductive, repetitive sameness, Bergson insists that all experiences are altered through repetition because repetition alters the nature of the experience. Using the analogy of love, Bergson shows how time works to unfold consciousness in dynamic growth:

> A violent love, a deep melancholy invades our soul, provoking a thousand diverse elements that melt together, interpenetrate, without definite contours, without the least tendency to separate themselves one from another. Their originality is at this cost. A moment ago each one of them borrowed an indefinable

76. Ibid., 97.
77. Ibid., 96.
78. Ibid., 98.
79. Ibid., 98.

coloration from the milieu where it was placed. Now it is bleached out and ready to receive a name. . . . Feeling is a living being, which develops, and is therefore always changing . . . when we separate those moments out, *unfurling time into space*, the feeling loses its color.[80]

Bergson sees in one emotion a multiplicity of interpenetrative, cross-pollinating elements. To translate any one of them—i.e., to name it—brings these emotional elements outside the realm of time and hurls them wrongly into the quantifiable paradigm of spatial thinking. Because "feeling is a living being," the only appropriate medium to manifest those living feelings is the force of time. The effect of falsely parsing out inner states is a removal from the medium of time, leaving one with only a shadow of self.[81]

Bergson's notion of the force of time is expounded on most fully in the third chapter of *Time and Free Will*. One of Bergson's main concerns is the debate over human freedom versus a philosophy of determinism. Above all, Bergson champions the dynamism inherent in life, consciousness, and duration; therefore, to claim any form of determinism would be a negation of Bergson's entire worldview. Just as Bergson opposes the reduction of the internal to the rules of physical science, so he claims that submitting the human consciousness to the model of mechanistic science only eliminates the possibility of free will. Though Bergson's advocacy of freewill is a major motif in *Time and Free Will*, it is not in itself relevant to this study on Lewis, Eliot, and Auden's use of Bergsonian duration.[82] Nevertheless, Bergson's discussion of free will versus determinism does foster another characteristic dualism that is relevant to his theory of the force of time.

Unlike the scientific theory of conservation, which holds that the energy of inanimate, material objects remains the same over time, Bergson holds time to be the type of energy guiding the progress of the animate. Indeed, time cannot touch the world of the inanimate: "The vague and instinctive belief in the conservation of one identical quantity of matter, and of force, depends on the fact that inert matter does not seem to exist in time (duration) or at least does not conserve any trace of past time.

80. Ibid., 98–99.
81. Ibid., 99.
82. For more on Bergson's treatment of free will, see: Guerlac's concise summary in *Thinking in Time*, 77–93; Deleuze's chapter "Elan Vital as Movement of Differentiation," 91–113; John Crane's "Golding and Bergson," 136–41; and the very early article by D. Basillie, "Prof. Bergson on Time and Free Will," 357–78.

But this is not the case in the realm of life."[83] Duration is reserved for the world of the living, for the élan vital, and acts on inner states causally, shaping and forming the multiplicity of intuitive thoughts: "duration in time seems to act as a cause, and the idea of putting things back in their place after a certain period of time is absurd, since this kind of regression in time has never occurred in a living being."[84] Unlike the principle of conservation, time is its own form of energy that leaves nothing the same.

If time is a force, an energy acting on inner states, then its implications for human experience are important. All human experience, all feelings, and all conscious activity can hardly be understood outside of time. Time is the primary domain of human experience, and experience the sphere in which time is made manifest. The fact that experiences always change and never completely replicate themselves testifies to the force of time on human consciousness. According to Bergson, time leaves nothing the same ("the same does not remain the same here").[85] Time acts according to the nature of life, and life itself always "progresses and endures in time."[86] Time is not just a force; it is also a transformative agent. It leaves nothing as is. Rather, time transforms consciousness and experience. Whereas time neither harms nor helps inanimate objects, "it is a gain . . . for a conscious [being]" as the animate progresses through time.[87] This gain is the growth of consciousness through and in time. According to Bergson, time's concern is with the living. Its "gain" is lost on the inanimate, but on the animate time has transformative properties. Bergson uses the example of the sensation of pain as an example of time's transforming work.

According to Bergson, a sensation cannot move back in time, cannot be un-experienced in the realm of consciousness. Therefore, pain, as a symbol of durative force, "changes to the point of becoming unbearable."[88] In change the sensation "reinforces itself and seems to fill and enlarge itself with its whole past."[89] What Bergson means here is that the force of time is strengthened by the past. According to Bergson in his most seminal work, *Creative Evolution*, past time moves into the present, and by exten-

83. Bergson, *Time and Free Will*, 115.
84. Ibid., 115.
85. Ibid., 115.
86. Bergson, *Creative Evolution*, 34.
87. Bergson, *Time and Free Will*, 116.
88. Ibid., 115.
89. Ibid., 115.

sion the future, in a manner comparable to the increased intensifying of energy constantly increasing. The present is the dynamic *now* charged by the energy of the dynamic *then*. And it is "the continuous progress of the past which gnaws into the future and which swells as it advances."[90] The future as a continuation of the durative act, like the past and present, demonstrates the virtually endless working of the force of time.

The culmination of Bergson's theories on the force of real duration calls the individual back to a state of introspection. Because, "real duration [time] is that duration which gnaws on things, and leaves on them the mark of its tooth," and if, according to Bergson, "everything is in time," then "everything changes inwardly, and the same concrete reality never recurs."[91] One whose consciousness is yoked with duration will experience the inward changes brought about by the force of time. But, as Bergson has already cautioned in his articulation of the superficial selves and the two kinds of time, many people forego the inward changes that time brings because they have traded durative thinking for shallow social thinking. Those whose worldviews are more informed by the socially external than by their internal states will confuse the true nature of duration with the mere passing of moments. Thus, they miss the intuitive connection with duration and so remain superficially connected with the transformative force of time.

According to Bergson, "we are not accustomed to observing ourselves directly but instead perceive ourselves through forms borrowed from the external world, we end up thinking that real duration, the duration lived by consciousness, is the same as the duration that slips inert atoms without changing anything."[92] Here again is Bergson's dualistic notion of duration. Real duration with its dynamic force on the individual's inner states is often mistaken for the social construction of time that impotently moves through the material world. Bergson reiterates his theory of two types of time and challenges the individual to consider the role of time in relation to the inner life. Real duration is always flowing and consciousness is always progressing through this flow. To recall, fundamental to immediate consciousness is the role of lived experience. Bergson radically opposes scientific rationalism or any other epistemology antithetical to human nature's inner states. Time is the manifestation of immediate consciousness because they both share the same dynamic nature. Lived

---

90. Bergson, *Creative Evolution*, 11.
91. Ibid., 31.
92. Bergson, *Time and Free Will*, 116.

experience is equally as dynamic and equally contributory to the development of consciousness in time.[93] In Bergson's theory, the force of time as duration is the realm of the inner life. Duration's force is one of becoming, of transformation. To experience true time is to share in its dynamism and be transformed at the deepest level of inner consciousness. Indeed, transformative change through knowing and experiencing in dynamic time is the culmination of Bergson's theory of intuition and duration.

From Duration to Theological Articulation

Creating Theologies of Time from Bergson's Theories

The three most important implications of Bergson's theory of duration for Lewis, Eliot, and Auden are the idea that time is a force, the belief that any one moment contains the eternal, and the notion of dualism. There is never a moment in time that is not deeply, dynamically transformative. Time works on the intuitive individual's immediate consciousness to enact inward change. The past works into the present through memory and intuition, thereby giving present time an infinite amount of energy, which greatly influences the future. The consciousness flows with the force of time, growing as time progress, and the individual is changed through time. A second implication is that any moment in temporal time is a conduit for the eternal, real duration. Bergson's idea of duration breaks down quantitative notions of a successive past, present, and future by showing that all epochs of time are qualitatively one. Time as experienced day-to-day cloaks the deeper world of real duration. All of temporal time is the medium for all of eternal duration, "Eternity no longer hovers over time, as an abstraction; it underlies time, as a reality."[94]

The last implication of Bergson's philosophy important for this study is the dualistic theoretical design so pervasive in his thinking. Bergson presents two ways of knowing (distinct multiplicity and confused multiplicity), two forms of consciousness (reflective and immediate), two selves (superficial and fundamental), and two types of time (temporal time and real duration). At the heart of Bergson's dualism is the belief that both man

---

93. It is at this point that Bergson turns to the second primary subject of *Time and Free Will*, the reality of free will. For Bergson, the force of time is made most manifest in the exercise of free will. While vital Bergson's meta-philosophical agenda in *Time and Free Will*, the role of free will is not within this study's purview.

94. Bergson, *Creative Evolution*, 159.

and his experiences in the world are divided into the existentially empty and the existentially meaningful. As this chapter has shown, what Bergson values most is a manifestation of man's inner states, which leads to a way of experiencing life in time. Deeper meaning, metaphysical meaning, comes from the connection of immediate consciousness with time, and whatever experiences do not come from this connection are subsumed by the superficial.

Lewis, Eliot, and Auden take Bergson's ideas about time and experience and from them form their own theologies of time. Like Bergson, who saw time as a vitally important topic for the development of twentieth-century ideas about reality and human experience, Lewis, Eliot, and Auden were equally invested in the idea of time. Where Bergson held the study of time in conjunction with the *élan vital* ("vital impulse") of life itself, Lewis, Eliot, and Auden held their theologies of time in close relationship to God's own relationship to man. Whereas Bergson stops short of theological propositions about time and experience, Lewis, Eliot, and Auden advance theological articulation. The force of time to transform, the function of time as vehicle for the eternal, and a dichotomous belief in man's inner state are all themes implemented by these three twentieth-century Christian thinkers. Lewis, Eliot, and Auden find a middle way between their Christian faith and twentieth-century ideals in Henri Bergson's thinking. The system that Bergson creates is one of openness to the metaphysical, and with that motif Lewis, Eliot, and Auden construct a theory of time ideologically akin to Bergsonism. Precluding the idea that mechanistic determinism and human experience in a closed system in which the material is all there is, Bergson expands the temporal world into a world beyond, a world of transformative agency and eternal influence, and in so doing creates a philosophy that Lewis, Eliot, and Auden can poetically theologize.

3

Meeting the Eternal

Bergsonism and the Theology of Present Time in C. S. Lewis's The Great Divorce

In this chapter I intend to do two things: show C. S. Lewis to be a Christian thinker intensely interested in secular philosophies of twentieth century and analyze Lewis's theories of time in conjunction with those of Henri Bergson's. C. S. Lewis is arguably the most preeminent Christian writer of the twentieth century, a writer whose theological writings eclipse those of Eliot and Auden in popularity, in number of theological publications, and in influence on twentieth-century Christian theology. Thus, his place in this book is central. Lewis is also important because his work, even more so than Eliot's and Auden's, aims to articulate theological themes through creative literature and so stands as one of the best examples of theologized literature from the first half of the twentieth century. Whereas Eliot and Auden had prominent pre-conversion careers and continued in their post-conversion careers to write poetry unrelated to Christian theology, Lewis's popular career did not begin until after his conversion. Indeed, apart from his relatively unknown collection of atheistic poetry *Spirits in Bondage* (1919) and his long narrative poem *Dymer* (1926), all of Lewis's publications, which number over fifty, came after his conversion to Christianity. Almost the entirety of Lewis's career spanned his post-conversion life, and the majority of his writings were devoted to communicating Christian theology to a twentieth-century audience.

Lewis's theological and apologetic works were often in conversation with what he deemed to be worldviews counter to the Christian faith. And with these competing philosophies, Lewis conversed from the vantage point of Christian theology. Lewis's affinity for philosophical engagement is no doubt an important contributor to his adoption of Bergsonism. Largely philosophical and theological responses to Bergsonian thinking, delineated in the previous chapter, Lewis's theories of time were so influenced by early twentieth-century thinker Henri Bergson that without Bergsonian duration *The Great Divorce* as Lewis fans now know it would not exist.

Indeed, there is no other twentieth-century thinker that influenced Lewis's theology of time as much as Bergson's secular philosophy. Seen in the light of both Bergson's theories and Lewis's Christian faith, Lewis's novel *The Great Divorce* is a construction of a Christian theology of time on the ideas of Bergsonian duration. The novel's Bergsonian duration shows that the force of time transforms human consciousness, that life dynamically changes in a process of ever becoming, and that the spiritual world behind the material comprises ultimate reality. Lewis combines his Christian faith with Bergson's philosophies to produce a theme of redemption—a redemption revealed through and enacted by duration, and particularly revealed by the theme of the present moment. Indeed, in Lewis, it is in the present moment that all eternity comes to bear on the human experience of time.

Lewis the Creative Theologian

C. S. Lewis—Christian apologist, literary critic, medievalist, mythologizer, theologian, fantastic world maker—most fiercely pushed against the subjectivities and fragmented ideologies of modernism, yet it was against the context of twentieth-century philosophies that he established his prolific literary and theological career. Indeed, the modernist era in which he lived was the single most dominant, powerful, and formative force in Lewis's life because he so frequently combated its ideals. In her popular work, *The Emperor's Clothes*, British poet, novelist, and critic Kathleen Nott rightly charged Lewis with trying to "make theology paramount again" in the modern age.[1] By "again" Nott implies that religious devotion in the twenti-

---

1. Nott, *The Emperor's Clothes*, 254.

Meeting the Eternal

eth century had shifted from the theocentric to the anthropocentric. This was a shift Lewis sought to undo through his significant body of theological works. Lewis was keenly aware of the difficult position of the theological thinker in the twentieth century. As his famous work, *God in the Dock*, declares, modern man does not readily accept the tenets of the Christian faith. And in 1954, in his inaugural lecture at Cambridge, Lewis would claim that the greatest shift in the history of human society occurred early in the nineteenth century, which ushered in modernism and the dawning of what Lewis would deem as the post-Christian era.[2]

As a Christian thinker, Lewis expressed no shortage of concerns about the twentieth-century world's antithetical stance towards Christianity. The world had changed with the advent of modernism, and Lewis was profoundly affected by a world that caused, as Rabate puts it, "either a sharp division or a slower splintering of the old self."[3] And while Lewis remained in constant conversation with twentieth-century ideologies, he frequently indicted the modern age for the dissolution of universal morality, a crisis in belief in universals, and brood of destructive ideologies, particularly subjectivism, a philosophical system that holds the individual's subjective experience as fundamental for all worldview and morality. In one discussion Lewis identified the shortcomings of this philosophy before he even named it:

> One cause of misery and vice is always present with us in the greed and pride of men, but at certain periods in history this is greatly increased by the temporary prevalence of some false philosophy. Correct thinking will not make good men of out bad ones; but a purely theoretical error may remove the ordinary checks to evil and deprive good intentions of their natural support. An error of this sort is abroad at present . . . I am referring to Subjectivism.[4]

According to Lewis, Subjectivism characterized his present age. Lewis saw in the "false philosophy" of Subjectivism the problem of the autonomous self whose devotion is given to the authority of subjective experience, rather than to any notion of absolute morality. This self-derived authority was an ideological error from Lewis's Christian perspective, and an error that he thought characterized the early to mid-twentieth century. Against this and other philosophical branches of twentieth-century

2. Lewis, "De Descriptione Temporum" in *They Asked for a Paper*, 18–21.
3. Rabate, *1913*, 141.
4. Lewis, *Christian Reflections*, 72.

ideology, Lewis produced theological works that argued that every aspect of thought and life pertain to God.

As Lewis insists in *Mere Christianity*, "The whole purpose for which we exist is to be taken into the life of God. Wrong ideas about what that life is will make it harder."[5] To communicate the message of right theological thinking and to warn against wrong thinking about God is the responsibility of the theological writer, and Lewis believed that conveying this message was especially important for his day. He firmly maintained that the times he lived in were spiritually empty and the modern world bereft of universal moral standards. Indeed, he found the culture of the early twentieth century to be spiritually impotent because man had lost the ability to enliven society with moral meaning. Lewis believed that secular philosophies like Subjectivism and movements like modernism had bifurcated mankind from morals, divorced beliefs from meaning, and separated God from man. Lewis negatively delineated the state of twentieth-century morality in *The Abolition of Man*:

> we continue to clamour for those very qualities we are rendering impossible. You can hardly open a periodical without coming across the statement that what our civilization needs is more "drive," or dynamism, or self-sacrifice, or "creativity." In a sort of ghastly simplicity we remove the organ and demand the function. We make men without chests and expect of them virtue and enterprise. We laugh at honour and are shocked to find traitors in our midst. We castrate and bid the geldings be fruitful.[6]

For Lewis, twentieth-century ideology—in its subjectivities—inverted a natural order, further breaking an already splintered world that had once adhered to a unifying theologico-moral code. In his view, the belief that God was man's authority was a crucial tenet of premodernist society that had been tragically lost. Man had become the end of all things, had turned inside himself for meaning, and had discarded God's presence in life and art, so that Lewis pronounces modern man's problem as one of spiritual inversion. According to Lewis, an exaltation of the self over divinity—a paradigm discussed in chapter 1—is the distinct condition of twentieth-century thought. In his critique of modern man's unwillingness to submit to a higher entity, Lewis says,

---

5. Lewis, *Mere Christianity*, 161.
6. Lewis, *The Abolition of Man*, 26.

> The ancient man approached God (or even the gods) as the accused person approaches his judge. For the modern man the roles are reversed. He is the judge: God is in the dock. He is quite a kindly judge: if God should have a reasonable defence for being the god who permits war, poverty and disease, he is ready to listen to it. The trial may even end in God's acquittal. But the important thing is that Man is on the Bench and God in the Dock.[7]

The twentieth century, according to Lewis, brought with it an inverted understanding of humanity and divinity, in that God was no longer the arbiter of human morality. Modern man has become the judge, displacing God as the ultimate authority in human experience. Lewis's concept of spiritual inversion, man's situating God as the defendant, is also depicted in his novel *Till We Have Faces*, a mythic retelling in which the protagonist levels accusations at the gods for what she perceives to be ill-treatment. This prosecuting of God is an important part of Lewis's diagnosis of the modern condition: man has usurped divine authority, putting both God and commonly held moral precepts under man's discretion. *Till We Have Faces* narrates an example of this moral inversion and will show that even man's best efforts result in perversions: "Now mark [yet again] the cruelty of the gods. There is no escape from them into sleep or madness. . . ."[8] Orual, the novel's narrator, displays antagonism, hostility, and even rebellion toward the gods, which attitudes Lewis intimates are all symptomatic of twentieth-century morality.[9]

It is important for my purposes here to emphasize that though Lewis held to the tenets of the Christian faith that he saw threatened by twentieth-century ideology, Lewis's articulations of the faith were inescapably influenced by that ideology. Many of his theological works (*The Screwtape Letters*, *The Abolition of Man*, *The Weight of Glory*) and all of his apologetic works (e.g., *Miracles*, *Mere Christianity*, *The Four Loves*) engage non-Christian ideas prevalent in his day.

In the last few decades, Lewis scholars have increasingly connected the man with twentieth-century currents of thought. Prolific biographer

---

7. Lewis, *God in the Dock*, 244.
8. Lewis, *Till We Have Faces*, 80.
9. *Till We Have Faces* is replete with what Lewis describes elsewhere as the "God in the dock" paradigm, which he believed exemplified twentieth-century morality, e.g., Orual's confession of alienation from the divine, "I was like a condemned man waiting for his executioner, for I believed that some sudden stroke of the gods would fall on me very soon" (ibid., 183).

A. N. Wilson asserts that Lewis experienced sustained, thriving popularity because his writings, "while being self-consciously and deliberately at variance with the twentieth century, are paradoxically in tune with the needs and concerns of our times."[10] Sanford Schwartz, who writes about Bergson's influence on Lewis, likewise situates Lewis in his philosophical milieu amidst the most influential twentieth-century conversations about reality and time.

Sanford Schwartz's reading of Lewis's work reconciles it with the modernist world in which it was published. For instance, Schwartz says of Lewis's popular sci-fi work, *Perelandra* (1943), "we may begin to look at Lewis's novel less as an irreconcilable struggle between an old-fashioned Christian humanism and a newfangled heresy than as the effort of a modern Christian intellectual to sustain and enrich the former through critical engagement with the latter."[11] Behind Schwartz's words is discontent with how the majority of Lewis scholars cannot reconcile him with twentieth-century ideas, a position held, for instance, by James Como (*Branches of Heaven: The Geniuses of C. S. Lewis*), Bruce Edwards (*Further Up and Further In: Understanding C. S. Lewis's The Lion, the Witch and the Wardrobe*), Joseph Pearce (*C. S. Lewis and the Catholic Church*), and Clyde Kilby (*The Christian World of C. S. Lewis*). While debate about how Lewis's theology and writing fit into his twentieth-century context has been dominated by scholars who hold Lewis hostile to his modern world, Schwartz calls for an interpretation of Lewis as an engaged, *twentieth-century* Christian thinker.

Schwartz's argument mirrors my approach to Lewis's work by reading Lewis alongside his modernist contemporaries. Like the twentieth-century Lewis that Schwartz's work highlights, my portrait of Lewis is one of a Christian author, whose work is responsive to the philosophies of his time, perennially yet diversely an engaged answer to twentieth-century, non-Christian ideologies. It is time to situate Lewis's theological writings in some of the most prominent philosophical discourses of the twentieth century, like those of Bergson, which so shaped the imaginative writer's theological thinking. To see Lewis's ideas among the modernist ideologies that so surrounded his work, one need not look any farther than the theme of time and Lewis's assimilation and employment of Bergsonian duration.

I have long thought that to detect a line of thought in one of Lewis's works is to gain an understanding of all of Lewis's writings. Lewis scholar David Downing makes a similar argument, when he says, "one always

---

10. Wilson, *C. S. Lewis*, ix.
11. Schwartz, "Paradise Reframed," 571.

senses in Lewis's books 'the one in the many.' His singular way of looking at things, his characteristic habits of thought and speech, developed early in his life and remained remarkably constant. So there is a fascinating interconnectedness in all the books Lewis wrote: reading any one of them casts light upon all the others."[12] Like Downing, who argues that one element in Lewis's work reflects a larger pattern, I see a pattern: that the engaged attention to ideologies contemporary to him displayed in works like *God in the Dock*[13] and *The Problem of Pain* takes on a new attentiveness in his adoption of Bergsonism in *The Great Divorce*.

Because he is Christian thinker influenced by his twentieth-century context, Lewis formulates narratives that speak to ideologies influential in his time, and he does so through theological themes he deems relevant to the philosophical context in which he writes. While works like *Till We Have Faces* and *The Great Divorce* are Lewis's responses to the inherent subjectivity of the twentieth century and its departures from the Christian faith, they are examples of Christian theology engaging, even absorbing, non-Christian ideology. A superb example of Lewis's relationship to secular philosophy is his employment of the ideologies of Henri Bergson. Lewis's novel *The Great Divorce* focuses remarkably on Bergsonian understanding of time within a Christian paradigm. As is the case with Eliot and Auden's use of Bergsonism, Lewis's reliance on Bergson's theory of time in *The Great Divorce* employs an acute use of twentieth-century ideology as well as attempts to subsume that ideology within Christian theology.

Bergson's Influence on Lewis

In his spiritual autobiography, *Surprised by Joy*, Lewis chronicles the thinking that led to his conversion. One particular catalyst for Lewis's spiritual journey toward the Christian faith came in 1918, when Lewis first engaged Bergson's ideas:

> The other momentous experience was that of reading Bergson in a Convalescent Camp on Salisbury Plain. Intellectually this taught me to avoid the snares that lurk about the word *Nothing*.

12. Downing, *Planets in Peril*, 8.
13. *God in the Dock* is a collection of essays that address various non-Christian ideas and belief systems from an apologetic Christian worldview. *The Problem of Pain* addresses the question often posed by skeptics of Christian theology, which Lewis thought was characteristic of twentieth-century Western man's response to Christianity, "If God is all-good and omnipotent, then why is there pain in the world?"

> But it also had a revolutionary effect on my emotional outlook. Hitherto my whole bent had been toward things pale, remote, and evanescent; the water-color world of Morris, the leafy recesses of Malory, the twilight of Yeats. The word "life" had for me pretty much the same associations it had for Shelley in *The Triumph of Life*. I would not have understood what Goethe meant by *des Lebens goldnes Baum* ("The Golden Tree of Life"). Bergson showed me. He did not abolish my old loves, but he gave me a new one. From him I first learned to relish energy, fertility, and urgency; the resource, the triumphs, and even the insolence, of things that grow. I became capable of appreciating artists who would, I believe, have meant nothing to me before; all the resonant, dogmatic, flaming, unanswerable people like Beethoven, Titian (in his mythological pictures), Goethe, Dunbar, Pindar, Christopher Wren, and the more exultant Psalms.[14]

Arguably, Bergson's greatest influence on Lewis is revealed in this passage. From Bergson, Lewis developed a love for dynamism and all of its inclusive "energy, fertility, and urgency"; the spiritual world of *The Great Divorce* will showcase this Bergsonian-inspired affinity for "things that grow." Juxtaposed to the vitalistic idea Lewis was being drawn to was the perilous idea of *Nothing* from which he was steadily converting. While Lewis never officially ascribed to Nietzschean nihilism, his atheism precluded that notion that there was something beyond the material world. In *Surprised by Joy*, Lewis chronicles the months at Oxford leading up to his conversion, stopping to focus on a particular intellectual phase in which he resolved to take a "New Look" at his existence in the world.[15] Lewis recounts:

> There was to be no more pessimism, no more self-pity, no flirtations with any idea of the supernatural, no romantic delusions. . . . I formed the resolution "of always judging and acting in future with that greatest good sense." And good sense meant, for me at that moment, a retreat, almost a panic-stricken flight, from all that sort of romanticism which had hitherto been the chief concern of my life.[16]

Lewis goes on to say that one of the several causes for this new look "was of course Bergson."[17] In Bergson, Lewis says, he found an alternative

14. Lewis, *Surprised by Joy*, 198.
15. Ibid., 201.
16. Ibid.
17. Ibid., 204.

to Schopenhauer's notion that the universe "might not have existed."[18] Lewis describes finding a "Divine attribute" of necessary existence in Bergson's work, though whereas Bergson applied this theory to the universe, Lewis applied it to the subject of God.[19] As discussed in the previous chapter, what Bergson brought to Lewis's pre-conversion thinking was the conviction that there was indeed a world behind the material. In *Creative Evolution*, Bergson argues that concepts like "nothingness" are derivative notions from the refusal of original idea of creation. In other words, there is no *nothing* without the original *something* from which it derives. Behind every concept of a penultimate nothing is the ultimate something.[20] Lewis took from Bergson's latent metaphysical ideas a view of necessary existence that countered the "absurd notion" that reality is an "arbitrary alternative" to a view of the universe as nothing.[21]

Once Lewis decided that there was a universal truth concerning divine and natural reality, he found it impossible to maintain a pessimistic view of life. Under the influence of Bergson's ideas, this stage of Lewis's thinking marked a greater acceptance of both universal truths and the world in which Lewis existed.[22] The ultimate reality, the existence of which Bergson insisted, became an object of Lewis's spiritual affection. This was an important step toward Lewis's conversion and was, Lewis confessed, "the nearest thing to a religious experience which I had had since my

---

18. Ibid., 204. In book two of *The World as Will and Representation*, titled "Ontology," Schopenhauer claims the physical universe and its natural properties to be forces of the human will. The natural world itself is an expression of the human's "will to life."

19. For more on Lewis's engagement with Bergson's ideas, see Schwartz's "Paradise Reframed."

20. Lewis, *Creative Evolution*, 91–106.

21. Schwartz expands on this connection between Bergson's affirmation of ultimate reality and evidence of its influence on Lewis, "Paradise Reframed," 577–79.

22. It is fitting to mention one of his contemporaries and fellow philosophers on time, Samuel Alexander (*Space, Time and Deity*), who, like Bergson, would be influential in Lewis's immediate pre-conversion thinking. Indeed, Alexander is underestimated in regards to his important to both Lewis's pre-conversion relationship to modernist philosophical theories of time and, later, to Lewis's Christian theorizing of time. Alexander's theories directly dispelled the last bits of Lewis's aforementioned "New Look" by forging an inseparable bond between a desire and its object, a bond previously underdeveloped in Lewis's thinking. Alexander's theories of "enjoyment" and "contemplation" bifurcated enjoyment from pleasure and contemplation from the contemplative life. Lewis says, "when you see a table you 'enjoy' the act of seeing and 'contemplate' the table. Later, if you took up Optics and thought about Seeing itself, you would be contemplating the seeing and enjoying the thought" (*Surprised by Joy* 217). From this logical distinction, Lewis realized "that essential property of love, hate, fear, hope, or desire was attention to their object" (ibid., 218).

prep-school days."[23] Lewis's entire life was guided by a mercurial desire for what he called he called "Joy," or an otherworldly desire for the numinous. Lewis became convinced that if Joy were like all other desires (i.e., hunger, affection, or sexual desire), then it would have a *real* object, and that if nothing in this world can satisfy that desire, then its satisfaction must lie in something outside of this world. Although Lewis described the desire for that something as Joy, Bergson's writing helped him to refocus on an ultimate objective reality that lay behind Joy, rather than on the mere desire for Joy itself. Lewis, having ended "any idea of a treaty or compromise with reality," found Bergson's confirmation of ultimate reality to be indisputable, resulting in his own surrender to the object behind Joy.[24] Lewis realized that his lifelong pursuit of "Joy" was a thirsting for an ultimate reality, which he later associated with the divine. It was after his conversion from theist to Christian that Lewis believed that the ultimate object of Joy was God, and that object quenched his lifelong hunger for Joy.[25]

There is more evidence of Bergson's influence on Lewis. For example, Lewis appreciated Bergson's stance against Darwinian evolution and repeatedly attests to Bergson's capability to counter the predominant mechanistic science of his day: "the Bergsonian critique of orthodox Darwinism is not easy to answer."[26] Lewis also asserts that of the divergent forms of creative evolution, "the wittiest expositions of it come in the works of Bernard Shaw, but the most profound ones in those of Bergson."[27] But while the younger, pre-Christian Lewis found Bergson's philosophy invaluable, the older Christian Lewis did not always look back favorably on it. For instance, though, early Lewis considered Bergson's vitalism thoroughly influential to his spiritual development, Lewis would be clear in his later apologetic works that Bergson's theories were no substitute for

23. Ibid., 205.

24. Ibid., 205.

25. Unsurprisingly, Lewis's main work on "Joy" is his autobiographical *Surprised by Joy*. About Joy in regards to his imminent conversion to Christianity, Lewis says, "It may be asked whether my terror was at all relieved by the thought that I was now approaching the source from which those arrows of Joy had been shot at me ever since childhood. Not in the least. No slightest hint was vouchsafed me that there ever had been or ever would be between God and Joy" (ibid., 230). However, after his conversion, Lewis says, "But what, in conclusion, of Joy? for that, after all, is what the story has mainly been about. To tell you the truth, the subject has lost nearly all interest for me since I became a Christian.... It was valuable only as a pointer to something other and outer" (ibid., 238).

26. Lewis, *Weight of Glory*, 89.

27. Lewis, *Mere Christianity*, 35.

spiritual beliefs. Looking back on Bergson's theory of creative evolution, Lewis would describe it as a distinctly modern idea, an essentially false and "modern form of nature religion."[28] In the previously mentioned *Pelelandra* (1943), the second volume of Lewis's Space Trilogy, Lewis ascribes Bergson's theory of creative evolution to the novel's diabolical antagonist, Professor Weston, who uses the expression *emergent evolution*. Later on the novel's protagonist, Ransom, also refers to Weston's doctrine as "Creative Evolution."[29]

While the later Lewis did not subscribe wholesale to Bergson's beliefs, he was indelibly influenced by them. The connections between Bergson and Lewis are not just in the direct influence Bergson had on Lewis's thinking. The two are connected by their common interest in time. Beyond *The Great Divorce*, his most focused treatment on time, Lewis's corpus reveals an intense interest in the subject of time's theological nature. In *The Pilgrim's Regress* (1933), Lewis says about finite man's ability to fully enjoy God, "The human soul was made to enjoy some object that is never fully given—nay, cannot even be imagined as given—in our present mode of subjective and spatio-temporal experience"[30] Here Lewis limits the ability of temporal time to do spiritual work. Spatio-temporal experience, which brings about limited subjectivity, hinders one's experience with the eternal. Not only is this a Bergsonian idea about two selves in two times, as discussed at length in the previous chapter, but it is an idea plausibly attributed to another thinker on time important in Lewis's philosophy.

Friedrich von Hugel's *Eternal Life* (1912) further informs Lewis's theology of time. Lewis had been familiar with von Hugel's work since shortly after his conversion, and he often referred to von Hugel's work and most often when speaking of time.[31] Von Hugel's work deals with the eternality of God in juxtaposition to known space and time. Von Hugel's ideas predate Lewis's but possess remarkable similarity. According to von Hugel, and according to Lewis when he was writing some thirty years later, eternal time exists because of the presence of an eternal God, and that eternality makes impossible temporal time's ability to contain eternal life. Indeed,

28. Lewis, *God in the Dock*, 86.
29. Lewis, *Pelelandra*, 121.
30. Lewis, *Pilgrim's Regress*, 10.
31. Lewis mentions von Hugel in several letters. In his well-documented correspondence with Sheldon Vanauken, Lewis speaks at length about the ontology of eternal life. And, on several occasions, Lewis refers his recipients to von Hugel's work, i.e., he instructs Vanauken with, "Read von Hugel's *Eternal Life* . . . ," *Collected Letters* 3.616.

von Hugel claims, "Eternal Life precludes space and clock-time because of the very intensity of its life. The Simultaneity is here the fullest expression of the Supreme Richness, the unspeakable Concreteness, the overwhelming Aliveness of God; and is at the opposite pole from all empty unity, all mere being—any or all abstractions whatsoever."[32] The nature of the temporal stands in polarized relationship to the nature of the eternal. Eternal life is by its very nature antithetical to measurable time and space. While Lewis will present a theology of time in *The Great Divorce* through which the eternal subsumes the temporal to the point of conflation, the novel still maintains an ontological difference between the temporal and the eternal. The temporal can transmit the eternal, can make known the eternal, and can take on the salvific importance of the eternal, but it cannot take the place of the eternal. The two types of time remain ontologically distinct.

Almost as frequently as Lewis discusses time, he deals with the theology of the present, the spiritually charged *now*. This is true in *The Great Divorce*, but also elsewhere. In a letter to a fan named Gilbert Perleberg, who is contending with Lewis's view of time, Lewis responds:

> This is v. [very] odd. All the arguments you advance as objections to my theory of eternity seem to me to show that you are in exact agreement with me. A doctrine that God "was" more creative "at the beginning" than "now" is absolutely excluded by my view—"was" and "at the beginning" being meaningless when applied to the Timeless Being. As I say in *Screwtape* the total creation meets us at every moment.[33] The distinction between miracle and natural even is *not* between what God *once* did and what He *now* does: it is always NOW with Him.[34]

Lewis's local retort reveals a more important global theme in his thinking about time, the theological preeminence of the present moment. Every temporal moment houses an eternal element. The miraculous, the divinely creative, the very economy of God's time all fill the punctilious present. Though Timeless in being, God's inhabitation of time defines the moment. Part of the idea at work in Lewis's view is that God's timelessness means being both outside and *in* every moment. Because He transcends time, any temporal moment that He inhabits is privileged as *present*.

---

32. Von Hugel, *Eternal Life*, 383.

33. From *Screwtape*, letter 15: "The Present is the point at which time touches eternity. Of the present moment, and of it only, humans have an experience analogous to the experience which our Enemy has of reality as a whole; in it alone freedom and actuality are offered them," 61.

34. Lewis, *Letters* 2.847.

Therefore, the frame of reference for understanding time is not contingent on a distinguishable past, present, and future.

In His timelessness, God is the frame of reference for measuring time, and points in time are eternally present to Him. Thus, any moment that God occupies is made the present, and the present is always "the point at which time touches eternity."[35] According to Lewis, God desires mankind to be "continually concerned either with eternity (which means being concerned with Him) or with the Present."[36] God desires this because to dwell on the eternal is to dwell on God, Himself. And for one to dwell on the present involves issues fundamental to relating to God, like "obeying the *present* voice of conscience, bearing the *present* cross, receiving the *present* grace, giving thanks for the *present* pleasure."[37] In Lewis's theology, the business of the present is the business of eternity, and to know the latter one must go through the former. This theme of the preeminent present is at the center of Lewis's theological agenda in *The Great Divorce*, which depicts the present as the harbinger of an individual's entire spiritual fate. The novel oscillates between, even toys at a conflation of, the temporal and the eternal present.

The temporal present and its eternal antecedent is a bifurcation of two times in Lewis's thought that promotes a hierarchy of being. Eternal time, God's time, is superior to man's finite time. Indeed, temporal existence is not only inferior by nature of its being non-eternal; it is also a defect in reality, according to Lewis, "I firmly believe that God's life is non temporal. Time is a defect of reality since by its v. [very] nature any temporal being loses each moment of its life to get the next—the moments run through us as if we were sieves! God forbid that we shd. [should] think God to be like that."[38] Whereas temporal man must acquire a new moment at the expense of losing a past moment, God's non-temporality forbids any successive accumulation of moments.[39] God, and therefore the eternality He defines, exists beyond the temporal in a greater ontological state.

On this point of God and time, Lewis's belief is clear: God stands supreme over time. Not only is God by nature superior to time in being,

---

35. Lewis, *Screwtape Letters*, 61.
36. Ibid.
37. Ibid.
38. Lewis, *Letters* 2.915.
39. On God's timelessness in comparison to the possibility of Christian believers have timeless beings, Lewis also writes, "I am not at all sure that blessed souls have a strictly timeless being (*a totum simul*) like God. Don't some theologians interpose *aevum* as a half-way house between *tempus* & *aeternitas*," *Letters* 3.1239.

but He is over time in operation as well. Lewis speaks of God's presence as sovereignly enveloping all elements of temporality, claiming that God is "already in tomorrow and still in yesterday."[40] As every moment in God's economy is an eternal present, God's occupation of every moment compresses notions of experience in successive time. God operates throughout time past, present, and future by fully occupying all moments within past, present, and future. While He operates through them, the epochs of past, present, and future do not apply to God's experience with time, as He transcends temporal succession or distinguishable periods of time. Lewis maintains that because of God's transcendent existence outside of time *and* his immanent involvement in time, God uses time as an agent of personal and theological change. In other words, because God uses it, time is a force.

The Great Divorce explores thoroughly the theme of time as a force in relationship to the individual's potential spiritual transformation. In the novel, time's function as a divine force is particularly relevant to the theological phenomenon of salvation, and the ongoing effects of that force function dynamically in each character, as some progress in time to redemption and some to damnation. In a letter discussing the process of salvation in the individual's life, Lewis expounds on the theologically primary role of the force of time in God's salvific action:

> The best I can do about these mysteries is to think that the [New Testament] gives us a sort of double vision. A. Into our salvation as eternal fact, as it (and all else) is in the timeless vision of God. B. Into the same thing as a process worked out in time. Both must be true in some sense but it is beyond our capacity to envisage both together. Can one get a faint idea of it by thinking of *A*. A musical score as it is written down with all the notes there at once. B. The same thing *played* as a process in time? For *practical* purposes, however, it seems to me we must usually live by the second vision "working out our salvation in fear and trembling" (but it adds "for"—not "though"—but "for"—"it is God who worketh in us").[41]

While Lewis charges his recipient with the Pauline practical admonition to work out one's own salvation with fear and trembling, even while God accomplishes the work of salvation (cf. Phil 2:12–13), he also acknowledges that the biblical idea of salvation in and through time is

40. Ibid. 3.1014.
41. Ibid. 3.1337.

defined by God's own timelessness. Because God is beyond time and salvation is a spiritual act, his salvific work is inaugurated transcendentally before the process is worked out in the individual's temporal life. God inhabits all moments, sees all "future" moments in his timeless vision, and works outside of time to accomplish the individual's salvation.[42] Though God's timelessness does not change the chronological conversion experience of the average person, it exists behind conversion's temporal events as a timeless fact. *The Great Divorce* will take up in full this theme of time as salvific force, applying a Bergsonian sustained theology of the present as the perennial intersection of the eternal.

Bergsonian Ideology in *The Great Divorce*

Bergsonism is evident in Lewis's theological novel in three thematic ways: dualism, dynamism, and the durative force. As previously discussed, dualism is a distinguishing characteristic in Bergson's thought. Dualisms of the self, of types of time, and of modes of experience in time are all dichotomies that Bergson proposes as ways to understand human experience in time. Another of Bergson's ideas, dynamism is one of the strongest thematic threads, one that runs throughout every part of his philosophical tapestry. All elements of life and human experience and every aspect of duration are defined by vitalistic dynamism. The themes of dualism and dynamism operate in accordance to a Bergsonian concept of the force of time. *The Great Divorce* constructs its theology of time on a Bergsonian concept of durative force, and it is through durative force that the eternal works in and with the present to transform the individual. It is essential to note that the tropes of dynamism and dualism are useful global approaches to Lewis's thought. Lewis is, in fact, writing a novel about alterity—a display of the alienation and otherness of a spiritual world far beyond the material. One major point of Lewis's novel, however, is to reveal a world behind the world, and in doing so to show that thoughts, actions, and lifestyles in one world reach far into the other. This two-dimensionality permeates the book's treatment on the force of time.

 The Great Divorce tells the story of a protagonist, a fictitious version of Lewis himself, who takes a bus that transports passengers from hell,

---

42. See the New Testament's claims of God's timelessness: "Jesus Christ is the same yesterday, today, and forever" (Heb 13:8); "I am the alpha and omega, the first and the last, the beginning and the end" (Rev 22:13). All scriptural references are taken from the New American Standard.

depicted as an infinitely expanding grey town without borders, to heaven, which is by contrast a mountainous, green, and Edenic highland. Lewis writes himself into the story as both narrator and character. From his first person point of view, he narrates the bus ride and subsequent series of events that take place once the bus arrives in the high heavenly countries and the passengers find that they have seemingly lost their human corporality. In this new world and by comparison to its reality, they are mere ghosts. Almost immediately after arrival the ghosts witness what look like gods coming toward them. In contrast to the ghosts' ethereal states, the approaching group is solid, radiant, and seemingly perfect in their physicality. The story's plot is facilitated by Lewis's perception of the choices made by his fellow bus passengers, the "ghosts." The ghosts have choices to make. Each ghost must choose heaven or hell, as the redeemed, glorified "solid people" confront him or her. Each solid person identifies and approaches a ghost known to him/her in their former earthly lives, which creates an episodic series of conversations, in which "This conversation also we overheard" is a common narrative transition.[43] The novel develops scene by scene with these conversations—most of them religiously apologetic in nature—as the glorified people attempt to persuade the ephemeral bus riders to stay in the high countries.

The conversational structure of the story's plot reveals the afore-argued themes of dynamism and dualism by keeping the plot in continual flux, an ever-moving plot comprised of the various interlocutors taking various polemical positions. Indeed, the conversations serve as microcosms of the novel's larger shape: the solid people embody their messages of redemption as well as representing ultimate reality while the ghosts present a self-centered damnation belonging to a lesser reality. In fictional form, Lewis has adopted Bergsonian ideas of dualism and dynamism. Lewis has taken and mobilized Bergson's ideas of superficial and fundamental self, of distinct multiplicity of unintuitive thinking and the confused multiplicity of intuition, and the construct of time and real duration, creating a novel comprised of dualistic depictions of time, self, and theological doctrine.

Lewis begins to mobilize Bergsonian dualistic doctrines in the novel's very preface. Here Lewis explains that the novel's title, a play on words referencing William Blake's *Marriage of Heaven and Hell*, counters the idea that time itself will resolve spiritual conflicts rather than our having to make any hard choices. That is, he attacks the belief that reality

---

43. Lewis, *Great Divorce*, 89.

never presents anyone with so absolutely harsh a choice as an either-or, but rather that "granted skill and patience and (above all) time enough, some way of embracing both alternatives can always be found; that mere development or adjustment or refinement will somehow turn evil into good without being called on for a final and total rejection of anything we should like to retain."[44] Lewis takes this idea to be a disastrous error for a thoroughly Bergsonian reason: the force of time is too strong to leave moral choice to co-existing static alternatives. Just as Bergson's claim that for a conscious being time is a gain,[45] the Bergsonian message of *The Great Divorce* is that the force of time moves moral and spiritual states down ever differentiating paths. Time leaves no moral condition the same from one moment to the next, no spiritual state unchanged, and no theological dichotomy in an un-evolving stasis. Time moves all. The theological categories to which one adheres, one's personal opinions about life, and the choices one makes are all sticks being rushed down the river of time.

But as Bergson states and Lewis fictionalizes, time and the self in time are essentially split. According to Bergson, the external world is more important that inner states, and so the "social life has more practical importance for us than our individual, inner experience."[46] Thus, inner states, which are in a "perpetual mode of becoming" (duration), are confused with external objects (the construct of time), "just as the fleeting duration or our inner self fixes itself by projecting itself into homogenous space."[47] The dichotomy that Bergson is making is not only between external thinking and inner experience, but rather between external time (homogenous space) and real duration. In the *Great Divorce*, moral conditions (Lewis uses the language "good" and "evil") leading to final spiritual states (heaven and hell) demonstrate dualistic time's dynamic effect best of all. If there seems to be a conflation between dualism and dynamism in both Bergson's and Lewis's language, that is because there really is one. In remarkable similarity to Bergson's ideological construction, Lewis's dualism is shown within his theme of dynamism.

For example, Lewis's discussion of the divergent, dualistic progressions of good and evil in the prefatory quotation cited above reveal an acute interest in the dynamism of morality: "that mere *development* or *adjustment* or *refinement* will somehow *turn evil into good* without our

44. Ibid., vii.
45. Bergson, *Time and Free Will*, 115.
46. Ibid., 89.
47. Ibid., 69.

being called on for a final and total *rejection* of anything we should like *to retain*."[48] In the novel, moral states develop throughout the narrative in destabilizing ways as characters either progress or regress spiritually.

According to Lewis, this movement happens as it were on a road split into two paths that move away from each other, because good and evil change dynamically in further and further isolation from one another. Indeed, the novel posits that morals do not exist statically, but move, grow, and change in the text in ways that destabilize the character's understandings and possession of them. Far from static states of being, good and evil develop, mature, morph, and ever push against one another in competition for primacy in the individual. Lewis says analogously in the preface:

> You cannot take all luggage with you on all journeys, on one journey even your right hand and your right eye may be among the things you have to leave behind. We are not living in a world where all roads are radii of a circle and where all, if followed long enough, will therefore draw gradually nearer and finally meet the centre: rather in a world where every road, after a few miles, forks into two, and each of those into two again, and at each fork you must make a decision.[49]

For Lewis, the divorce between heaven and hell is not mere bifurcation, but moral magnetic repulsion, as good and evil diverge perpetually throughout time, a process stretching into eternity. In addition to its theological nature, this notion is distinctly Bergsonian. According to Bergson in *Creative Evolution* (which, again, does not refer to mechanistic evolution, which Bergson strongly opposed), the evolutionary process is one of forking roads in life that constantly divide to create new roads in a dynamic change,[50] and the individual's entire moral self moves along these roads in the same way as biological life divides in its dynamic development. Lewis's use of the journey analogy for spiritual change works nicely with Bergson's notion of divided biological change; and it is on such a Bergsonian model that the Christian writer Lewis creates a poetics of time wrapped in a theology of moral dualism. Beginning in the preface and moving throughout the narrative, moral conditions in *The Great Divorce* are always depicted as dynamic, either progressing or devouring themselves, transforming or in the process of stagnation, being glorified or condemned as characters move through the plot. The best example of

48. Lewis, *Great Divorce*, vii.
49. Ibid., viii.
50. Bergson, *Creative Evolution*, 35.

this moral dynamism is the way each conversation unfolds in the novel. Each ghostly character's moral state changes in the course of its conversion with a solid person. One sees in each conversation a microcosmic process of sanctification or damnation, as each ghost decides to accept or reject theological salvation.

It might be helpful to explore Lewis's affinity for dualism and dynamism before moving on with a close reading of *The Great Divorce*. One good source on Lewis's thought is the work on the Christian writer by Owen Barfield, longtime friend and fellow Inkling. In an essay on Lewis entitled "Either: Or," Barfield argues that one basic element of anyone's imagination is polarity, the dualistic act of countering one thing against another. Polarity is particularly fertile for the imagination because it creates a dialectic in which the polar opposites are generative of each other and generative of a new product. I find it helpful to apply Barfield's notion of polarity to my current study. For example, in Lewis, Eliot, and Auden's work, the theme of temporal time and its polar opposite, eternity, actually generate an intersection at which man may meet God. The polar opposites create a charged, dynamic relationship. According to Barfield, "polarity is dynamic, not abstract."[51] One of Barfield's main arguments in the essay is that Western rationalism has created an "either/or" fantasy, and that polarized thinking is the core of imagination. "Moral imagination is the dialectic," Barfield states, "or the polarity, of love."[52] Barfield argues that this type of polarized thinking defines artists like Coleridge and Lewis.

In an even more seminal essay for my study, "Some Reflections on *The Great Divorce*," Barfield argues that an accurate reading of C. S. Lewis's thinking must be dualistic. According to Barfield, what defines Lewis and *The Great Divorce* is his universal tendency for ideological dualism. Barfield argues that there are fact "two Lewises," one who thinks atomically with unbending logic and one who thinks mythopoetically with wild imagination.[53] In *The Great Divorce* one encounters both Lewises. For example, the novel's depiction of salvation is in accordance with Lewis's own beliefs about salvation, as the choice of salvation is clearly presented to each ghost, and each will face the rewards or consequences of their moral choice. But not only does one see a logical Lewis, whose moral world is ordered according to the tenets his Christian faith. One also sees a wildly

---

51. Barfield, "Either: Or," 42.
52. Ibid., 59.
53. Ibid., 87.

imaginative world, in which fallen humanity takes apparitional form, waterfalls speak, and lizards become stallions.

Barfield argues that in *The Great Divorce* the atomically rational Lewis and the mythopoeic Lewis "join hands."[54] So joined are the two Lewises, but yet so distinctly operational in the novel, that Barfield implies that the titular "divorce" is really occurring in Lewis.[55] It is *The Great Divorce* among Lewis's works that contains the most "vividly imagined, *qualitatively* imagined landscapes of heaven and hell."[56] Barfield also argues that in this dualistic world of heaven and hell, created by an author with a dualistic mind, one sees a world where, instead of cause and effect, we find a sequence of shapes and patterns gradually changing into each other."[57] "It is a world where everything flows," Barfield says.[58]

The dualism that Barfield claims is so fundamental to Lewis's *The Great Divorce* is also heavily employed in the structure of much of his literary criticism. For example, in *An Experiment in Criticism*, a theoretical look at divergent judgments readers make about literature, Lewis declares about himself, "I am writing about literary practice and experience from within, for I claim to be a literary person myself and I address other literary people."[59] Here Lewis interestingly positions both himself as a literary critic and others as recipients of his criticism inside a literary guild of sorts, a discourse community of criticism. Lewis's assertion of authority is in part based on his self-proclaimed role as an insider—the position of writing "from within"—as well as his emphasis on the subjective *experience* of reading literature. This authoritative stance is extremely important for Lewis's overall rhetorical purpose since the very nature of his criticism and the underlying premise proposed in his literary critical experiment ("I propose to try an experiment"),[60] hinges on the polarized roles of the self and the other, as well on the dichotomization of divergent reading experiences. In the epilogue to *An Experiment in Criticism*, Lewis says, "Literature as Logos is a series of windows, even of doors. One of the things we

---

54. Ibid., 87.
55. Ibid., 90.
56. Ibid., 87.
57. Ibid., 88.
58. Ibid., 88. For more on how Lewis develops themes similar to those Barfield notes, see also Michael Raiger's "The Place of the Self in C. S. Lewis's *The Great Divorce*," 109–31.
59. Lewis, *An Experiment in Criticism*, 130.
60. Ibid., 1.

feel after reading a great work is 'I have got out'. Or from another point of view, 'I have got in.'"[61]

In *Experiment*, Lewis, perhaps unbeknownst to himself, reveals how one can move in and out of his most paradigmatically important philosophical agendas and most employed literary tropes of dynamism and dualism found throughout his entire body of work. *Experiment* is an investigation of both how readers of divergent types of literature produce divergent readings of texts and of the unconscious consequences of divergent readings. Lewis divides readers by their approach to texts, claiming that a reader is either unliterary or literary depending on how cursorily or deeply they interpret a text. *Experiment* also moves dualistically in argument, beginning with a hermeneutical stance comprised of Lewis's self-placed position as a reader juxtaposed to other readers and continuing with the juxtaposition of types of readers/reading. Furthermore, the dichotomies Lewis constructs become a thematic as well as a structural framework that consistently perpetuate more polarities: good taste versus bad taste,[62] the very presentation of the two kinds of literary people, "few" and the "many," the reading of the unliterary[63] and the misreading of the literary,[64] and the logos and the poiema.[65] In *An Experiment in Criticism*, I think, it is precisely the dualistic combination of Lewis's positioning himself as a "literary person" (the self) amongst *other* literary people along with his emphasis on the subjectivity of reading (good and bad) that allows one to understand Lewis's meta-approach to fiction, to literary criticism, and arguably to apologetics. Lewis anchors his argument through this meta-element of bipolarity, constantly reminding the reader of the interplay between various dimensions of his rhetorical dualism:

> Admittedly, we never quite get out of our own skins. Whatever we do, something of our own and of our age's making will remain in our experience of all literature. Equally, *I can never see anything exactly from the point of view even of those* whom I know and love best. But I can make at least some progress towards it. I can eliminate at least the grosser illusions of perspective.

---

61. Ibid., 138.
62. Ibid., 1–4.
63. Ibid., 27–39.
64. Ibid., 74–87.
65. Ibid., 132.

> *Literature helps me to do it with live people*, and live people help me to do it with literature.[66]

Here Lewis bifurcates his view of literature from others' reading of literature. The juxtaposition of self against other readers reinforces a dualistic construction in the text. Lewis's nuanced negotiation of self and other in the act of reading becomes significantly greater in importance when placed in conversation with Lewis's larger literary (and philosophical) schema. In *An Experiment in Criticism*, dialectical dualism is essential for Lewis's articulation of both morality and literary aesthetics. What *Experiment* explicitly sets out to do on a small scale, i.e., to conduct a critical experiment on divergent types of reading of diverse texts, becomes crucial for understanding Lewis *in toto*. He creates a critical agenda through which one can best navigate by dealing in polarizing oppositional constructions. I can hardly think of another theme, approach, or hermeneutical tactic that best characterizes what Lewis attempts on a meta-literary level than this dualistic formulation.

This bifurcated relationship brings me back to the fundamental dualism at play in *The Great Divorce*. In *An Experiment in Criticism*, Lewis's most explicit manual on how to interpret literature, a dualistic pattern emerges that can help us understand his fiction. It seems that positioned in the oscillation between self and other, between good reading and bad, and the subjectivity of the reader's experience, Lewis lays out a blueprint for reading his other works of fiction, particularly *The Great Divorce*. In establishing the ideological connection between Lewis's dualism and Bergsonism in *The Great Divorce*, I have demonstrated just how pervasive are Bergson's dualistic formulations to Bergson's philosophy. In *Time and Free Will* alone, Bergson espouses two types of multiplicity (distinct and confused), two notions of duration (time and pure duration), two modes of subjective experience (social and intuitive), and two kinds of self (superficial and fundamental). A sound understanding of Lewis should be just as aware of his pervasive dualistic thinking as an understanding of Bergson is necessarily aware of that philosopher's dualism.

Lewis's dualism transcends the genres of fiction and literary criticism and helps shape his apologetics as well. Some examples of Lewis's dualistic patterns are the dualistic elements in *The Problem of Pain* (physical and non-physical pain, the paradoxical problem of reconciling divine omnipotence and divine goodness, human pain versus non-human pain); the bipolar logic often used in *Mere Christianity* ("But a Christian must

---

66. Ibid., 101.

not be either a Totalitarian or an Individualist");[67] and even the biformity of the rhetoric used in describing Christian sanctification in *The Weight of Glory* ("poetry replaces grammar, gospel replaces law, longing transforms obedience").[68] What these diverse examples show is that polarity is the key to unlocking Lewis' thematic/schematic agenda in *Experiment* as well as the template by which we can understand Lewis's fictional and critical thinking. I want to briefly offer one other example from Lewis's literary criticism to substantiate my position before returning to *The Great Divorce*.

His essay collection *Rehabilitations*, though published over twenty years before *Experiment*, anticipates the dualism so critically important to *Experiment*. *Rehabilitations* demonstrates Lewis's early thinking about literary classification and value. Like *Experiment*, *Rehabilitations* engages literature through a polarized lens; for example, in the chapter "High and Low Brows," Lewis distinguishes types of books and readers in two classes, "A" and "B," rhetorically working to define each by their differences as well as possible likenesses, "the more I look into it the more I am convinced that any contrast of weighty and frivolous, solid and slight, deep and shallow, must cut right across the A and B distinction."[69] In order to define one thing, Lewis must present an opposite thing; in order to define a virtue, Lewis must describe a vice; in order to say what good literature is, he must say what it is not. This programmatic approach of *Experiment* is representative of Lewis's fictional and critical corpus.

Like Lewis's approach in *Experiment*, where he writes himself into his theoretical model (a placement of the self against other literary and nonliterary types) and like his polarized approach to literature in *Rehabilitations*, his approach in *The Great Divorce* equally fosters the contraposition of the self among other souls. *The Great Divorce* fictionalizes what *An Experiment in Criticism* theorizes, as divergent souls follow their "tastes" to the utmost ends of teleological polarization: "As the *solid people* came nearer still *I noticed* that they were moving with order and determination as though each of them had marked his man in our *shadowy company*."[70] Just as in Lewis's other polarized works, *The Great Divorce* morally divides characters, plot, and setting.

---

67. Lewis, *Mere Christianity*, 186.
68. Lewis, *The Weight of Glory*, 28.
69. Lewis, *Rehabilitations*, 103.
70. Lewis, *Great Divorce*, 25.

Perhaps more importantly, *The Great Divorce* adheres to the same polarized schematic as the later *Experiment* in its emphasis on the importance of dualistic relationships, "Good, as it ripens, becomes continually more different not only from evil but from other good."[71] It is precisely on this dualistic opposition—on the differing ends of the ideological spectrum that exist in relation to and define one another—that Lewis relies in *Experiment* for the *poiema*, which means the thing *made*, or the making of a text. Like the distinction between good and bad literary taste, and like that between good and bad reading, the subjective expression of good and bad in *Divorce* is most strongly defined by the elements' opposing of each other, thereby *making* the polarized relationship both an extremely important theme as well as the key arrangement of the soteriological fiction. Indeed, soteriology in *The Great Divorce* is a matter of polarity, in that each ghost must choose between two spiritual opposites. And the choice is never unrelated to the polarity. Thus, each character simultaneously stands in close proximity to both heaven and to hell, to good and evil, to self-enslavement and belief in the other. The choosing of one spiritual state is always made in reference to that state's polar opposite.

Having established that dualism is as fundamental to Lewis's thinking as it is to Bergson's, let us now look at how that dualism functions dynamically in Lewis's novel on time. As previously discussed, the preface has established the themes of moral dualism and spiritual dynamism in the narrative. The novel proper fictionalizes the preface's theories of dualistic, dynamic morality. Lewis begins his novel with the presentation of a superficial reality in the "Grey Town," a vast city of spiritually and personally isolated citizens, whose existence is seemingly suspended outside of time. In this superficial reality, twentieth-century concerns for man's isolation and the material world emerge. Of course, the city is a perennial modernist motif. *Mrs. Dalloway*'s London, *Ulysses*' Dublin, and *Crime and Punishment*'s Saint Petersburg all reveal a modernist concern with the role of the city in man's life. While cities in twentieth-century novels often animate the character rather than the other way around, they also reveal that the characters are very much isolated from each other. The city is often the stage on which man is most desperately paraded and most drastically depicted as alienated from the world around him. Lewis begins his theological novel in the "Grey Town," which projects outward indefinitely because of its inhabitants' desire *for* alienation. One of the novel's ghostly figures says to Lewis concerning the grey town,

71. Lewis, *Great Divorce*, viii.

the trouble is that [the town inhabitants are] so quarrelsome. As soon as anyone arrives he settles in some street. Before he's been there twenty-four hours he quarrels with this neighbor. Before the week is over he's quarreled so badly that he decides to move. . . . Finally he'll move right out to the edge of the town and build a new house. You see, it's easy here. You've only got to *think* of a house and there it is.[72]

The setting is Lewis's play on twentieth-century tropes and themes of man's alienation. Instead of a typical city that forces people into some sort of community, however disunified that community might be, Lewis's city by its very nature forces them out of community, and so carries the twentieth-century trope to its logical conclusion of isolation. In order to show man's control of his socio-material world (though how "material" it actually is will be up for debate as the novel progresses), Lewis gives the town's inhabitants the power to think up a physical structure all in service to their desires for isolation. Lewis virtually creates a city out of twentieth-century anxieties, a town built out of man's self-imposed state of alienation. Inhabitants only have to think of moving and a dwelling materializes, and of course they always think of moving to rid themselves of the very community that the city provides—a modernist paradox at its best. It is the citizens' choice for isolation that makes this Grey Town a paradoxically dynamic spiritual limbo. Their selfish natures have made them discontented with their primary world, so they create other dwellings *ad infinitum*. The citizens of this Grey Town mistakenly think that theirs is a world of ultimate reality. Though some citizens live millions of miles from others at the borders of the city, and some have lived there for thousands of year, they all still maintain the illusion of reality and human relationships lived in real community.[73] The citizens' illusion is aptly described by Bergson, who warns that the superficial self "touches the external world by its surface."[74] Contentment with the external world, which for Bergson is not ultimate reality due to its externality, is "why our superficial psychological life unfolds in a homogenous milieu."[75] The citizens of the Grey Town have done precisely that, infinitely unfolding their superficial lives across the homogeneity of the Grey Town.

---

72. Ibid., 10.
73. Ibid., 11.
74. Bergson, *Time and Free Will*, 93.
75. Ibid.

Once the plot moves forward, the quasi-physical world of the Grey Town gives way to the real world of the high countries furthering the ghosts' state of alienation from their own city as well as introducing them to a world to which they are invited to live, but rarely do.[76] In this overarching theme of polarized worlds, the novel's focus is always dualistic—ever focused on the distinction between the finite and infinite. The textual movement is also dynamic, as the finite earthly moves into and up against the ultimate reality of the high country. The novel proper begins with the narrator's positioning himself in a place of transit, a bus station, where the novel's characters anticipate departure.

Lewis further reveals that prior to the novel's beginning, he had already been walking through the city, "always in the rain and always in evening twilight," in a world where time seems to have stood still.[77] Historical figures long dead by the time Lewis penned the novel still exist in the Grey Town, living with citizens contemporaneous with Lewis in a state of timelessness, though time has unceasingly passed. The narrator's language of dynamism, which was so prominent in the preface and will be throughout the novel, is suspended in the opening scene, in which the theme of time is first introduced, "Time seemed to have paused on that dismal moment when only a few shops lit up and it is not yet dark enough for their windows to look cheering. And just as the evening never advanced to night, so my walking had never brought me to the better parts of the town."[78] Here dynamism gives way to stasis, as the narrator finds himself in a spatial, chronological limbo, where time itself is described in terms of its suspended motion. The "not yet" of the narrator's experience seemingly suspends narrative action; the tone of motion creates a dynamic quality that enlivens the sense of the story's movement and anti-movement, "evening never advanced . . . my walking had never brought me."[79]

In the Grey Town's conflation of time and space one detects a strong Bergsonian presence. What Bergson most opposes, indeed, and what he argues is most unrealistic, is an understanding of time tainted by a conflation with the spatial. Because space is homogenous and time is heterogeneous, it is the conflation of the spatial with time that distorts a dynamic view of time.[80] Time in the Grey Town does not operate dynamically, and

76. Cf. MacDonald's statement is that "Heaven is reality itself. All that is fully real is Heavenly," 63.
77. Lewis, *Great Divorce*, 1.
78. Ibid.
79. Ibid.
80. Bergson, *Time and Free Will*, 93.

Meeting the Eternal

therefore, according to Bergsonian theory, does not coincide with the complex reality of the human condition. The world of the Grey Town is a void in which time passes without culminating in dynamic inner change. This stagnation is antithetical to both the vital impulse of Bergsonian duration and the transformative way time functions in the High Countries. In the Grey Town, the ghosts' spiritual states are as static as the time they inhabit. But time works very differently in the High Countries, where one's spiritual state must either progress or regress. The dualism between the static time of the Grey Town and the dynamic of the High Countries is central to the novel's theology of time, and so the plot hurries from the Grey Town to reach the High Countries just five pages into the work.

The motif of dynamic movement only becomes more obvious as the plot moves from the Grey Town to the high, green countries:

> Hullo! We've left the ground . . . the wet roofs of the town appeared, spreading without a break . . . and still the light grew . . . a cliff loomed up ahead. It sank vertically beneath us so far that I could not see the bottom, and it was dark and smooth. We were mounting all the time . . . presently we glided over that top . . . we were losing height now . . . then, suddenly we were at rest.[81]

The metaphor of the omnibus serves the novel's theme of dynamism. Every character, including Lewis himself, is in a constant state of flux. Not only are they moving from one kind of time to another, but, as suggested by the preface, they are moving spiritually, either to a state of salvation or to a state of damnation. Indeed, the characters inside the bus are moving away from the immoral world of their making and moving to a new realm of morality, but still one that will further exasperate their alienated condition. For all of the ghosts who do not accept salvation in the High Countries, their alienation will be all the more dynamic as they have left the timeless static of the Grey Town only to reject the dynamic duration offered by the High Countries. The device of the bus epitomizes the theme of dynamic motion—leaving the station, transporting souls—themselves in a state of dynamic moral flux—traveling to a destination filled with spiritual characters, who in turn invite further movement throughout the landscape of the text.

Upon arriving at the High Countries, Lewis the character realizes that he and his ghostly co-passengers are not only in a different place, they are in a different kind of place.[82] It is also upon arrival that the passengers

81. Lewis, *Great Divorce*, 5, 19.
82. Ibid., 20.

realize that they are ghosts, as it takes a juxtaposition of the passengers against the reality of the High Countries to reveal ultimate reality: "The men were as they had always been; as all the men I had known had been perhaps. It was the light, the grass, the trees that were different; made of some different substance, so much solider than things in our country that men were ghosts by comparison."[83] Lewis's dualism of worlds reveals his theological belief that the spiritual world is more real than the physical, for the materiality of the Grey Town and its inhabitants pales in comparison to the glorified world of the High Countries. So real is this new spiritual world that Lewis and company cannot handle its true materiality: the leaves weigh hundreds of pounds, the grass feels like nails, flowers are as hard as diamonds.[84] I contend that Lewis is proceeding from both a Christian theological position, which believes that the spiritual is more real than the physical, and a Bergsonian position, which holds that the world of durative time brings with it a more true reality.[85] In durative time, the individual feels reality rather than measures it,[86] the human soul truly progresses in accordance with durative reality,[87] and human expression most truly coheres with life.[88] In the move from the Grey Town to the High Countries, Lewis draws the same lines of delineation as Bergson, in that Lewis presents a superior reality in which true existence is enabled.

The dynamism involved in the text's polarization of realities is made most manifest in the story's aforementioned conversational structure. Once arrived at the High Countries, the ghosts are approached by the glorified solid people, and the episodic conversations ensue, comprising almost all the plot other than the movement of Lewis the character to the next conversation. It is also upon arrival at the High Countries that Lewis intensifies his treatment of the theme of time. What the novel immediately introduced as a theme in the Grey Town's static time becomes a pervasive concentrated treatment of time in the High Countries. Indeed, on the thematic level, references to time—either in an explicit reference to a period of time ("In about half an hour"), adverbially ("momentarily, presently,

---

83. Ibid., 21.

84. Ibid.

85. Lewis's view of reality is both Christian and Platonic. E.g., Upon entering Aslan's kingdom, Lord Digory exclaims, "[The reality of another metaphysical, spiritual world beyond the material is] all in Plato, all in Plato: bless me, what do they teach them at these schools!" *The Last Battle* 212.

86. Bergson, *Time and Free Will*, 93.

87. Ibid., 97.

88. Ibid., 136–37.

Meeting the Eternal

suddenly"), or as a transitional expression ("a moment later, in the meantime")—appear some eighty-two times throughout the novel's 146 pages. From the arrival at the High Countries and throughout the rest of the plot, the theme of time is amalgamated with the themes of spiritual dynamism and dualism.

The very first conversation that Lewis witnesses reveals the novel's theological agenda concerning time, dynamism, and dualism. A solid person approaches a ghost ("the Big Ghost," as he is called), who was the solid person's former employer. As is the case with every encounter in the text, the conversation turns to some detail of their relationship from the past. In this case, the solid person killed a man, and the Big Ghost holds him in contempt, hurling judgmental statements at the solid person throughout the conversation.[89] The solid person immediately reveals his purpose for coming, and it is the same purpose that every solid person has in approaching their ghostly acquaintances: to plead with the ghosts to accept salvation and stay in the High Countries.

This plea is met with a selfish obstinacy on the part of ghosts in all but one of the plot's conversations. In the case of the Big Ghost, the solid person's invitation is met with prideful resistance to any form of spiritual help. The Big Man barks at the solid person, "What do you keep arguing for? I'm only telling you the sort of chap I am. I only want my rights. I'm not asking for anybody's bleeding charity."[90] To which the solid person replies, "Then do. At once. Ask for the Bleeding Charity. Everything is here for the asking and nothing can be bought."[91] In this and every subsequent conversation lies Lewis's theology of the present moment. The solid person is offering the Big Ghost the opportunity for redemption, but that redemption must take place in the durative force of the present ("At once"). Because the force of time always works to empower the present moment, it is only in the present that one can experience time's transforming agency. Indeed, each conversation is a reiteration of ongoing, present time decision-making. Each conversation presents a spiritual choice enabled only by the present. The solid people reiterate the urgency of the present to the ghosts in almost every conversation as they repeatedly announce that the time for spiritual transformation is the *now*.

In what is arguably the novel's most superb example of Lewis's theology of the present, a ghost with a little red lizard on his shoulder is

89. Lewis, *Great Divorce*, 25–27.
90. Ibid., 28.
91. Ibid.

approached by a flaming, radiant solid person. The ghost has a strained, spiritually unhealthy relationship with the lizard, a metaphor for the ghost's besetting sin of lust. Lewis catches sight of the ghost and noticed that "he turned his head to the reptile with a snarl of impatience. 'Shut up, I tell you!' he said. It wagged its tail and continued to whisper to him."[92] Lewis then narrates the solid person's reply, "Would you like me to make him quiet' said the flaming Spirit—an angel, as I now understood."[93] Once the ghost admits that he would like to be rid of the lizard, the flaming Spirit announces, "Then I will kill him."[94] Shocked and afraid, the lizard-clad ghost defers, "Well, there's time to discuss this later." The flaming Spirit announces, "There is no time."[95] The ghost complains, "It would be most silly to do it now. I'd need to be in good health for the operation. Some other day, perhaps." To which the solid person replies, "There is no other day. *All days are present now.*"[96] This line from the flaming Spirit best reflects Lewis's Bergsonian theology of the present.

The entire exchange between the Spirit and lizard-beset ghost is also figure of duration. Bergson argues that pure duration is "the form taken by the succession of our inner states of consciousness when our self lets itself live, when it abstains from establishing a separation between the present state and anterior states."[97] For Bergson, the power of the durative is the power of the present, when the individual ceases to measure out or separate the flow of time. When the individual ceases those things and surrenders to the force of time, then pure duration is consciously realized. Lewis inserts this Bergsonian notion of the durative present with a theology of God's ever-present "nowness"—all days are present now.

Another example of Lewis's theology of the present is a letter Lewis wrote to a Ms. Breckenridge on the subject of prayer and God's foreknowledge of a supplicant's request, Lewis says,

> Don't bother about the idea that God "has known for millions of years exactly what you are about to pray." That isn't what it's like. God is hearing you *now*, just as simply as a mother hears a child. The difference His timelessness makes is that this *now* (which slips away from you even as you say the word *now*) is for Him

92. Ibid., 106–7.
93. Ibid., 107.
94. Ibid.
95. Ibid., 108.
96. Ibid., 109.
97. Bergson, *Time and Free Will*, 74–75.

infinite. If you must think of His timelessness at all, don't think of Him having looked forward to this moment for millions of years: think that to Him you are always praying this prayer.[98]

In the angel's statement about time in *The Great Divorce*, Lewis emphasizes God's eternally inhabiting the present. For Lewis, as for Bergson, true spiritual life comes through God's working through time. Because God inhabits every present moment, time transforms those who choose to consciously know it. Lewis's theology of the present is an echo of Bergson's belief that for those choose it, "we are always capable of placing ourselves in pure duration."[99] Once one is in duration, once experiencing the transformative force of the present as the ghost with the lizard did, one can achieve a new metaphysical level of consciousness according to Bergson. The whole of durative force is in the present moment, if only chosen: "for if the moments of real duration [are] perceived by an attentive consciousness.... We should know ourselves absolutely."[100] The problem with the ghosts in Lewis's novel is the same problem Bergson sees in the superficial self: they choose not to perceive the moments of real duration provided them in their conversations with the solid people.

The very plot of the novel seems fragmented and episodic, consisting of one conversation after another between two opposing moralities, but this structure shows how the dynamic force of time works in the present moment. The novel's solid people and the ghosts coexist but in temporary tension, in that each ghost will have to cease to be a ghost and so put to death its selfhood in order to remain in community with the solids, or each ghost will cease to be transformed by time's power.[101] Once the ghost with the lizard surrenders to God's working in the present moment, he is marvelously transformed:

> Then I saw . . . unmistakably solid but growing every moment solider, the upper arm and the shoulder of a man. Then, brighter still and stronger, the legs and hands. The neck and golden head materialized while I watched, and if my attention had not wavered I should have seen the actual completing of a man—an immense man, naked, not much smaller than the Angel. What

---

98. Lewis, *Letters* 2.962.
99. Bergson, *Time and Free Will*, 175.
100. Ibid., 176.
101. Lewis's idea that the ghost must cease to be a ghost is akin to the biblical concept of dying to the self. Cf. Luke 9:23, "And he said to all, "If anyone would come after me, let him deny himself and take up his cross daily and follow me."; Gal 5:24, "And those who belong to Christ Jesus have crucified the flesh with its passions and desires."

distracted me was the fact that at the same moment something seemed to be happening to the Lizard . . . what stood before me was the greatest stallion I have ever seen, silvery white but with mane and tail of gold. . . . The new-made man turned and clapped the new horse's neck . . . . Then, still like a star, I saw them winding up . . . they vanished, bright themselves, into the rose-brightness of that everlasting morning.[102]

Lewis's theology of the present goes even further than Bergson's notion of transformative time. Lewis takes a Bergsonian model of dynamic time and theologizes it to construct his own model of durative force. As with the ghost and his lizard, time works as a transformational mode of experience. The transformed ghost acts freely by choosing the salvific act of self-surrender, and to act freely is "to retake possession of oneself" in the form of surrender to the durative present.[103] Likewise, in *The Great Divorce*, to experience soteriological transformation is "to place oneself in pure duration," as Bergson describes.[104]

The glorified ghost attests to the theme that human emotion, moral, virtues, the blackest vice, all must, will, and do change in the imagined world of *The Great Divorce* through the force of time. It is precisely this unceasing, metaphysical movement that invites a dynamist reading, as the ghosts embody—or perhaps disembody—animated morality or immorality through the Bergsonian duration represented by the novel's action. As Lewis scholar Clyde Kilby notes, one of the most predominant themes in Lewis is that "every living being is destined for everlasting life and that every moment of life is a preparation for that condition."[105] Kilby connects everlasting life with the temporality of moments, claiming that for Lewis the latter composes the former. Every present moment is a preparation for an eternal state, as each present moment holds an individual's choice of either salvation or damnation. Each choice, always made in the present, determines the spiritual state, whether heaven or hell, in which one will eternally abide.

Another example of this dynamic becoming in time is the encounter between the obsessive ghostly mother Pam and her glorified acquaintance Reginald. Pam lost her son Michael, who now resides in the High Countries, some time ago. All that Pam selfishly wants from the present

---

102. Lewis, *Great Divorce*, 111–12.
103. Bergson, *Time and Free Will*, 174.
104. Ibid.
105. Kilby, *The Christian World of C. S. Lewis*, 180.

conversation with Reginald is to take Michael back for herself. Reginald tells Pam that her obsessive love for her son while he yet lived on earth "was uncontrolled and fierce and monomaniac.... [W]hen that first kind of love was thwarted, then there was just a chance that in the loneliness, in the silence, something else might begin to grow."[106] The glorified Reginald's message about Pam's merely instinctual "love" is one of dynamic morality, identifying the kind of *bad* that Lewis said in the preface grows to full *evil*. Reginald explains that what started as a simple desire, Pam's love for her son, had to by its very essence grow into something else. In Pam's case, her love grew to a self-serving, selfish possessiveness masked as love (much like Orual's love for Psyche in *Till We Have Faces*). Pam's bent love could not endure, as the conversational present reveals. In the High Countries' durative time, there is no static state for human emotion; all must move, change, and be transformed.

In view of Pam's dynamically regressive spiritual condition, the character Lewis asks his guide, the Christian fantasy writer George MacDonald (1824–1905), also a character in the novel, to explain further. MacDonald tells him, "There's something in natural affection which will lead it on to eternal love more easily than natural appetite could be led on" and further explains, "Every natural love will rise again and live forever in this country: but none will rise again until it has been buried."[107] Again, Lewis's idea that life predicates a death is biblical, for example, Jesus's words in John 12:24, "I tell you the truth, unless a kernel of wheat falls to the ground and dies, it remains only a single seed. But if it dies, it produces many seeds." Much like Jesus's description that spiritual transformation only occurs after the self figuratively falls and dies, love as Lewis imagines it acts in motion, oscillating between its most natural human expression and its most idealized, spiritual state. Lewis imagines natural love being transformed into an eternal counterpart through a surrender to God's working on the individual in time ("none will rise until it has been buried").

Here again we come up against a Bergsonian notion in *The Great Divorce*, for according to Bergson, all inner states, love especially, grow in accordance to their inherent vital impulse. "Feeling is a living being, which develops, and is therefore always changing," Bergson states.[108] It is when one fails to consciously allow one's inner states to grow in duration that "feeling loses its animation," leaving the individual to be only a shadow

---

106. Lewis, *Great Divorce*, 100.
107. Ibid., 104–5.
108. Bergson, *Time and Free Will*, 132.

of himself. Much like Lewis's ghosts, who are given the ever-important choice of present moment, in Bergson's thinking the transformation of internal states happens in duration or not at all.

This transformation through duration is manifest in yet another revealing passages about Lewis's use of Bergson dynamism in time. Upon first meeting George MacDonald, the confused Lewis asks him to explain what keeps spiritually taking place in the conversations he has been witnessing. In a particularly didactic fashion, MacDonald explains that good and evil, as dynamic states, operate through time and motion in the individual's life: "not knowing that Heaven, once attained, *will work backwards and turn* even that agony into a glory . . . little dreaming *how damnation will spread back and back* into their past and contaminate the pleasure of sin. *Both processes begin* even before death."[109] Not only does MacDonald's explanation reveal just how dynamic morality operates in Lewis's world, it also reveals Lewis's dependence on a Bergsonian system of thought. Heaven in *The Great Divorce* is most certainly a place, and its spatial qualities are often the narrator's focus. But, when MacDonald speaks of heaven's working backwards, he is not speaking of heaven's broadening its boundaries. Rather, heaven as an epoch of time "will work backwards." Likewise, hell, or the state of damnation, "will spread back and back into their past."[110]

Both heaven and hell are kinds of times. Good and evil move like personalized cosmic forces back through time and eternity to shape earlier actions. Good deeds do not exist concretely like moral mountains, but rather move like meteors through the temporal and spiritual worlds, acting as forces of change. Likewise, evil pierces back through time as both moral cause *and* effect, perpetuating itself unless suspended by some choice of the individual. As articulated in the preface, good and evil—both described in perpetual movement away from one another—dynamically change the moral, spiritual, and narrative space of the novel. *The Great Divorce* is more about the dynamic process of damnation and salvation *in time* than the final states associated with good and evil; indeed, heaven and hell (or the High Countries and the Grey Town) function as animated realms in which dynamic spirituality can operate. Though he was likely not applying a cosmological template to the imagined world of *The Great Divorce*, Lewis seems to be perpetuating a theologically informed version of dynamism—a contrived world in which humanity itself moves, grows,

---

109. Lewis, *Great Divorce*, 69.
110. Ibid.

and finds its essence in dynamic activity, "Redeemed humanity is still young, it has hardly come to its full strength...."[111]

The last passage on time that I want to look it is perhaps the most theologically important in the book. At the end of the novel, still confused about the dynamic relationship between a present moment and eternal states, still questioning how eternal salvation plays out in a present moment, Lewis asks MacDonald to explain the theology of all he has seen. MacDonald's answer is a dichotomous explanation about the nature of time: "If ye put the question from within Time and are asking about possibilities, the answer is certain. The choice is always before you. Neither is closed. Any man may choose eternal death. Those who choose it will have it."[112] MacDonald explains that for the ghosts facing the present moment of each conversation, the decision is clear enough. In time, the choice to have eternal life is always present in the moment. One has only to choose it. But, MacDonald warns that if one is trying to answer the question from an eternal perspective, then one asks "what cannot be answered to mortal ears."[113] MacDonald tells Lewis that "Time is the very lens through which ye see—small and clear, as men see through the wrong end of a telescope—something that would otherwise be too big for ye to see at all."[114] Though it provides only a limited view, the lens of time is necessary to understand the workings of eternity.

MacDonald says that what men cannot understand and what time allows them to perceive is freedom, "the gift whereby ye most resemble your Maker are yourselves parts of eternal reality."[115] Freedom manifests Lewis's theology of the present in that it enables eternity to meet the temporal. Through freedom expressed in temporal time one is allowed to partake of an eternal reality that is duration. One half of Bergson's *Time and Free Will* is devoted to this concept of freedom in duration. According to Bergson, freedom *is* the force of durative time in that freedom allows the individual to know duration, if he/she chooses: "there is a conscious force or free will, which, subject to the action of time and storing up duration, would, by this very fact, escape the law of the conservation of energy."[116] In his typical refutation of scientific thinking about time, Bergson says that free will

---

111. Ibid., 120.
112. Ibid., 140.
113. Ibid.
114. Ibid., 140–41.
115. Ibid., 141.
116. Bergson, *Time and Free Will*, 116.

builds up over time, dynamically increasing in the consciousness as time passes. Unlike a conservational theory, which holds that energy remains the same over time, Bergson says that freedom flows with time's force. Bergson would go on in *Time and Free Will* to say that freedom is how duration is experienced, and that both freedom and duration "are in a continual state of becoming, like real living beings."[117] Bergson presents freedom as that which accesses durative force, the two coming together like intersecting lines, and in its high view of freedom as the way to eternal reality, the concluding treatment of time in *The Great Divorce* unfolds along these Bergsonian lines.

What every conversation in *The Great Divorce* demonstrates is that freedom is a channel for duration and that durative time meets temporality if one chooses to experience the eternal force of the present moment. The assumption is that behind time is an eternal reality and that free choice is the way to know the eternal through the temporal. In the novel, when one chooses salvation, that person experiences the power of the eternal through the temporal moment. Those characters who do not choose salvation remain trapped in temporality, never knowing the eternal. Thus, not only do the conversations serve as rhetorical devices that foster the novel's theme of present time, but the two types of characters involved in every conversation create an intersection of the text's two types of time: temporal and eternal.

The novel ends with a sudden transformation of worlds. Lewis records that "suddenly all was changed," and in the place of the High Countries was a giant chessboard.[118] Lewis observes that the chess pieces are really "men and women as they appear to themselves and to one another in this world," and the chessboard was really time itself.[119] Surrounding the chessboard were "the immortal souls of those same men and women" who were actually moving on the chessboard. Bewildered, Lewis asks MacDonald, "is all that I have been seeing in this country false? These conversations between the Spirits and the Ghosts—were only the mimicry of choices that had really been made long ago?"[120] To which MacDonald cryptically responds, "Or might yet not as well say, anticipation of a choice to be made at the end of all things?"[121] The analogy of the chessboard along with Mac-

---

117. Ibid., 137.
118. Lewis, *Great Divorce*, 143.
119. Ibid.
120. Ibid., 144.
121. Ibid., 144.

Donald's words reaffirm the novel's theme of cosmological dualism. Each choice made in time creates an eternal reality, and the choice made in the present moment anticipates an ultimate spiritual decision.

MacDonald intimates that free choice mediates eternity in such a way that successive events coalesce. MacDonald says that in time free will is easy enough to understand. But from an eternal perspective, free will carries with it another reality. In the same way that the preface presented the theme of moral dynamism—how good and evil grow in time, and how heaven and hell will work backwards through time—MacDonald says that the present moment dynamically expands beyond itself by the eternity it carries. In other words, the present is no longer just the present. It is now the eternal. This interplay between the temporal and eternal is another Bergsonian idea. According to Bergson, "A perpetuity of mobility is possible only if it is backed by an eternity of immutability, which it unwinds in a chain without beginning or end."[122] Bergson sees the exercise of free will in time ("perpetuity of mobility") as a possibility only if it is backed by a constant flow of the eternal. Eternity empowers the present to so profusely that each moment enables an almost infinite amount of choices. Time unwinds the eternal through durative force and free choice, but only because a dualism exists that empowers the temporal. In other words, if there is no eternal, there is no temporal. *The Great Divorce* endorses this belief that there is a temporal and an eternal world, and, while distinct, the two mutually penetrate one another in durative force.

An eschatological event concludes the work, echoing the novel's overall theme of the temporal being interrupted by the eternal: the arrested sun finally rises, initiating "the sunrise that shoots Time dead with golden arrows."[123] Most abruptly, the eternal that has knocked on the door of the present for the duration of the book finally breaks through. The novel's end reinforces the theme of the force of time by depicting eternity as a power that must inevitably pierce the present. "The sunrise" is an image of inevitably (of course the sun will rise) that fosters the novel's central idea that the eternal infuses the temporal, even to the point of eventually overtaking the temporal. For the theme of time in *The Great Divorce* exists to manifest the eternal. Once the eternal overtakes the temporal, time in the novel ceases to be. In the end, the medium of time is removed and the characters are faced with a final eternal state. Whether that final state be

---

122. Bergson, *Creative Evolution*, 63.
123. Lewis, *Great Divorce*, 145.

eternal salvation or eternal damnation depends on how one has chosen to experience the temporal.

Conclusion

The Great Divorce is a novel about spiritual and cosmological dualism, moral dynamism, and the theology of durative force. To treat those themes, Lewis employs Bergsonian ideas. It is this employment of Bergsonian philosophy that most shapes Lewis's theology of time. One could say that *The Great Divorce* is a "baptized" twentieth-century philosophical work in that it shares the themes of dynamism, dualism, and assumptions about how time operates. But Lewis goes beyond Bergson's ideas. *The Great Divorce* uses Bergson's philosophy to frame a theology of time, draws spiritual implications from Bergson's duration, and ultimately reaches for a redeemed resolution that presents time as the way to know the eternal.

Not only is *The Great Divorce* about time, but it is a work built on a Bergsonian foundation about how time works as a transformative theological force. Like Bergson, Lewis imagines two kinds of time experienced by two kinds of self. Like Bergson, Lewis sees inner states as dynamic, ever-changing entities that move with the force of time. And, like Bergson, Lewis sees time as the revealer of one's inner states, the intersection when the eternal meets the temporal, and the ultimate instrument of transformation for the individual's consciousness.

4

T. S. Eliot's Bergsonism "Always Present"

Incarnation and Duration in Four Quartets

In this chapter, I will argue for a theological reading of time in *The Four Quartets* modeled on the Bergsonian idea of duration, previously detailed. Eliot chose to employ a Christian reading of time by incorporating Bergson's influential ideologies, rather than drawing from biblical statements of time or on the theories of past or contemporary prominent theologians. The *Four Quartets* is a poem that promotes, through its reliance on Bergsonian ideas, a theological understanding of time. *Four Quartets* demonstrates an absorption of twentieth-century philosophy for the purpose of constructing theology. Like Bergson, Eliot will emphasize the themes of human experience in time, time's ability to reveal deeper personal meaning, and the power of time to transform human inner states, or what Bergson called *intensities*. While Bergson is not known as a Christian thinker, he certainly is a twentieth-century thinker, and his ideas provide a sort of "middle ground" between secular modernism and Christianity on which Eliot constructs a redemptive view of time. As Bergson saw real duration as the conduit for deeply meaningful human experience, so Eliot sees theological time as a medium for the salvific Christian doctrine of the Incarnation. But Eliot also furthers Bergson's notion of time as a force by depicting it as a salvific force. This chapter will show that the *Four Quartets* poeticizes Bergsonian intuition and duration to create a theology of experience in time. Through my Bergsonian reading the following ideas in Eliot will emerge: to experience the force of the past and the future, one must experience the spiritually charged present; to experience the redemptive that is metonymically depicted in the poem as the eternal, one must experience time; and to experience spiritual transformation, one must surrender to the workings of the divine in time.

The critical conversation on Eliot's *Four Quartets* to which I am going to contribute has not yet adequately treated the relationship between Eliot's theology and Bergsonian philosophy. In my reading of *Four Quartets*, I will engage the scholarship most pertinent to my analysis of the topic, and in so doing I will argue that Eliot relies on secular philosophy to articulate his theology, an argument not made by many. In order to clearly articulate my argument that Eliot framed Christian theology in Bergsonian terms, I will first survey the few scholars who have written on the relationship between Eliot and Bergson as it relates to Eliot's depiction of time in *Four Quartets*.

A good preliminary reading of Eliot's reliance on Bergson has been performed by Mary Ann Gillies, though she does not engage specific texts by Bergson. Mary Ann Gillies has written extensively on Bergson and his influence on twentieth-century thought. In her book *Henri Bergson and British Modernism*, Gillies devotes a chapter to Bergson's influence on Eliot. In her chapter, "T. S. Eliot: The Poet," Gillies argues that her discussion of Eliot's poetry will "demonstrate its dependency on Bergson's philosophy and will also illustrate how Eliot's gradual movement toward Christianity is foreshadowed by those elements Eliot borrows from Bergson's theories."[1] Gillies then goes on to examine the following categories where Bergson's influence on Eliot is most apparent: time, self, consciousness, and memory. Among the poems Gillies examines, *Four Quartets* receives significant attention.

Gillies begins her analysis of *Four Quartets*, rightly I think, by considering Eliot's conversion to the Christian faith in 1927. Gillies insists that Eliot's conversion was a solution to his growing problem of living in a world "without absolutes."[2] Eliot turned to the Christian faith as an epistemological and spiritual counter to all of the early twentieth-century's scientific theories and the widespread skepticism in religion. Gillies argues

1. Gillies, *T. S. Eliot*, 78.
2. Ibid., 96.

that the "fundamental link between Bergson and the Christian faith that Eliot so enthusiastically embraced" is the notion of process.³ It is Bergson's emphasis on the process of conscious development in time, Gillies insists, that Eliot found so attractive. Gillies relates Bergson's emphasis on process to the Christian's belief that God designs, even ordains, those events of an individual's life that development him or her spiritually.⁴

Providing a brief overview of Eliot's *Four Quartets*, Gillies's treatment of Bergson and Eliot calls special attention to the poem's emphasis on how humans understand and relate to God in time. Understanding God in time necessitates making God "material" through the lens of temporal thinking. The paradox, according to Gillies, is that the God humans must know through the temporal and material world is an infinite, eternal, and transcendent being.⁵ In her reading of *Four Quartets*, Gillies intimates that Eliot connects Bergson's notion of duration with the time that God enters in order to make Himself known. As I will do in my analysis, Gillies emphasizes the importance of the Incarnation for Eliot, arguing that the concept of Bergson's duration and the Christian notion of eternity must meet at the point of Incarnation in which the eternal God enters temporal time.

However, unlike Gillies, who claims connection between Eliot and Bergson but as previously mentioned does not engage specific texts by Bergson, I will read *Four Quartets* for its connections with *Time and Free Will* and other selected Bergson texts. A more important difference between Gillies's contribution and my own is that I will trace the entirety of Eliot's theology of time in *Four Quartets*, demonstrating a thorough, multivalent reliance on Bergsonism. Not only does Eliot rely on Bergson's theory of duration as a force of change, but he also depends on Bergson's depictions of superficial and fundamental human experience in time as well as on how an intuitive knowledge of time can transform human inner states, or intensities, as Bergson calls them. Gillies, while helpful in showing the connection between Bergson and Eliot, does not account for the particulars of Eliot's dependence or the reason why Eliot employed Bergsonism. I will examine the Bergsonian framework for Eliot's theology of time, demonstrate the many connections between *Four Quartets* and Bergsonian duration, and show Eliot to be a theological writer in the vein of Lewis and Auden, one who saw fit to draw on the common currency

---

3. Ibid., 97.
4. Ibid., 96–98.
5. Ibid., 98.

of Bergsonian thought in order to articulate his theology to a twentieth-century audience.

Another scholar who treats Bergson's relationship with Eliot is Staffan Bergsten, in his *Time and Eternity*. Bergsten explores the theological and philosophical underpinnings of Eliot's depictions of time, placing Eliot in the larger group of modernist writers who were concerned with the same theme. The decades leading up to *Four Quartets* were characterized by a larger preoccupation with time, which characterized early twentieth-century Europe. As evidence of this preoccupation, Bergsten cites philosopher Samuel Alexander, a figure briefly discussed in the last chapter, who asserted in 1921:

> If I were to name the most characteristic feature of the thought of the last twenty-five years, I should answer, the discovery of Time. I do not mean that we have waited until today to become familiar with Time; I mean that we have only just begun, in our speculation, to take Time seriously, and to realize that in some way or other Time is an essential ingredient in the constitution of things.[6]

Bergsten uses Alexander's statement to emphasize the heightened sense of and interest in time during the years in which Eliot wrote. Throughout the 1920s, debates about time abounded. Twentieth-century writers such as Gertrude Stein (*Composition as Explanation*, 1926) and Wyndham Lewis (*Time and Western Man*, 1927) created a discourse on time that could not help but influence Eliot. Bergsten describes this discourse about time by literary figures as a symptom of a larger philosophical problem of time (partly attested to in this dissertation in chapters one and two), to which Bergson would be one of the twentieth-century's most formative contributors.[7]

Bergsten insists that Bergson's thinking, along with Einstein's, was one of the greatest influences on Eliot's conceptions of time, but this general claim is as far as Bergsten goes in his argument for a Bergsonian influence on Eliot's work. While Bergsten rightly asserts that "Eliot's conception of the timeless is as much religious as philosophical," he offers very little connection between Bergson's philosophy and Eliot's theology.[8] Bergsten attributes Eliot's theology of time in *Four Quartets* to a variety of sources:

---

6. Bergston, *Time and Eternity*, 28.
7. Ibid., 30.
8. Ibid., 33.

the nature of time is clearly what interests Eliot, and in so far as his conception of time and the timeless in the *Four Quartets* is derived from philosophy, it is derived from the Platonic, Idealist tradition in metaphysics, and the modern theories have worked as a strong but negative stimulus, directing his attention to the treatment of time in classical philosophy.[9]

Bergsten here attributes Eliot's theology of time to pre-modern philosophical systems, going so far as to attribute to modern theories a negative influence on Eliot's thinking. Bergsten further insists that Eliot rejects the "current philosophical and theological approaches to the problem of time" (e.g., Bergsonism), because they did not cohere with the traditions of Eliot's Christian faith.[10] Bergsten devotes some two hundred pages analyzing *Four Quartets*, often attributing Eliot's theology of time to historically monumental Christian texts like Dante's *Divine Comedy*.[11] Unlike Bergsten, I will argue that Eliot was positively influenced by Bergson's theory of duration, and that the poet employs Bergson's thinking more than that of any other thinker on time to complete his theology. Thus, the relationship between Eliot's theology and Bergson's philosophy is one of ideological dependence, and attention to that dependence is key to elucidating Eliot's theology of time.

One scholar who does mention a connection between Eliot's concept of time and Bergson's philosophy is Morris Weitz, who notes, "it is often said that Eliot's conception of time is derived from Heraclitus, and is consequently similar to Bergson's."[12] It is remarkable, however, Weitz

9. Ibid., 33.
10. Ibid., 34.
11. Ibid., 22, 35, 53–59, 70, 77, 87, 140–53, 212, 237, 244. Because Bergsten argues that Eliot's theology of time comes primarily from Dante, I should provide some reasons why I do not hold this same view. While Christian writers are often influenced by several thinkers from various periods of time, while Dante's *Divine Comedy* is a major work in the Christian literary tradition, and while Eliot alluded to Dante in his poetry, an argument for Dante as Eliot's primary influence does not account for the dissimilarities between Dante and Eliot. The force of time as imagined by Eliot has no counterpart in Dante, nor does Dante emphasize spiritual growth through duration as Eliot does. Dante also has little to do with the twentieth-century philosophical context in which Eliot wrote, and his ideas were certainly not thought to be prominent counters to twentieth-century philosophical systems like positivism or scientific mechanism. Finally, when comparing the similarities between constructions of time in Eliot and Bergson or Eliot and Dante, one sees that Eliot's and Bergson's depictions of time share remarkable commonalities, while Dante and Eliot have far less coherence on the subjects of time and human consciousness.
12. Weitz, "Time as a Mode of Salvation," 139.

provides no basis for his claim that Eliot's and Bergson's treatments of time are similar. Rather, Weitz argues for a neo-Platonic notion of time in Eliot that results in a "repudiation of the Heraclitean with its insistence upon the ultimate character of time as flux."[13] Weitz focuses on the two Heraclitean quotes at the beginning of *Four Quartets*, arguing that Eliot "changes the Heraclitean theory of time [i.e., that temporal time is always in flux] into a Christian theory of value," in which time must be seen as more than flux if it is to be congruent with Eliot's Christian faith.[14]

Like Bergsten's, Weitz's reading of *Four Quartets* dismisses Bergson's influence on Eliot. Indeed, Weitz spends most of his time on *Four Quartets* contending against a Bergsonian or Heraclitean reading, yet he offers no alternate theory to account for Eliot's complex theology of time. Thus, one is left to imagine Eliot's ideological sources instead of being provided those philosophies (e.g., Bergson's) that do account for Eliot's theological articulations. My argument contributes to Eliot studies in that it not only accounts for the philosophical source of Eliot's theological content, but it also places Eliot in the same literary category as fellow Christian authors Lewis and Auden, all of whom treated time in terms of secular philosophy.

Eliot: A Christian Thinker's Concern for Time

T. S. Eliot epitomizes the intersection of twentieth-century ideology and Christianity. Modernism's preeminent poet, Eliot had what Ackroyd calls a "monumental reputation" well before his most ambitious Christian work, *Four Quartets*, was published in installments from 1936 to 1943.[15] Unlike his contemporary, Christian writer C. S. Lewis, whose relationship to modernism is tenuous, Eliot's position in literary modernism need not be argued.[16] Indeed, Eliot is one of the literary figures from the first quarter of the twentieth century most associated with and representative of high modernism, a literary giant whose pre-Christian label by Wyndham Lewis

13. Ibid., 139.
14. Ibid., 142.
15. Ackroyd, *T. S. Eliot*, 291.
16. It should be noted that Lewis and Eliot shared a unique relationship. Neither very fond of the other, the two mostly differed on literary tastes, though they agreed on the essential soteriology of the Christian faith. Indeed, Lewis says, "I agree with Eliot on matters of such great importance that all literary questions are trivial in comparison," *Preface to Paradise Lost*, 9. For more on their relationship, see Tetreault's "Parallel Lines: C. S. Lewis and T. S. Eliot," 256–69; see also Spurr's Appendix, "T. S. Eliot and C. S. Lewis," 254–56.

as a "man of 1914" connoted a strong association with modernism's most bold artists (Woolf, Joyce, Pound, and Wyndham Lewis himself).

"Prufrock" (1915) made Eliot a known literary figure in England. *The Waste Land* (1922) made him an international figure, and by the end 1922 Eliot had already launched his own literary journal, the *Criterion*.[17] Eliot would eventually become the loudest voice of the Christian intelligentsia. For that reason, Eliot's post-conversion corpus is perhaps one of the most important bodies of literature if one wishes to study the marriage of literary modernism and the Christian faith. Before taking a focused look at *Four Quartets*, I will discuss some pertinent ideological implications of poetry that stemmed from Eliot's Christian ideology, briefly look at Eliot's treatment of time in selected pre-conversion works, including *The Waste Land*, and discuss the poet's connections with Henri Bergson.

Eliot was intensely invested in the marriage of writing and faith. The poet's conversion to the Christian faith in 1927 brought with it new ideas about the role of art and the artist. Though "conversion" is the term most applied to writers like Lewis, Eliot, and Auden, it is not always exhaustive enough to encompass its many implications for the Christian artist. Barry Spurr, whose *Anglo-Catholic in Religion* (2010) looks at Eliot's relationship to the Anglo-Catholic faith, argues,

> the term *conversion* in Eliot's case tends to diminish the importance of all the diverse elements that led up to his baptism and confirmation over so many years . . . in relation to the reading and interpretation of Eliot's poetry and plays, *conversion* is a term best avoided, having practically no relevance at all . . . to the understanding and appreciation of his verse.[18]

Spurr cites some of Eliot's earliest post-conversion works, like "Journey of the Magi" (1927), as examples of "the difficulties of faith and the elusiveness of transcendental experience."[19] Spurr's point is that Eliot's pre- and post-conversion works do not cleanly break on the line of conversion. Rather, the difficulties that defined Eliot's early works like *The Waste Land* (1922) continued to define his post-conversion writing, like his themes of fragmentation in human experience or the difficulty of transcending the social through the metaphysical.

---

17. For more on Eliot's pre-conversion literary legacy, see Gordon's *Eliot's Early Years*; Matthieson's *The Achievement of T. S. Eliot*; and Pinion's *A T. S. Eliot Companion*.
18. Spurr, *Anglo-Catholic in Religion*, 112–13.
19. Ibid., 113.

However, some new questions emerge because of Eliot's conversion. One such question is the nature and function of Christian art, a subject about which Eliot was interested his entire post-conversion life. Christian literary theorist Michael Edwards says that for Eliot the "question of writing Christianly was paramount,"[20] and it is that question that drove much of Eliot's post-conversion verse as well as his criticism. In a post-conversion preface to his pre-conversion collection of essays, *The Sacred Wood* (1920), Eliot highlighted the relationship between poetry and religion, claiming that a poem "in some sense, has its own life."[21] The poem's "life" is its philosophical message, its overall ideology, which transcends the poem itself. Eliot connects this life of a poem with its relationship to religious belief, concluding the preface with the claim that "poetry certainly has something to do with morals, and with religion."[22] The relationship between belief and poetry would be more articulated in Eliot's more concentrated critical works.[23]

The question of art and the Christian faith is also a central theme in his 1935 essay "Religion and Literature," where Eliot addresses the relationship of theology and poetry. Eliot's main argument in the essay is that the modernist Christian should judge literature with theological criteria, rather than by literary criteria alone. Given the lack of Christian standards in modernist art, Eliot declares, "it is the more necessary for Christian readers to scrutinize their reading, especially of works of imagination, with explicit ethical and theological standards."[24] Eliot's interest in upholding a Christian reading is directly related to his low view of modernism's morality. Eliot accuses modernist literature of an inability to apprehend the supernatural. Eliot calls this inability Secularism, claiming that "the whole of modern literature is corrupted by what I call Secularism, that it is simply unaware of, simply cannot understand the meaning of, the primacy of the supernatural over the natural life: of something which I assume to be our primary concern."[25] Eliot goes on to clarify that what he means by modernist literature's secularism is not that it is immoral or amoral,

---

20. Edwards, *Towards a Christian Poetics*, 99.
21. Eliot, *The Sacred Wood*, viii.
22. Ibid.
23. Eliot's *After Strange Gods* (1933) and other critical works like "The Idea of a Christian Society" (1939) are important examples of how Eliot's Christian faith overlapped with his views of modernism, but neither deal most directly with Eliot's view of Christian art.
24. Eliot, *Selected Prose*, 97.
25. Ibid., 104–5.

but that it is ignorant of any fundamentally important issues regarding Christian theology.

Eliot's critique of modern Secularism was more intensely expressed some ten years before "Religion and Literature," when critic and rhetorician I. A. Richards published "A Background for Contemporary Poetry" in *Criterion* in 1925, sparking a debate between Richards and Eliot on the relationship of poetry and belief that would last well into the 1930s. As Richards described modern man's worldview, "A sense of desolation, of uncertainty, of futility, of the baselessness of aspirations, of the vanity of endeavor, and a thirst for a life-giving water which seems suddenly to have failed, are the signs in consciousness of this necessary reorganization of our lives."[26] By "necessary reorganization, Richards is referring to the rapidly growing acceptance of a scientific world. He leaves no doubt as to how some artists saw modernism's morality. Particularly interesting is his biblical allusion to modernist man's "thirst for a life-giving water" (cf. Jesus's words in John 7:37–39),[27] which reveals a particularly religious element in Richards's diagnosis of the modernist condition. Modernism created a spiritual thirst that was quenched by nothing spiritual. One could say that the solution to Richards's diagnosis was taken up in Eliot's post-conversion work, where Christian theology and a high view of art meet. To post-conversion Eliot, the problem with modernist literature, as with modernism as a whole, was its skewed morality, though for post-conversion Eliot, the answer to modernism's moral apathy was the Christian faith.

By his religious turn in 1927, Eliot saw the Christian faith, and by extenstion the Christian church, as the solution to Richard's failed "thirst for a life-giving water." Indeed, the problems of modern society as post-conversion Eliot saw them were rooted in their removal from the Christian church. To Eliot, the importance of the Christian church could not be overstated as a crucial catalyst for social change. As John Xiros Cooper says about Eliot's relationship to the Christian community:

> Church gave him a thoroughly historical social locus, which neither the notion of myth nor the dehistoricized Hegel of Bradleyan idealism contact. Yet the church, also, offered a transcendental signified that raises the Church's spiritual and cultural

---

26. Richards, "A Background for Contemporary Poetry," 520.

27. "On the last and greatest day of the festival, Jesus stood and said in a loud voice, 'Let anyone who is thirsty come to me and drink. Whoever believes in me, as Scripture has said, rivers of living water will flow from within them.' By this he meant the Spirit, whom those who believed in him were later to receive. Up to that time the Spirit had not been given, since Jesus had not yet been glorified."

significance beyond mere contingency: it is both of the world and not of the world in a way that can adequately illuminate the relation of the historical and transcendental in a single visible unity.[28]

According to Cooper, what Eliot found in the Christian church was a paradoxical yet fulfilling answer to the question of socio-historical place in the world. Unlike some other philosophies (i.e., those of Hegel and Bradley), Christianity offered Eliot a real social space to encounter the transcendent in a "single visible unity." The church combined the transcendental and the visible. This combination metaphorically manifested the intersection of supernatural and social, of spiritual and physical, and of faith and art.

When one considers Eliot's art, one can appreciate this appeal of the Christian church. Eliot's post-conversion verse often mirrors this dynamic of the theologically transcendent meeting the local in a work of "single visible unity." For example, there are not many better examples of the transcendent touching the socio-historical than Eliot's early post-conversion poem "Journey of the Magi" (1927). The poem recounts the journey of the Magi to see the newborn Christ. The poem's speaker is unaware of the journey's exact purpose and unaware of his own spiritual depravity, as the poem builds to the moment of spiritual awakening. Upon seeing the Incarnate Christ, the Magi pass over from spiritual death to life. The poem is remarkably void of spiritual language, is much more descriptive and local in scope than the majority of Eliot's work, and never explicitly Christological, though the subject matter centers on the Advent. What the poem does provide, through its localized imagery and plot of physical journey, is a theological theme of death to self, leading to spiritual salvation.[29] The poem's speaker is keenly aware that despite the seemingly mundane events involved, a transcendental act has occurred:

> were we led all that way for
> Birth or Death? There was a Birth, certainly,
> We had evidence and no doubt. I had seen birth and death,
> But had thought they were different; this Birth was
> Hard and bitter agony for us, like Death, our death.[30]

---

28. Cooper, *T. S. Eliot and the Ideology of the Four Quartets*, 9.
29. Pinion, *A T. S. Eliot Companion*, 71–73.
30. Eliot, "Journey of the Magi," lines 34–39.

The speaker's ambiguous understanding of his conversion coheres with Eliot's opinion in "Religion and Literature" of what Christian art should do. While it can and should be thoroughly theological, Christian literature should not be overtly Christian. Indeed, besides explicitly religious writing, which is not Eliot's main concern, Eliot calls for a literature that "should be *un*consciously, rather than deliberately and defiantly, Christian."[31] Here Eliot reveals the philosophy that Christian art should be theological—for that is part of Eliot's agenda in the essay, to show theology's place in literature—but not explicitly "Christian." While Eliot is thoroughly invested in the theological (*Four Quartets*, *Ash Wednesday*, *The Rock*), he has no interest in proselytizing. What is most important for Eliot is a work's artistic and theological integrity, not its ability to convert. "Journey of the Magi" navigates this polarity between the theological and the overtly Christian, by presenting the former but refusing the latter. The *Four Quartets* will uphold its Christian identity in this same way, not by being overtly Christian in language or rhetorical appeal, but by the theology interwoven in its verse.

Theological prowess, and somewhat inaccessible theology at that, is certainly the philosophy behind the *Four Quartets*, a poem unmistakably theological but resistant to any easy Christian interpretation that might lead to religious decision. Perhaps Helen Gardner's classic work *The Art of T. S. Eliot* (1949) captures it best:

> If *Four Quartets* shows skepticism integrated into faith, it shows skepticism none the less; and in a skeptical age it speaks to those whose skepticism stops at the question, and to those who are led to denial, as well as those who are led to believe. It is not the poet's business to make us believe *what* he believes, but to make us believe *that* he believes.[32]

Gardner's discussion of the poem's skepticism is not a promotion of unbelief. Quite the opposite, Gardner sees skepticism as an honest, authentic sign of the poet's belief. And while that belief is not impervious to doubt, it is a belief nonetheless. This promotion of skepticism within belief is only one of element of *Four Quartets*' complex theology. Indeed, portions of *Four Quartets* like "Dry Salvages" seemingly undoes the poem's theological work by exploring the experience of spiritual isolation. Despite the poem's treatment of spiritual regression, what one sees in *Four Quartets* is a poet steeped in theological belief. Indeed, what one sees in

---

31. Eliot, "Religion and Literature," 100.
32. Gardner, *The Art of T. S. Eliot*, 68.

the *Quartets* is a concentrated attention to the poeticizing of theology, unprecedented in Eliot's career in terms of both scale and scope.[33] Eliot's post-conversion verse is the best evidence of the poet's beliefs in the presence of theology in art.

The impact of Eliot's conversion on his art cannot be overstated, and it is in his art that one best sees how completely Eliot's faith informs his poetry. The marked presence of theology in Eliot's verse has been noticed by many and criticized by some as a retreat from modernism's problems. In his review of Eliot's post-conversion poem "Ash Wednesday," Allen Tate criticizes Eliot's verse for its theological theme: "The reasoning that is being brought to bear upon Mr. Eliot's recent verse is as follows: Anglo-Catholicism would not at all satisfy; therefore, his poetry declines under its influence."[34] Tate charges that Eliot's post-conversion verse is "'not contemporaneous,' not solving any practical problems, and unable to do the public any good."[35] As F. O. Matthiessen notes about Tate's diagnosis of the nature of the problem of theology in Eliot's work, the issue is not whether one agrees or disagrees with the poem's Christian ideology.

Matthiessen himself is far less concerned by the religious motifs in Eliot's poetry, but he recognizes their undeniable presence. Indeed, "the question of our own acceptance or rejection of his doctrine remains irrelevant" Matthiessen proclaims in his authoritative study, *The Achievement of T. S. Eliot*.[36] Rather, what one must remember is that Eliot's theology is constitutionally a part of his post-conversion poetics, an organic extension of the poet's ecclesiastical life. Matthiessen quotes an anonymous reviewer's estimation of Eliot's theological writings, an estimation that captures this relationship between Christianity and art in Eliot's work: "To accept the poetry seems to amount to accepting an invitation to join the Anglican Church. For the assumption is that the poetry and the religious positions are identical."[37] According to the reviewer, to read Eliot's verse is to read the fullest expression of his Christian philosophy. While this reviewer

---

33. In *T. S. Eliot and the Ideology of Four Quartets*, John Xiros Cooper situates *Four Quartets* as an important work in a larger Christian literary revival: "[The apologetic that Eliot's Sweeney poems promotes] bristles with the code-words and notional idiom of the neo-conservatism that appeared as the important ideological force in a Christian literary revival in the 1940s, of which *Four Quartets* was then seen as forming a principal part," 112.

34. Tate, *The Poetry Reviews*, 117.

35. Ibid., 108.

36. Mathiessen, *The Achievement of T. S. Eliot*, 108.

37. Ibid.

mistakenly conflates Anglicanism with the Christian faith as a whole, the review underscores the significance the church had for Eliot and that his devotion to the faith finds expression in his theologized literature.

Because the important personal meaning that Eliot found in the church was matched only by what he considered the importance of theology in art, Eliot's verse and critical works are often the most complete pictures of Eliot's theological ideas. As his work attests, Eliot's Christian faith permeated every facet of his worldview, and very few issues remained outside of the jurisdiction of his Christian thinking. For example, works like "The Pensees of Pascal" (1931), "The Use of Poetry and the Use of Criticism" (1933), "The Aims of Education" (1950), and "To Criticize the Critic" (1961) all are amalgamations of Eliot's Christianity, his literary criticism, and his social commentary. Indeed, Christianity provided Eliot with a new view of personal and poetic life and art that would encompass all of his intellectual endeavors. Eliot's use of Bergson is a prime example of the poet's intellectual subjugation of secular philosophy for the Christian faith. In his use of Bergson, Eliot will fuse philosophical concepts of time with a dominant theological agenda of showing time as the medium for salvation. Through his new theological understanding, Eliot would come to contextualize issues of social and literary morality in the Christian faith.

According to Eliot, the task of the Christian thinker is to engage philosophical systems and ultimately to interrogate them, all under the auspices of the thinker's Christian faith. The Christian thinker is one who, after having sampled the world's systems of thought, resorts to Christianity in utter commitment to its doctrine. To truly reconcile himself with the world, the thoughtful Christian must stay "inexorably committed" to Christian doctrine:

> The Christian thinker—and I mean the man who is trying consciously and conscientiously to explain to himself the sequence which culminates in faith—proceeds by rejection and elimination. He finds the world to be so and so; he finds its character inexplicable by any non-religious theory: among religions he finds Christianity, and Catholic Christianity, to account most satisfactorily for the world and especially for the moral world within . . . he finds himself inexorably committed to the dogma of the Incarnation.[38]

Eliot's firm language suggests that the Christian thinker is best equipped to handle the world, as long as he is a "Catholic" Christian, that

38. Eliot, "The Pensees of Pascal," 113.

is, a Christian devoted to tenets of the universal Christian church, and wholly committed to the doctrine of the Incarnation. The importance of Eliot's denominational allegiance is beyond the scope of this study, but Eliot's specific mentioning of the Incarnation is not.[39] For Eliot, the act and doctrine of the Incarnation is of utmost importance, and much more will be said about this when looking at *Four Quartets*. As an introduction to the *Four Quartets*, the doctrine of the Incarnation is important because it reveals the theme that caused Eliot to write such a Bergsonian work, that theme being about time.

If poeticizing the theology of the Incarnation most informs Eliot's treatment of time in *Four Quartets*, which I will argue is the case, then it is not improbable that Eliot maintained some interest in the subject of Incarnation and time before his conversion. Indeed, while Eliot draws no Christian conclusions about time in works like *The Waste Land*, his pre-conversion interest in time is closely tied to theology as a whole and to the Incarnation (which I will define below) in particular.

Eliot's most seminal work, *The Waste Land*, written pre-conversion some twenty years before *Four Quartets*, already reveals the poet's concern for the theme of the theological in time. One can see in *The Waste Land* the seeds of inquiry about the meaning of time. In fact, after the publication of *The Waste Land*, novelist and critic Malcolm Cowley described Eliot's poetic message as a "simple" one: "The past was dignified; the present is barren of emotion."[40] As Cowley explains, in *The Waste Land* "the past was a landscape nourished by living fountains; now the fountains of spiritual grace are dry...."[41] Eliot would deny this, saying that he regarded no epoch of time as better than another and that all periods in time should be seen as qualitatively the same as the present.[42] Eliot's dismal view may be attributed to a pre-conversion perspective that saw no spiritual meaning in time.

Concerning Eliot's pre-conversion perspective, Edmund Wilson, editor at *Vanity Fair* and *The New Republic*, writes in a letter to American

---

39. Cf. Cooper's claims, "For Eliot, the church will remain the paramount social institution, the primary ideological state apparatus, even though it does not coincide entirely with the power elite or with the Community of Christians." Cooper, *T. S. Eliot and the Ideology of Four Quartets*, 97. For more on Eliot and his denominational association, see Spurr's *Anglo-Catholic in Religion*.

40. Cowley, *Exile's Return*, 113.

41. Ibid.

42. For more on Eliot's opinion of the moral states of historic epochs, see Longenbach, "Mature Poets Steal," 42.

poet John Peale Bishop that *The Waste Land* is "nothing more or less than a most distressingly moving account of Eliot's agonized state of mind during the years which preceded his nervous breakdown." Wilson also calls the poem a "cry *de profundis* if ever there was one" from a "sensitive man in the modern city chained to some work he hates and crucified on the vulgarity of his surroundings." The poem's profound cry is no doubt partly due to the soteriological emptiness it betrays, for the poem imagines time without Incarnational power and transformative theological meaning. Literary critic Claude Edmonde Magny claims that in *The Waste Land*, "we are in the bleak even time before the Incarnation, before the unique, exceptional event took place, that which, moreover the cards are unable to predict, because it is outside time."[43] Magny's comment calls attention to a prominent theme in *The Waste Land*, the inability of the present time to reveal salvific spiritual truth.

The poem advances this theme in several ways, some of which are the diction of broken time and the imagery of disrupted personal meaning. An example of present time's inability to reveal theological truth is in book two, "A Game of Chess," where Eliot employs Ovid's story of Tereus and Philomela, in which the mythic king Tereus rapes Philomela, who in some versions of the story is turned into a nightingale, and cuts out her tongue. This mythic allusion to the reduction of articulate meaning fosters the poem's greater theme of disruption in any knowable higher meaning. Ovid's myth is used to show that philosophical and/or theological meaning is reduced through the use of language, and that reduction is associated with time. Constant in *The Waste Land* is the reiterated theme of the mythic not providing a soteriology. The poem's myth does not communicate meaning in any discernable way, but rather offers a

> "Jug Jug" to dirty ears.
> And *other withered stumps of time*.[44]

The incommunicable "jug jug" of the mythic figure lands on ears unfit for hearing, or "dirty ears." This disruption in language and meaning is coupled with the "withered stumps" of deteriorated time. Not only is the articulation of meaning reduced to an inhuman "jug jug," but time itself is likened to Philomela's foreshortened tongue, cut off and unable to convey meaning about human experience.[45] The meaning of mythic history is met

---

43. Magny, "A Double Note on T. S. Eliot and James Joyce," 214.
44. Eliot, "The Waste Land," 1, lines 103–5.
45. "Jug jug jug jug jug jug" and the Tereus myth occur again in "The Fire Sermon,"

by the inefficacy of time to transmit that meaning. The poem's voracious appetite for divergent form and allusion collapses genre and intermeshes themes in destabilizing ways—i.e., by the myth that can no longer articulate truth and the withered time that cannot convey its meaning.

This textual dismantling facilitates the poem's underlying irony about the disillusionment of modern man in the foundational myths of Western society.[46] The poem's intertextual and ideological scope is vast, encompassing numerous genres (e.g., myth, homily, biblical texts) and even more philosophical categories (e.g., reality, space-time relationship, human experience). Time is one philosophical category that is frequently in the poem's purview. The speaker in "A Game of Chess" echoes the announcement of a pub at closing time, "HURRY UP PLEASE ITS TIME / HURRY UP PLEASE ITS TIME"[47] in the context of a cryptic Shakespearian allusion to mad Ophelia's last words before her death, "Good night, ladies, good night, sweet ladies, good night, good night."[48] Again, the poem's treatment of time is informed by the allusion in which it is couched, in this case a Shakespearean allusion that connotes time's imminent end, a permanent cessation of time in the poem's personal, spiritual, and social worlds. Whereas *Four Quartets* will give meaning to time, *The Waste Land* dismantles time's meaning through broken collages of allusion and fragmented diction, symbolized by "a heap of broken images."[49]

The theological meaning missing from *The Waste Land*'s treatment of time is that which the *Four Quartets* uses to give time its ultimate meaning: the Incarnation, the act of God's entering temporal time by taking on humanity. It is not space or abstract consciousness into which Eliot writes the Incarnation. The conduit for the Incarnate is time. The Incarnation defines the theological meaning of time in the *Four Quartets* by giving time its identity as the theological instrument of divine revelation. For example, in "Burnt Norton," the speaker says, "only through time time is conquered."[50] The Christian view of the Incarnation is that Christ, the eternal logos, entered history by taking on human flesh and that the eternal logos overcame time itself by so entering it. This line ("only through time time is

---

2, lines 204–6. The second occurrence of "jug jug" is situated in the bleak context of the poem's description of London as the "Unreal City," a place of social disillusionment.

46. For more on this idea of disillusionment and myth, see Young 24–25.
47. Eliot, "The Waste Land," 2, lines 141, 153, 165, 169.
48. Shakespeare, *Hamlet*, 4.5.71–72.
49. Eliot, "The Waste Land," 1, lines 22.
50. Eliot, "Burnt Norton," line 89.

conquered"), and indeed the entire poem, is an extension of an underlying theology in the poem that privileges the Incarnate act. As with Auden's "Kairos and Logos," Eliot's *Four Quartets* holds the Incarnation to be *the* pivotal moment in human history. According to Eliot, at the Incarnation the temporal was breached, inhabited, and forever changed by the eternal. In other words, time temporal was conquered by time eternal. As will be shown in a later section, *Four Quartets* is Eliot's most pronounced work on the Incarnation. In it Eliot depicts the Incarnation as the event that visits time, creating a theological crossroads between the historical moment and its theological interruption. However, while thoroughly theological, the *Four Quartets* resists easy exegesis as an expression of Christian doctrine. Rather than following the dictum to "deliver something clearly and richly Christian," as Michael Edwards wishes Eliot to do, the poet often conceals explicit Christian allusion and creates a Christian theology of spiritual seeking centered on the theme of time. I take the presence of Bergsonian ideas in the poem as a primary reason for its theological difficulty. Just as Eliot joins Christian theology together with literary criticism and social commentary in some of his post-conversion critical work, as for instance in "Religion and Literature," in *Four Quartets* Eliot smoothly poeticizes incarnational theology by means of Bergsonian theory.

So far in preparation for examining *Four Quartets*, I have considered Eliot's interest in time and the importance he placed on the Incarnation. Now I want to briefly trace the known evidence of Eliot's exposure to Bergson's ideas. Philip Le Brun has written on Bergson's influence on Eliot. In Le Brun's "T. S. Eliot and Henri Bergson," the critic argues for such a significantly Bergsonian influence on Eliot that without it, Eliot's poetry as now known could not have been written. Although Le Brun claims that Bergson's theories heavily affected Eliot's work, he also and paradoxically raises a formidable objection to claiming such an influential relationship between the philosopher and the poet: "Eliot was openly hostile to Bergson."[51] Le Brun traces how Eliot's attitude toward Bergson that grew from ambivalence to opposition. While visiting the Sorbonne in 1910–11, Eliot wrote an essay that declared Bergson's theory of time merely to be "simply not final."[52] But between 1917 and 1920, Eliot became more hostile in his comments about Bergson, accusing the French philosopher and his disciples with wrongly blending the genres of philosophy and art.[53]

51. Le Brun, "T. S. Eliot and Henri Bergson," 10.
52. Mathiessen, *The Achievement of T. S. Eliot*, 183.
53. For a more detailed account of Eliot's critiques of Bergson, see Le Brun, 149–50.

By the late twenties, Eliot objects to Bergson's ideas of change as being inherently valuable and critiques the relativism in Bergson's philosophy of time.[54] Eliot also holds Bergson's notion of intuition to be a restriction of human intelligence.[55]

But for all Eliot's grumblings against Bergson, Eliot's work betrays strong influence of Bergson's philosophy.[56] I will discuss the Bergsonian debts in *Four Quartets* more fully below, but even a cursory look at the poem in comparison to Bergson's work reveals similarities. The poem's interrogation of the meaning of a moment results in the concept of dynamic new experiences in each new moment. One such extraordinary moment is metamorphosized in "Burnt Norton," the moment in the rose garden that represents the entrance into a present time that is charged with the presence of the eternal:

> What might have been and what has been
> Point to one end, which is always present. . . .
> and immediately moves into a journey,
> towards the door we never opened
> Into the rose-garden.[57]

Eliot's opening meditation on time becomes a consideration of every step *in* time and a perceptive realization that moments are culminations of eternal interruptions in the ever present. The present is not merely present but is the place to which all other possible epochs and experiences of time point. Here the poem is moving into the unknown, previously unexperienced "always present," through which the "logos common to all" will manifest itself.

The opening of "Burnt Norton" leads the reader throughout time. The reader enters the poem and is immediately ushered through time past into time present. One of the ways in which the poem moves the reader through time is by evoking memory as that which brings the past into the present and beyond. The speaker contemplates memory, and in

---

54. Le Brun, "T. S. Eliot and Henri Bergson," 11.

55. For more on Eliot's opinion of Bergsonian intuition, see, "Mr. Middleton Murry's Synthesis," 340–47.

56. Le Brun draws connections between Eliot and Bergson that, while helpful for situating Eliot against the context of Bergson's ideas, are beyond the scope of this study, such as Bergson and Eliot's view of language and society. Le Brun, "T. S. Eliot and Henri Bergson," 151–53.

57. Eliot, "Burnt Norton," lines 9–10, 12–14.

contemplation follows the "footfalls," which "echo in the memory."[58] In contemplating memory, the speaker asks what memory's purpose is, as the poem moves through its opening garden scene. The first section in "Burnt Norton," culminates—as does the speaker's contemplation of memory—in an affirmation of the "always present." Thus, memory is coupled with the speaker's realization that all time outside the present points "to one end, which is always present."[59]

Bergson not only deals with the same phenomenon of memory being contextualized in a temporal moment, but like Eliot, he uses the image of the rose garden as the catalyst for memory. In his discussion in *Time and Free Will* of the intuitive view of dynamic experience inherent in every moment, Bergson says, "I smell a rose and immediately confused recollections of childhood come back to my memory. In truth, these recollections have not been the perfume of the rose: I breathe them in with very scent; it means all that to me."[60] Bergson philosophizes the meaning of a simple event in a simple moment. For Bergson, the role of memory is wrapped up in the power of time. The rose is secondary at best for Bergson; more important to him is the moment in which one smells the rose. For it is time, not physical objects, that "means all" to one's intensities.

Eliot's thinking also seemingly shares some commonalities with Bergson's about the dynamism of inner states (intensities) and language. Bergson's dynamic views of human life and intensities is well documented here in chapter 2, where I noted that Bergson describes thought as a "living thing" and announces that language should ideally be "the translation of thought, should be just as living."[61] By living, Bergson means dynamic development, a process of ever becoming. Eliot echoes Bergson in his essay "The Writer as Artist" (1940), where Eliot proclaims that "A living language is constantly changing."[62] In an address delivered at Washington University and published as *American Literature and the American Language* (1953), Eliot asserts that "a living literature is always in process of change," and that "language should be in constant change. If it is changing it is alive."[63]

---

58. Ibid., line 11.
59. Ibid., line 48.
60. Eliot, *Time and Free Will*, 161.
61. Bergson, *Comedy*, 137.
62. Eliot, "The Writer as Artist," 773.
63. Eliot, *To Criticize the Critic and Other Writings*, 49, 57.

Other similarities between Eliot and Bergson have also been documented. Le Brun points out that Eliot's view of poetry coincides with Bergsonian thinking on the development of ideas over time, i.e., that ideas morph into new ideas, evolve, and change collective thinking about issues. Bergson, in speaking about how the introduction of any single idea can change entire philosophical systems, claims, "the supervening of each term brings about a new organization of the whole."[64] Bergson's view is reflected in Eliot's own thinking on how ideas in a single text can change understandings of literature as a whole. When discussing in his 1919 essay the function of time in the shaping of a literary tradition, Eliot claims that:

> What happens when a new work of art is created is something that happens simultaneously to all the works of art, which preceded it. The existing monuments form an ideal order among themselves, which is modified by the introduction of the new work of art among them. The existing order is complete before the new work arrives; for order to persist after the supervention of novelty, the whole existing order must be, if ever so slightly, altered.[65]

Eliot here conflates the present and past of literary history in his claim that any new text essentially works backwards to reshape one's perception of an entire literary tradition. Any new text creates an alteration of whatever previous artistic canon existed. The past is changed by the present, which alters the "whole existing order" by its very presence. It could be that this connection between Eliot and Bergson concerning the theme of time is one of the most revealing, as Eliot goes on to state that, "whoever approved this idea of order . . . will not find it preposterous that the past should be altered by the present as much as the present is directed by the past."[66] In his own discussion of literature delivered at Oxford in 1920, Bergson actually referred to Eliot's literary theory of the present being altered by its past. In what was eventually published as *The Creative Mind: An Introduction to Metaphysics* (1934), Bergson posits that new creations work backwards to influence perceptions of past creations, thereby changing past art itself.[67]

This mutually influential notion of past and present finds its fullest expression in Bergson's theory of time. Time is a force that resists

64. Bergson, *Time and Free Will*, 124.
65. Eliot, "Tradition and the Individual Talent," 38.
66. Ibid., 39.
67. Bergson, *Creative Mind*, 110.

T. S. Eliot's Bergsonism "Always Present"

categorization of past, present, and future and that moves seamlessly to act on itself, creating a flow of interpenetrative moments. In other words, past, present, and future are so interconnected and so dynamically intergenerative that all that exists is the power of experiencing the present time, which past and future empower. The Bergsonian idea of a mutually reciprocal force that acts from the past to the present and present back on the past will be one of the structuring motifs in *Four Quartets*, a poem to which I now turn. Having surveyed Eliot's post-conversion affinity for theological verse, having taken note of Eliot's interest in the theme of time, and having demonstrated connections between Bergson's and Eliot's thinking, I will now provide a Bergsonian, theological reading of Eliot's opus on time.

Theologizing Bergsonian Time in *Four Quartets*: "Burnt Norton"

The first of the four books that comprise *Four Quartets* is "Burnt Norton," based on an actual manor of that name in Gloucestershire, England that T. S. Eliot had visited in 1934 during a weekend getaway with longtime, close friend, Emily Hale. Burnt Norton quickly became a place of great affection, of personal meaning, and of poetic inspiration for the poet. The poem "Burnt Norton" would appear one year later, in 1935. Eliot and Hale found the garden, rather than the house, a romantic place on which Eliot would look back in longing memory. The poem "Burnt Norton," much like the actual place, invites entrance. The reader is asked to "walk" the lines of the poem with the imagery of personal journey. Phrases like "footfalls echo in memory" and "towards the door we never opened" intimate entrance and movement through the landscape of the poem.[68] The poem's movement through the garden is initially depicted as partly a matter of memory ("echo in memory," line 11); thus, the poem's larger relationship of time present to time past is contextualized in the speaker's conscious state ("thus, in your mind," line 115). Time and one's experience of time, then, is inseparably linked to consciousness. This relationship between conscious perception and time will be an important Bergsonian theme through the poem, as Eliot continually adjoins the spiritual reality of time with one's conscious awareness (e.g., memory) of that reality.

"Burnt Norton" includes two introductory quotes that serve as the poem's epigram, both by the pre-Socratic Greek philosopher, Heraclitus:

---

68. Eliot, "Burnt Norton," lines 11–13.

"Although the Logos is common to all, we live as if by our own wisdom" and "The way up and the way down are the same." The key to the two quotations is the term "logos," a thematic key to the entire poem because of its theological focus on the Incarnation. As will be explained below, in the Christian tradition *logos* can be used christologically to connote the incarnate Christ in time. Understanding the theological importance of the logos is an approach to the poem's overall theological meaning, as the logos of the epigraph becomes the Incarnation of the poem proper. The poem depicts the experience of the eternal in temporal time as an experience of the christologically signified logos. At the logos, time and eternity intersect.

The intersection of ideas is a guiding principle in *Four Quartets*. Intersections of time and eternity, memory of the past and experience of the present, superficial and salvific experiences in time are all examples of the kinds of themes that intersect through the books of *Four Quartets*. I agree with Eliot scholar Kenneth Kramer, who begins his own study of the poem with the prefatory claim that "what concerned Eliot in structuring *Four Quartets* was the way that the poem supported intersections between ideas and themes."[69] Indeed, the intersection of the ideas of spiritual meaninglessness and salvific time is enabled throughout the entire poem. Besides the immediate example of the Heraclitean quotes explained below, there are several instances in the poem where time is given salvific qualities, thus creating an intersection of a spiritual phenomenon and time. I will explain further below several examples of how time and Eliot's theology intersect in what he calls the theological "still point of the turning world" that is manifest in temporal time.[70] The still point is that which does not move in time, as it is beyond time because of its eternality. Another example of ideological intersection and perhaps one of the most theological moments in the poem occurs in the speaker's contemplation of "the point of intersection of the timeless / with time."[71] The intersection of the timeless with time is the moment of the Incarnation:

> The hint half guessed, the gift half understood, is
> Incarnation.
> Here the impossible union
> Of spheres of existence is actual . . .[72]

69. Kramer, *Redeeming Time*, 22.
70. Eliot, "Burnt Norton," line 62.
71. Eliot, "Dry Salvages," lines 201–2.
72. Eliot, "Burnt Norton," lines 114–17.

Not only does the speaker call this paradoxical intersection of eternity and temporal time an "impossible union," but he also comments on the difficulty of spiritually perceiving the Incarnate moment. The Incarnation of the eternal in time is a "hint half guessed" and "half understood" by individuals experiencing temporal existence.

One of the poem's Bergsonian themes is that of perception of the spiritual in time. Bergson asserts that there are two selves, the superficial and the fundamental, who experience time in superficial and spiritual profound ways. *Four Quartets* will expound on Bergson's notion of the two selves and their respective perceptions of eternity. While every temporal moment possesses spiritual meaning, some individuals fail to see the intersection of eternity and time and thus experience time differently than those who perceive the eternal in the temporal. The prefatory claim that "although the Logos is common to all, we live as if by our own wisdom" will be a paradigm for experience of the spiritual through the temporal, as some fail to know the logos and so live by a wisdom unrelated to the spiritual. The logos of the Heraclitean epigrams, with its christological associations, is the intersection in the poem at which the two contrasting notions of time (perception of the logos and the "wisdom" of temporal) meet.

The Heraclitean quote is also an interpretive lens through which the poem's theology should be seen. The term *logos*, while used by Heraclitus, Plato, and Philo, is also associated with the Gospel of John (1:1, 1:14).[73] Scholars have debated the connotation of Eliot's use of *logos*, questioning its philosophical and theological implications for the poem.[74] Given the thematic importance of the Incarnation in the poem, I take the logos to be the eternal's entrance into the temporal, the Incarnate in time. In choosing the term logos, Eliot is employing a term most often associated with Christian theology, specifically the theological category of Christology (the study of the person of Christ). The association of Eliot's logos with the Johannine logos urges a theological reading, because, in his use of logos, Eliot is evoking a christological designation most often discussed in the context of the Incarnation. As previously mentioned, the Incarnation is the biblical doctrine that God became human. The New Testament

---

73. For more on the lexical meaning of "Logos," as used in John's Gospel, see Kittel's entry on "logos" in the *Theological Dictionary of the New Testament* 4:69–137 See also my discussion of the "logos" in the following chapter on Auden's "Kairos and Logos."

74. See Clubb 'Hereclitean,' 19–33; Smith's *Poetry and Plays*, 255–56; Reibetanz *Four Quartets*, 11–22; Weitz's "Time as a Mode of Salvation," 49–52, and Kramer's discussion in *Redeeming Time*, 28–32.

documents are replete with verses that describe the nature of the Incarnation. A few examples of such incarnational verses are John 1:1, John 1:14, and Philippians 2:5–11.[75] Had I more time, I would perform exegesis on each passage, but it is sufficient to say that the doctrine that Christ became flesh, that the eternal Christ would enter time and take on temporal flesh, is vital to both the Christian faith and to Eliot's *Four Quartets*. So important to the poem is the interruption of the temporal by the eternal that the first fragment becomes a commentary on the reality of the logos in temporal moments. This commentary will guide the entire poem toward Eliot's incarnational theology, which asserts that present time is inhabited by the eternal and therefore potentially experienced by an individual on a spiritual level.

While the logos is "common to all," as Heraclitus claims, it is often missed by human wisdom because that wisdom is bound by temporal limitations. I submit that this notion is Bergsonian. Bergson calls for an "attentive psychology" (i.e., the intuitive knowing) that goes beyond socially constructed wisdom or scientific rationalization. For Bergson, this intuitive epistemology discerns "a duration whose heterogeneous moments interpenetrate . . . beneath homogeneous duration."[76] The *Four Quartets* promotes a dualistic epistemology much like that of Bergson. As will be shown in my reading, to know the logos one must perceive in time; on the other hand, the great hindrance to knowing the logos is time itself. This is the poem's paradox: one must live in time but not be bound by the temporal. Because the temporal is the medium for the eternal, the eternal must be known through time, though the trappings of the temporal cause the eternal to be easily missed. This concept is one of Eliot's most Bergsonian and one on which he builds an entire poetic theology of knowing in time. Bergson espoused a theory of the temporal and the durative: the former all individuals inhabit, though the socially constructed self often misses the latter. In Eliot's *Quartets*, the logos is common to all moments, but not commonly perceived by all people.

In the epigraph, Eliot is trying to articulate a spiritual sensitivity that a theological understanding of time should possess. The second epigraphic fragment ("the way up and the way down are the same") alludes to the *via positiva* (the way up, a spiritual ascent) and the *via negativa* (the way down, a spiritual descent), identifying them both as necessary

---

75. For more on the doctrine of the Incarnation, see Marshall's *New Testament Theology*, 287, 292, 320, 409–10, 541–43, 595–96 and Hurtado's *Lord Jesus Christ*, 32, 36, 575, 644, 648.

76. Bergson, *Time and Free Will*, 95.

spiritual journeys in human experience.[77] The coupling of these epigraphic fragments with the poem's introduction of the logos, the logos being that which is common to all but missed by human wisdom, thematizes a cultivation of spiritual experience through communion with the logos. Since the logos is that divinely visited moment in time, the logos must be known in time. The ups and downs of the spiritual journey (*positiva* and *negativa*) are subjected to time. The way up and down are the same in temporal existence, but only possess spiritual meaning in their ability to reveal the logos. As Eliot scholar Morris Weitz argues about the role of the poem's epigrams and the use of the second Heraclitian quote, "Eliot does not mean that time . . . or that the temporal is the ultimate reality. Rather: that within the flux the choice is always the same, either death or God; and that, if we deny God, Who is Timeless, the Eternal, all experiences are the same in their value, that is, they are worth nothing."[78] Weitz explains that the primary reason that time is important for Eliot is because time is "where" God can be met, if He will be met at all. Eliot's *Four Quartets* identifies no other medium through which to know God than that of time.

Within that temporal complex, i.e., of individual choices lived out in time, what Weitz calls "the flux," spiritual choice is ultimately reduced to two ways, which are equally worthless if not lived in relation to the eternal. No human experience, whether it be an ascent to spiritual union with the logos or a descent, possesses meaning apart from the eternal logos. *Four Quartets* is largely concerned with finding spiritual meaning through temporal experience, and the poem laments spiritually meaningless experience, "we had the experience but missed the meaning."[79] As Kramer insists about the way up and the way down, the "second Heraclitian fragment embodies an existential demand that a person become disengaged from those satisfactions in life that curtail our ability to engage the common logos."[80] The poem's introductory admonishment is to know the eternal (the logos) through the temporal and in so doing to return from the "temporal confusion" of theologically empty time.[81]

After entering the poem, as it were, through the gate of the logocentric epigraphic quotes, one comes into a philosophical meditation on time.

---

77. Charles Williams, Christian novelist and contemporary to Eliot, depicts a *via negativa* in his novel *Descent into Hell* (1937).
78. Weitz, "T. S. Eliot: Time as a Mode of Salvation," 52.
79. Eliot, "Dry Salvages," line 97.
80. Kramer, *Redeeming Time*, 30.
81. Ibid., 31.

The first ten lines situate "Burnt Norton" and *Four Quartets* as a whole in the thematic context of time and timelessness.

> Time present and time past
> Are both perhaps present in time future,
> And time future contained in time past.
> If all time is eternally present
> All time is unredeemable.
> What might have been is an abstraction
> Remaining a perpetual possibility
> Only in a world of speculation.
> What might have been and what has been
> Point to one end, which is always present.[82]

The poem opens with four types of time: chronological time, eternal time, speculative time, and the time of the "always present." These four senses of time all work to construct the controlling theme of the relationship between the eternal logos and the temporal. The first line is chronologically simple enough but quickly moves into the possibility ("perhaps") that the present and past stretch beyond themselves into the future in a coexistent state. The future could even work backwards into the past in some mysteriously dynamic way. In the same way that both Bergson and Eliot imagine new art working back to change the way past art is understood, the present moment can alter perception of the past.[83]

The poem then addresses eternal time along with a question of time's redeemability: "If all time is eternally present / All time is unredeemable." According to Eliot, *if* all time is eternally present, then all time is unredeemable. The contingency of the "if" is key to what Eliot is doing here with speculative time. Kramer insists that the poem's initial treatment of time*s* is akin to looking through a prism of mutually constructive kinds of time. According to Kramer the "pluralities of time (present, past, and future) reflect and co-implicate one another. The unredeemable 'eternal present' (a perpetually speculative possibility) and the always present 'one end' (timeless moments in time yet not of time) visually conflict with, though at times complement, one another."[84] One part of *Four Quartets*'s prism of time is the notion of the speculatively imagined eternally present. The speculative present is not the same as the redeemable present, as the

---

82. Eliot, "Burnt Norton," lines 1–10.

83. For more on Eliot's theory of past and present in literary studies, see also Neilson's "T. S. Eliot and Walter Benjamin," 204–7.

84. Kramer, *Redeeming Time*, 36.

former is representative of temporal flux and the latter is the Incarnated moment, what the poem calls the "always present."[85]

The speculation that time might be "eternally present" is not the same as the poem's notion of the eternal being in the "always present." The speculative eternally present in the first lines of "Burnt Norton" conflicts with the poem's overall message of redemptive time. As will be shown, the poem depicts time as the medium of redemption through time's temporal succession. Like Bergson's idea of time's force, the poem's depiction of the force of time lies in the past flowing into the present through memory and experience. But *speculation* of past time's being condensed in the present is not the experience of the present that the poem privileges as the redemptive moment. It is in the always present, which is the only point in time in which one exists ("always present"), that one experiences the logos. Weitz comments on the difficult line: "'All time is unredeemable' has another meaning: There is no redemption if we recognize only the flux. Further, even the realm of pure possibilities, of things that might have happened, is no different from the temporal: Collapsing all time in the present would remove time's dynamic flow and its power to work on the individual."[86] Weitz notes a theme in *Four Quartets* that originates in Bergson, which is that the force of time is in the present, and that the present is a force because of its dynamic flow. One can see Bergson's notion of time and real duration here. The poem's suggestion of "unredeemable time" points to human experience that resides only in the flux of the temporal. To approach the present through speculation, to remove time's force by distorting time's flow, as suggested by the opening statement that "time present and time past / are both perhaps present in time future, / and time future contained in time past," is to only know the temporal, and so miss durative force.[87]

Bergson's socially constructed time, like Eliot's speculative time, exists alongside real duration as a false construct for the consciousness. As I discussed in chapter 2, Bergson warns that too often "consciousness . . . substitutes the symbol for the reality, or only perceives the reality through the symbol."[88] The temporal, depicted in the poem's opening speculative present, is a symbol of the poem's deeper reality of spiritual duration. And it is the reality of the spiritual logos that gives the symbol of temporal time

85. Ibid., 10.
86. Weitz, "T. S. Eliot: Time as a Mode of Salvation," 56.
87. Eliot, "Burnt Norton," lines 1–3.
88. Bergson, *Time and Free Will*, 96.

ultimate meaning. In *Four Quartets*, all considerations of the temporal and time as a symbol are themes employed in service to the eternal "always present," which the poem depicts as the ultimate intersection of eternity and human experience. The poem's prism of time culminates in the "one end" that reveals the logos, which the epigram declared is common to all through time.

The culmination of each of these kinds of time point to time's ultimate manifestation, which is the Incarnate, eternal, "always present." The "one end" (the common logos) that is "always present" will develop thematically as the poem's theology unfolds. Chronological time, eternal time, speculative time, and the always present Incarnate moment are interwoven as the speaker ponders the possibility of regaining the timeless from the temporality of the past.

> Footfalls echo in the memory
> Down the passage which we did not take
> Towards the door we never opened
> Into the rose-garden.
> My words echo.[89]

The poem revisits the speculative while inviting entrance into the theological. The poem's garden is filled with echoes that animate the text with theological possibility that evokes the theme of Edenic redemption. Indeed, Kramer asks, "Will [the garden] lead us to Edenic redemption?"[90] The garden's echoes and "other echoes" transcend the local through an interjection of the theological, and the reader is invited to follow the "other" voice of the spiritual: "Other echoes / Inhabit the garden. Shall we follow?"[91] In chapter 1, I discussed Charles Taylor's theme of the self and the idea of that self being filled with the "other," one of the poem's strongest displays of its Christian poetics is its promotion of the presence of the other. Indeed, the temporal, the local, the world of the self is perennially interrupted by the voices of the theological "other."

Not only do the footfalls of memory recall the past, leading as they do to the garden inhabited by other theological voices, but they also evoke different pasts, the prelapsarian past and the more immediate past of the speaker. The movement is from narration that focuses on the present to an Edenic past of echoed voices to a local memory of walking through the garden. This oscillation between past and present is a common trope in

---

89. Eliot, "Burnt Norton," lines 11–15.
90. Kramer, *Redeeming Time*, 36.
91. Eliot, "Burnt Norton," lines 17–18.

Eliot's poem and follows Bergsonian prescriptions of time. For Bergson, the recollection of the past is an accumulation of durative force. Indeed, memory itself is durative force in that it constantly fuels the present with the power of inner states. According to Bergson, "memory functions in two important ways. First, it interweaves the past into the present, such that memory is practically inseparable from perception. Second, it gathers together multiple moments of duration and contracts them into a single intuition."[92] In "Burnt Norton," the speaker brings the past into the present, the former enlivening the latter in such a way as to shape all experience of the present.

Here Eliot is playing with the force of time and its ability to shape experience. In bringing the past into the present, the poem demonstrates the malleable nature of experienced time. Not only is Eliot drawing on Bergsonian concepts of durative force between past and present, but he is also pulling from canonical theological themes. Eliot scholar Stephen Sicari argues that Eliot's theology of the past comes from Dante, that from Dante, Eliot learned "to consider memory not simply as the repository for images of the past, but as a power that allows us to reshape and interpret past experiences into a new and different form."[93] Sicari also argues that Eliot learned to give meaning to past experiences form of final spiritual states from Dante. Sicari argues moreover that the Quartets are "dialectically arranged meditation on 'the use of memory' as the faculty of the human mind that can liberate us from attachment to the world and bring us ever nearer to a revelation of the divine," though Sicari's argument does little to account for how the function of memory in *Four Quartets* empowers transformation of the consciousness in the present through the force of time.[94] Sicari also seems to miss the point that Eliot is not seeking liberation from the world as much as he is promoting knowledge of the divine through temporal world's time. What Sicari does not account for is how dependence on Dante helps Eliot construct a theology of the Incarnate present. Indeed, Eliot is constructing a relationship between the past and present that operates in a dynamic mutuality to foster a theology of the Incarnate present:

> Human kind
> Cannot bear very much reality.
> Time past and time future

92. Bergson, *Matter and Memory*, 73.
93. Sicari, "In Dante's Wake: T. S. Eliot's Art of Memory," 414.
94. Ibid., 413.

> What might have been and what has been
> Point to one end, which is always present.[95]

The conflation of past and present points to one end, which is "always present." The poem returns to the Heraclitean epigrams' pronouncement that though the logos is common to all, people have missed it due to their own "wisdom." Like Bergson's "superficial self," Eliot's characterization of human wisdom indicts mankind for its inability to know the theological through time. What humankind has failed to see is that all moments, all points in the flux of temporality, all speculative notions of the temporal ("what might have been and what has been"), all point to the Incarnate present. Herein lies the heart of Eliot's construction of a theology as it concerns time: the adoption of a modern philosophical framework to create a theology of time. Again, Eliot's theological move is Bergsonian; Bergson claims that "past, present, and future shrink into a single moment, which is eternity";[96] his duration collapses past, present, and future into an existential singularity. In a Bergsonsian model, time is the veil behind which exists duration. The dualisitic model allows for interplay between the temporal and the atemporal. In Eliot's *Four Quartets*, the flux of temporality veils the eternal while allowing access to the eternal, again the paradox of time being both the portal for the eternal and its greatest hindrance. To experience a "single moment" is to experience the eternal, and the place where and when the eternal can be met is the temporal.

Section II of " Burnt Norton" changes formally from a tightly metered iambic line to lines nearly twice in length and more lexically unfettered. For example, section I ends with the following terse lines:

> Below, the boarhound and the boar
> Pursue their pattern as before
> But reconciled among the stars.

And section II begins with the following lengthier lines,

---

95. Eliot, "Burnt Norton," lines 42–46.
96. Bergson, *Creative Evolution*, 160.

> At the still point of the turning world. Neither flesh nor fleshless;
> Neither from nor towards; at the still point, there the dance is,
> But neither arrest nor movement. And do not call it fixity.[97]

As the lines change, so the content moves from imagery of the patterned natural world to the axial "still point of the turning world," where time and space do and do not exist in a state that contains all paradoxes.[98] Eliot's love of the dialectical shows through here. At this still point of the turning world, empirical and physical properties cannot fully be and cannot completely cease to be: "neither flesh nor fleshless . . . neither from nor towards . . . neither arrest nor movement . . . neither ascent nor decline."[99] Amidst the assertions of being and non-being and despite the moving and not moving, the poem posits a "still point." While this still point is not a place of fixity—"do not call it fixity"—it is a moment of timelessness within temporal time.[100]

This "still point" is where the "dance is," the poet claims.[101] While some scholars have associated the metaphor of the dance with intuitive sensations,[102] I would add that the metaphor stands for intuitive sensations of a Bergsonian nature. Susan Guerlac, commenting on Bergson's analogy of melody as a figure for duration, states that:

> duration implies a mode of temporal synthesis that is different from the linear of the narrative development of past-present-future . . . Melody, which implies a certain mode of organization, is a figure for duration. The identification of a melody implies an act of temporal synthesis. Melody performs this work to the extent that it binds past, present, and future together in a radically singular way.[103]

Like the singularity of melody, the timelessness of the "still point" in "Burnt Norton" both furthers the breakdown of past, present, and future and privileges the always present. As Guerlac insists about the temporal synthesis that is bound up in a melody, the still point in "Burnt Norton" represents a temporal synthesis, in which timelessness becomes more important than temporality. In this still moment the appropriate response is

---

97. Eliot, "Burnt Norton," lines 60–66.
98. Eliot, "Burnt Norton," lines 60–62.
99. Eliot, "Burnt Norton," lines 62–70.
100. Eliot, "Burnt Norton," lines 66.
101. Eliot, "Burnt Norton," line 65.
102. Kramer, *Redeeming Time*, 48.
103. Guerlac, *Thinking in Time*, 66.

intuitive action, a dynamic reaction in a dynamic moment of timelessness. Indeed, if it were not for the still point, there would be no dance, and, the speaker asserts, "there is only the dance."[104] Eliot is not interested in time for time's sake, but in a theology of experience in time.[105] In its temporal nature alone, time allows no transcendent experience. But in the stillness of timelessness that the "always present" moment brings, one experiences intuitive knowing.

Eliot moves from the dance of timelessness to a juxtaposed image of temporal limitation.

> Yet the enchantment of past and future
> Woven in the weakness of the changing body,
> Protects mankind from heaven and damnation
> Which flesh cannot endure.[106]

Here the speaker contemplates epochs of time juxtaposed from the all-important always present. The past and future are futile flights of fancy, woven into the weakness of the flesh. Eliot scholar Anthony Flinn asserts that this speculative contemplation about time is a result of a dismissal of the logos and the spiritual comprehension so vital for knowing the logos. Futile thinking about time is the natural result for man, once logocentric thinking is abandoned.[107] "Protection" here carries a negative connotation. Because it originates in negative thinking about the logos, thereby missing the Incarnate present, speculative thinking about the enchanted past and future results in mankind's non-spiritual state, being unable to experience either salvation or damnation. Only in time, in duration, can one experience the logos. Hence, the poem promotes experience of the present and denounces conscious connection to past or future:

> Time past and time future
> Allow but a little consciousness.[108]

Here the poem offers one of its most important paradoxes involving the past, future, present, and timelessness. The poem asserts that consciousness is a timeless state, "to be conscious is not to be in time";[109]

104. Eliot, "Burnt Norton," line 71.
105. For more on the idea of Eliot's creating an experience of time, see Gardner's comments, 160–62.
106. Eliot, "Burnt Norton," lines 79–82.
107. Flinn, *Approaching Authority*, 115.
108. Eliot, "Burnt Norton," lines 80–81.
109. Eliot, "Burnt Norton," line 85.

however, consciousness that leads to redemption can only operate in time. A form of consciousness that the poem introduces as a way to achieve redemption is memory. The poem uses the image of the rose garden to incite memory: "But only in time can the moment in the rose-garden ... be remembered; involved with past and future."[110] Memory is here introduced as an agent of redemption, a way of retrieving from past moments redemptive meaning. Memory through smell, sight, and sound brings past experiences into the present. By bringing the past into the present through memory, the meaning from past experiences is transported to the always present, where ultimate meaning lies. This transfer of the past into the present is Bergsonian durative force.

Bergson states that because of the flow of time, the importance of the past is how it shapes the present.[111] Indeed, because of the flow of duration, "in actuality we perceive only the past, the pure present being the invisible progress of the past gnawing into the future."[112] According to Bergson, memory serves the present empowering it. The present, empowered by the past, becomes the future, creating an unending durative flow. This idea of durative flow is key to what Eliot is doing with memory in *Four Quartets*. Memory is a consciousness not in time (Eliot, "to be conscious is not to be in time"; Bergson, "consciousness is the note of the present"), because to be in time is to be in the present moment.[113] But because of durative force, consciousness through memory brings moments outside of present time (the past) and places them inside the "always present." Thus, the moments in the rose garden mean nothing outside of memory's ability to revivify them within the present. As Kramer says about the role of memory, "the 'moment in the rose garden'" and other past moments "are retrieved from time past and become a spirit-infused lens through which to engage the present."[114] He concludes, "By restoring these moments of 'immediate experience,' in which the enchainments of past and future are broken, if only temporarily, the soul, burdened by temporal limitations, is awakened to new life."[115] Kramer rightly notes the power of memory to recruit the past in order that the present be animated, but could have even gone further in his claim of memory's restorative affect on the past. Memory, and

---

110. Eliot, "Burnt Norton," lines 80–88.
111. Bergson, *Matter and Memory*, 166.
112. Ibid.
113. Eliot, "Burnt Norton," line 85; Bergson, *Matter and Memory*, 181.
114. Kramer, *Redeeming Time*, 50.
115. Ibid., 51.

therefore the past, is not merely restored to the present in *Four Quartets*, but it is also converted to the present. The past does not remain the past in the present. Instead, the past actually *becomes* the present, as it fills the present with the theological meaning of the logos.

Eliot climactically ends this section of "Burnt Norton" with another paradox about timelessness and time: "only through time time is conquered."[116] Eliot has built a foundation for this paradox up to this point in the poem. To conquer time is to transcend the temporal through an experience with the eternal, but it is only in time that the eternal can be met. It is only in the present that the eternal abides.[117] All conscious experiences with time outside of the present, like accessing the past through memory, can only be redemptive once brought into the present. Thus, temporal time can be conquered by eternal time because memory is a conscious act of bringing past time into the present, because the timeless eternality of the present defines the temporality of the present, and because experiencing the present is the way to experience the Incarnate. The conquering of temporality by eternality is the very nature of the Incarnation.

Much like the existence of the Grey Town in *The Great Divorce*, a "place of disaffection" is depicted in section III, line 90 of "Burnt Norton." The imagery has a limbo like quality, that of a place caught between "neither daylight" "nor darkness."[118] The estranged landscape empties the temporal of inner states and sensory experience; it is a spiritually ambiguous place of "neither plenitude nor vacancy."[119] The present is vacated in this state of disaffection as the poem only affirms, "time before" and "time after."[120] Here the poem's depiction of spiritual experience takes a more strained, disciplined turn as the speaker takes on the prodigal voice of a spiritual sojourner. The depiction of two spiritual experiences is an important example of Bersgonian dualism in *Four Quartets*. In the initial quotations about the logos common to all and the wisdom that has missed it,

---

116. Eliot, "Burnt Norton," line 89.

117. Cf. Davies, *The Mind of God*: "God the Creator, by his very nature, must transcend space and time . . . the coming into being of the physical universe involved the coming into being of space and time as well as matter. I can't emphasize this too strongly and so if we wish to have a God who is in some sense responsible for the origin of the universe or for the universe, then this God must lie outside of the space and time which is being created" (from an unpublished manuscript qtd. in Craig's *Time and Eternity*, 20–21).

118. Eliot, "Burnt Norton," lines 93, 96.

119. Eliot, "Burnt Norton," line 100.

120. Eliot, "Burnt Norton," lines 91, 107.

Eliot has set up a poem representing two selves. And here in "Burnt Norton," the poet meditates on two human conditions, a longing to experience the Incarnate through time and a deep dissatisfaction with temporality.

Eliot's presentation of human experience is thoroughly Bergsonian. Human experience operates in duration, "Words move, music moves / Only in time."[121] Time hosts human expression and provides *the* conduit for language. The adverb "only" negates other mediums for human expression. Much in the same way that Bergson negated spatial thinking in his espousal of an intuitive knowing through pure duration, the poem removes other mediums of expression, meaning, and knowledge. *Only* in time does communicable expression take place, and it is only in time that meaning is found. For the real movement in the four poems of *Four Quartets* is not a movement through space. It is a movement through time. But if bogged in temporality, dynamic movement can become a hindrance to what Bergson calls the fundamental self, for it is the fundamental self (rather than the superficial self) that seeks knowledge and meaning through duration.

To be entrapped by one's temporality and finitude, and so fail to experience durative transformation, is to threaten one's ability to transcend the superficial self. Bergson and Eliot are not the only twentieth-century century thinkers to espouse this idea. Influential twentieth-century theologian, Paul Tillich, expresses the spiritual problem occasioned by finite temporal existence: "Finitude is the possibility of losing one's ontological structure and, with it, one's self. But this is a possibility, not a necessity. To be finite is to be threatened. But a threat is possibility, not actuality."[122] Tillich here recognizes the implications of finitude on the human consciousness, and he warns that one can lose their very sense of ontological self, if limited by temporal thinking. But, as Tillich affirms, this sense of threat and ontological loss are mere possibilities, not necessities. Though the voice of "Burnt Norton" echoes Tillich's description of anxiety, the poem visits temporal disaffection in order to approach a possible redemption.

The poem moves from meaning and words in time back toward the theme of redemption through the Incarnate always present, which has always been and always will be:

> And the end and the beginning were always there
> Before the beginning and after the end.
> And all is always now.[123]

---

121. Eliot, "Burnt Norton," lines 137–38.

122. Tillich, *Systematic*, 201.

123. Eliot, "Burnt Norton," lines 137–38.

The "always there" and the "always now" before the beginning and after the end imply a perennial presence, because the logos inhabits every moment and because all moments point to the one end of the present. This move in the poem is one back towards the logocentric moment. Like Bergson's "there is only the present" motif, Eliot values the now as the agent of transformation. The Incarnate present of *Four Quartets* is always the destination. It is always where the poem's theology is headed and is where spiritual experience culminates. Once the poem moves back toward the always now of the logos, its poetics consist of brief lines, which all define the logocentric experience. Here Eliot, like Bergson, animates inner states (intensities) to demonstrate the force of the present:

> Desire itself is movement
> Love is itself unmoving
> Only the cause end of movement,
> Timeless, and undesiring
> Except in the aspect of time
> Between un-being and being.[124]

Experience in the always now translates into an inner dynamism. For the individual consciously connected with the logos, inner emotions, even "desire itself," move in time. However, Eliot makes an exception to his dynamic depiction of experience: "love is itself unmoving." Here Eliot theologizes dynamism's goal by ascribing a teleology of love. While the human soul seems to be caught between temporal limitations and theological ascent ("between un-being and being"), God's unconditional love assimilates that soul to itself. This assimilation, like all theological acts in *Four Quartets*, cannot happen "except in the aspect of time."

"East Coker"

A year before the start of World War II in 1939 and three years after the publication of "Burnt Norton" (1935), Eliot made what critic T. S. Matthews has called a "pious pilgrimage" to the Somerset village of East Coker.[125] Eliot's ancestral family had lived at East Coker before moving to the Massachusetts Bay Colony in the seventeenth century, and Eliot's visit helped inspire what would be the second part of the *Quartets*. The poem by the same name was published on Good Friday 1940. The poem also

---

124. Eliot, "Burnt Norton," lines 162–68.
125. Matthews, *Great Tom*, 131.

carries with it the feel of a personal pilgrimage as it moves beyond the first garden world of "Burnt Norton," with its mystical imagery and confidence in the eternal present, to a more concretely imagistic setting expressed in a more personal tone, though in no aspect less theological.

In "Burnt Norton" the poet contemplates timelessness and temporal time, but in "East Coker" the poet focuses on the seeming meaninglessness of cyclical patterns in time, in which nothing endures. The poem opens, "In my beginning is my end . . . In my beginning is my end" (lines 1 and 14), a refrain that speaks to the beginning and ending place for the soul, the cycles of birth and death, and the spiritual journey evoked throughout the poem. The poem couples its bemoaning of cyclical meaninglessness with biblical allusion. There is an Ecclesiastical refrain in "East Coker." Phrases like, "And a time for living . . . and a time for the wind . . . the time of the seasons . . . the time of milking . . . the time of coupling" echo the words of the Old Testament book of Ecclesiastes, in which the author envelopes all life experiences under the belief that only a relationship with God matters.[126] All else is "vanity of vanities."[127] The third chapter of Ecclesiastes employs an anaphora through the repetitive phrase "a time," which occurs in some form fifteen times in eight verses. What Eliot is most interested in his implementation of Ecclesiastes is the subversion of temporal existence by relational knowledge of the eternal, of God. The temporal experiences of man captured in metonymic times to live, die, etc., are contextualized by the larger theme of futile human existence apart from God. As in Ecclesiastes, the occasional "times of" are fragments whose only spiritual meaning comes from their absorption by the eternal.[128]

The lamentations that echo Ecclesiastes suggest that the speaker's soul is in time but not connected with the logos of "Burnt Norton." This spiritual disconnect with the Incarnate present identifies a *via negativa*: "I said to my soul, be still, and let the dark come upon you / Which shall be the darkness of God."[129] Life is still being lived in time, but at this point in the poem's depiction of spiritual progression, time is no longer perceived as spiritual force. The result is a fixation on the temporal and an unfolding of a confused psychological life. This confused temporal thinking is exactly what Bergson said happens when durative thinking is abandoned for

---

126. Eccl 3:1–8
127. Eccl 3:19
128. See also Lobb's treatment of Eliot's biblical allusion in "Limitation and Transcendence in 'East Coker,'" 28.
129. Eliot, "East Coker," lines 113–14.

superficially distinct multiplicity.¹³⁰ Outside of pure duration, the superficial self is refracted and subdivided, and so expresses itself in existential anxiety.

> The poem oscillates between superficial temporal thinking and theological hope:
> I said to my soul, be still, and wait without hope
> For hope would be hope for the wrong thing; wait without love
> For love would be love of the wrong thing; there is yet faith
> But the faith and the love and the hope are all in the waiting.
> Wait without thought, for you are not ready for thought:
> So the darkness shall be the light, and the stillness the dancing.¹³¹

Moving back and forth between virtues of hope, love, and faith, a reference to 1 Corinthians 13:13, the poet concludes that all virtues are found in the waiting.¹³² With the waiting comes a spiritual humility to the poem ("you are not ready for thought") that leads the speaker back to the types of paradox ("darkness shall be light, and the stillness the dancing") that characterized "Burnt Norton." As they were in "Burnt Norton," the paradoxes in "East Coker" are spiritually transformative. The speaker rises from temporal thinking to a spiritual wisdom that comes about through waiting in time.

The waiting here is akin to existence in Bergsonian duration. As one intuitively exists in time, one internalizes duration. Bergson says that for the individual consciously connected to duration, time is not measured, but is felt and becomes an internal part of one's thinking.¹³³ This growing in wisdom in time is the spirituality that "East Coker" describes. Indeed, David Moody, who writes about *Four Quartets*, describes the voice in "East Coker" as reminiscent of an Old Testament prophet calling for a spiritual awakening despite current depravity.¹³⁴ But if it a is spiritual wisdom that the poem calls for, then it is a spiritual wisdom built on paradoxes wrapped in polarities. In the poem's spiritual ascent, one has to traverse seemingly contradictory theological tensions, beginning from the prologue's version of "the way up is the way down" to the ambiguities of "East Coker":

---

130. Bergson, *Time and Free Will*, 93–97.
131. Eliot, "East Coker," lines 126–33.
132. "And now these three remain: faith, hope, and love. But the greatest of these is love," 1 Cor 13:13.
133. Bergson, *Time and Free Will*, 93.
134. Moody, *Four Quartets*, 145.

> Our only health is the disease
> If we obey the dying nurse
> Whose constant care is not to please
> But to remind of our, and Adam's curse,
> And that, to be restored, our sickness must grow worse.[135]

In "Burnt Norton," the speaker announced that time could be conquered through time, a reference to the Incarnation's entering time to overcome it. Here the poem announces that spiritual health is only possible once depravity has been recognized ("our only health is the disease"). The nurse whose constant care is not to please is a figure of the church, which as I have already noted was immensely important to post-conversion Eliot, who saw the church as an answer to modernism's moral depravity. Here, the church reminds humanity of its depravity and serves even to emphasize that depravity, so that in growing awareness of his spiritual need for God, mankind might turn to God for salvation. The spiritual wisdom promoted by the poem is grounded in the tension of depravity as the temporal man in pursuit of the logos must embrace temporality as the way by which the logos is known.

"East Coker" ends its spiritual progression where it began, pondering cyclical, temporal events. In its conclusion "East Coker" has arrived at new spiritual understanding of temporal existence. The speculations, limitations, and spiritual lows that come with temporal existence are subsumed in a theological affirmation:

> Here and there does not matter
> We must be still and still moving
> Into another intensity
> For a further union, a deeper communion
> . . . .
> In my end is my beginning.[136]

Gardner describes the final moment in "East Coker" as a movement toward something new, paraphrasing the conclusion as, "Every new moment is a new moment, and every new end a beginning—that the past is alive in the present, modifying it and itself being modified by it."[137] I think Gardner is right in detecting the sense of newness in "East Coker"; since the speaker has gone from bemoaning temporality at the beginning of the poem to a point of theological reaffirmation at the end of the poem,

---

135. Eliot, "East Coker," lines 152–56.
136. Eliot, "East Coker," lines 204–7, 210.
137. Gardner, *The Art of T. S. Eliot*, 117.

the feature of revived theological perspective is appropriate. Regardless of temporal finitude, the poem's charge is to keep with time's dynamism until something beyond the temporal is reached: "into another *intensity*," to use both Eliot and Bergson's term.

The poem culminates in a new spiritual insight into the same things, hence the ending repetition of the first line, "In my end is my beginning." Bergson presents this very theme of new insight in *Creative Evolution*. Bergson asserts that what the conscious man "perceives in reality, what he will succeed in effectively thinking of, is the presence of the old object in a new place or that of a new object in the old place"[138] (*Creative Evolution* 142). This new insight is the result of the vital impulse working through the individual in time: a new perspective about existence founded on experience in time. According to Eliot, who builds on this notion both Bergsonian and theological, that new perspective will result in a "deeper communion" with the Incarnate present.

"The Dry Salvages"

"Burnt Norton" begins in an English manor and garden, "East Coker" in a village from Eliot's youth, and "The Dry Salvages" draws from two landscapes from Eliot's youth: the Mississippi River in St. Louis, where Eliot was born, and the coast of Cape Ann, Massachusetts, where Eliot and family spent summers from 1893 to 1911.[139] Eliot's strong personal connections to these regions might be why time is humanized in the "Dry Salvages" more so than anywhere else in the *Four Quartets*. Indeed, in the "Dry Salvages," time is understood in terms of human experience and human experience in terms of time—each being the other's qualifier.

For example, the book opens with a personal admission about experience with the divine, "I do not know much about gods; but I think that the river / Is a strong brown god."[140] Here the speaker begins his mediation of the spiritual through the interpretive lens of experience. What the speaker has experienced with his natural surroundings informs his knowledge of the divine. "Dry Salvages" is also the portion that contains one of *Four Quartet*'s most important couplets, "We had the experience but missed the meaning, / And approach to the meaning restores the

---

138. Bergson, *Creative Evolution*, 142.

139. For more on Eliot's relationship to these two locations, see Gordon's *Eliot's New Life*, 114–24.

140. Eliot, "Dry Salvages," lines 1–2.

experience."¹⁴¹ The relationship between the spiritual meaning of time and human experience in time is privileged in this section of the poem, as the speaker contemplates particular experiential moments ("the moments of happiness" line 89) while also considering how past time effects present experience. Thus, "Dry Salvages" provides a fresh look at theological time, one from the vantage point of human experience, but in remarkable unity with the preceding "East Coker." For example, the sense of new sight that concluded "East Coker" becomes a theme of New World discovery in "Dry Salvages." I agree with scholars Moody and Kramer that the two middle quartets "East Coker" and "The Dry Salvages" are so thematically connected as to be one work.¹⁴²

The connection between "East Coker" and "The Dry Salvages" is thematic and progressive, for the end of "East Coker" calls for a new spiritual insight into the temporal so that the union with the spiritual can be possible, and "The Dry Salvages" will exercise that new sight through its humanized imagery of time. Indeed, "The Dry Salvages" promotes the most Incarnate depiction of time that the *Four Quartets* has to offer. The logos-inhabited "always present" is inherent in the poem's archetypes and images, as the speaker sees examples of Incarnation in the physical landscape: for example, the river thought to be the "strong brown god," the sea that possess divine voices, and the "ground swell" that is described in particularly christological language, "that is and was from the beginning."¹⁴³ While the speaker's experience still continues in temporality, it also remains spiritual. The speaker's initial thought, "I do not know much about gods; but I think that the river / Is a strong brown god," quickly represents time and personal experience: "the river is within us, the sea is all about us."¹⁴⁴ Kramer has asserted that the ocean represents prehistoric time, while the river represents personal time.¹⁴⁵ Unlike Kramer and other scholars like Helen Gardner, who takes the ocean as a metaphor for imaginative time, I take the ocean to be a metaphor for spiritual time, because the poem's depiction of theological time is that it pervades all human experience.¹⁴⁶ Like the ocean, theological time vastly expands to touch the shore of every

---

141. Eliot, "Dry Salvages," lines 93–94.

142. See Moody, *Thomas Stearns Eliot: Poet*, 222–34; Kramer's *Redeeming Time*, 103.

143. Eliot, "Dry Salvages," lines 1–2, 24–25, 48.

144. Eliot, "Dry Salvages," lines 1–2, 15.

145. Kramer, *Redeeming Time*, 105–8.

146. Ibid., 171.

human experience. As figures of time, the images of the river and ocean signify a furthering of the dichotomous theme of temporal and eternal time. The big brown river god of personal time moves through human experience, while the sea of spiritual time surrounds the speaker's world.

The two times in "Dry Salvages" are interwoven, as the speaker's spiritual progression consists in, "Trying to unweave, unwind, unravel / And piece together the past and future."[147] Here the speaker toils in temporal time while trying to discern spiritual time. The two times are confused for him, and he attempts to make sense of his temporality by trying to count time, to "calculate his future"[148]:

> Between midnight and dawn, when the past is all deception,
> The future futureless, before the morning watch
> When time stops and time is never ending . . .[149]

Here time is measured in the succession of moment. Between midnight and dawn, before morning, time continues indefinitely. For a moment, the theological time so important to the poem is lost in a purely temporal understanding of successive moments. A helpful interpretive framework is to look back on Bergson's campaign against the conflation of spatial and durative thinking. Bergson warns that a quantitative estimation of time destroys durative thinking. As it applies to durative thinking, a "conception of number ends up scattering in space everything that can be directly counted," in which case "it is presumed that time . . . is nothing but space."[150] Bergson warns that this calculated approach to time corrupts representations of internal states in duration, removing time's transformative force on the human conscious.[151] Eliot's warning against quantitative thinking is as strong as Bergson's; the speaker in "The Dry Salvages" is snared by a state of temporal anxiety. Thus, the speaker exclaims, "Where is there an end of it?"[152] This anxiety about temporality becomes a refrain that echoes throughout book II, being intensified by images and sounds of daily life: "Clamour of the bell of the last annunciation / Where is the end

---

147. Eliot, "Dry Salvages," lines 41–42.
148. Eliot, "Dry Salvages," lines 40.
149. Eliot, "Dry Salvages," lines 43–45.
150. Bergson, *Time and Free Will*, 67–68.
151. Ibid., 54–55.
152. Eliot, "Dry Salvages," line 48.

of them...."[153]; "There is no end of it, the voiceless wailing, / No end to the withering of withered flowers."[154]

The speaker's anxiety leads to what is perhaps the poem's most sober commentaries on temporality. The speaker contemplates the aging process, a prominent theme of "The Dry Salvages," and one that once reflected upon leads to a spiritual epiphany:

> It seems, as one becomes older,
> That the past has another pattern, and ceases to be a mere sequence—
> Or even development: the latter a partial fallacy
> Encouraged by superficial notions of evolution....[155]

Here the speaker realizes that the past, once subjected to memory, takes on a different form than the sequence he thought existed. The speaker reveals that one is prone to superficial thinking, encouraged by equally superficial notions of merely biological evolutionary development, and so apt to distort the meaning of the past. The speaker has misremembered the past and in misremembering has distorted the past's meaning for his present. He begins to realize that past moments of happiness, fulfillment, security, affection, "or even a very good dinner" are moments of temporal meaningless, and this realization of temporal meaninglessness leads to a "sudden illumination" that characterizes Eliot's entire theology of temporal time: "We had the experience but missed the meaning, / And approach to the meaning restores the experience."[156] The great sin in *Four Quartets* is to miss the logos common to all—i.e., to experience temporality but miss its spiritual meaning. Here, the speaker has inhabited time, experienced daily life, and known temporality, but he has missed the Incarnate timelessness that gives all moments meaning.

It is worth recalling that Bergson claimed the function of memory is to enliven the present. Memory brings the past into the present, thereby strengthening the transformative power of the present moment. Memory is how one accesses the power of the past so that the present can be animated with past time. That is memory's function, to restore the meaning to past experiences.[157] Eliot's themes are identical with Bergson's theories on this point. In Eliot's *Quartets*, one must approach the meaning by restoring

153. Eliot, "Dry Salvages," lines 66–67.
154. Eliot, "Dry Salvages," line 79.
155. Eliot, "Dry Salvages," lines 86–89.
156. Eliot, "Dry Salvages," lines 90–94.
157. Bergson, *Time and Free Will* 115; cf. Bergson, *Matter and Memory*, 72–76.

the experience, and "meaning" here partly means the function of memory to animate the present. Indeed, it is helpful to reiterate that what *Four Quartets* most promotes in its theory of time is the Incarnate force of the *present*, not the power of the past or future. To restore the experience of the past through memory, one must approach its meaning for the present. The theme that time without divine contact is merely an empty sequence is reinforced by the speaker's contemplation of temporality in this section of the poem: the future merely a "faded song" and experience with the present apart from the logos described as being "pressed between yellow leaves of a book that has never been opened."[158] The temporal, the past, and the superficial memory that distorts the past all suggest that temporal "time is no healer."[159]

The individual's sudden illumination of having had the experience of time but missing its theological meaning brings about a return to time's true meaning in the logos. The two themes of temporal existence and theological hope pervade "The Dry Salvages" and culminate in a final realization that time cannot be transcended by humanity. While time brings with it limitations and spiritual struggles, it is also all that man has through which to know God. Thus, while time cannot be transcended, it can be lived in, embraced, and ultimately surrendered to through spiritual union with God. The speaker begins the final discourse on time in "The Dry Salvages" by acknowledging man's habitually temporal thinking, "Men's curiosity searches past and future / And clings to that dimension."[160] As was also intimated in the first two quartets, man's tendency is to cling to the temporal without a theological understanding of the present's durative force.

Reaffirming man's failure to see God in time, the speaker asserts that to apprehend God in time is a theological endeavor: "But to apprehend / The point of intersection of that timeless / With time, is an occupation for the saint."[161] Not only is it the task for the theological consciousness ("occupation for the saint"), but seeking God in time is a lifelong process, "something given / and taken, in a lifetime's death in love,"[162] indeed such seeking is, "ardour and selflessness and self-surrender."[163] The kind of love

---

158. Eliot, "Dry Salvages," lines 127, 131–32.
159. Eliot, "Dry Salvages," lines 136.
160. Eliot, "Dry Salvages," lines 197–98.
161. Eliot, "Dry Salvages," lines 200–203.
162. Eliot, "Dry Salvages," line 203.
163. Eliot, "Dry Salvages," line 205.

described here is a matter of increasing intensity and is a matter of "prayer, observance, discipline, thought and action."[164] The development of emotion has a teleology, pointing to the one end that "is Incarnation."[165] The requirement in *Four Quartets* that love must intensify in one's spiritual life in time is closely akin to Bergson's belief that inner states in time must and will grow dynamically throughout one's life. According to Bergson, the immutable fact of duration is that "the same does not remain the same, but reinforces itself and seems to fill and enlarge itself with its whole."[166] For the conscious being, Bergson insists, time is a gain.[167] Eliot's dynamic view of surrendering to time until the point of death is the heart of logocentric living, for every moment is Incarnate and must be lived in apprehension of the eternal.

"Little Gidding"

Eliot began working on the last quartet, "Little Gidding," almost immediately after finishing "The Dry Salvages" in 1941. The name "Little Gidding" refers to a small, historical community of Anglican Christians, who began meeting in 1626 for worship three times a day at Little Gidding's parish church in Cambridgeshire. Eliot visited the humble chapel in 1936, and it remained a special place in Eliot's religious thinking.[168] Like the actual location, the poem "Little Gidding" represents a place of spiritual devotion. The last quartet brings about the end of a spiritual progression. Having passed through the garden of "Burnt Norton," through the village of "East Coker," along the river of "The Dry Salvages," the poem arrives at the spiritual province of "Little Gidding," a moment of theological intersection with the temporal. Here one finds an end in Eliot's theology of time that manifests in the logos of the poem's Heraclitian prologue. As do the previous three quartets, the final quartet presents its spiritual progression through time to the timeless Incarnate present by capturing an element of temporal existence, this time through natural imagery: "Midwinter spring is its own season / Sempiternal though sodden towards sundown,

---

164. Eliot, "Dry Salvages," line 213.
165. Eliot, "Dry Salvages," line 215.
166. Bergson, *Time and Free Will*, 115.
167. Ibid., 116.
168. For more on Eliot's personal relationship with Little Gidding, see Kramer, 135–37.

/ Suspended in time, between pole and tropic."¹⁶⁹ Existing between winter and spring, "midwinter spring" is a paradoxical representation of the state of being in between states. The poem has fostered this in-between state since the first quartet through its constant oscillation between the temporal, the eternal, and the human experience that facilitates an intersection of the two. Not only is the poem concerned with temporality (past, present, and future time) and eternal time (the always present), but it is also interested in the state between these two types of time. The time between two types of time is the state of being between the temporal and its eternal antecedent, "suspended in time." The poem is returning to the idea that the conscious being in time is in between the temporal and the eternal, a situation with a distinct purpose:

> You are here to kneel
> Where prayer has been valid. And prayer is more
> Than an order of words, the conscious occupation
> Of the praying mind, or the sound of the voice praying.¹⁷⁰

Existing between the temporal and eternal presents an opportunity to consciously seek union with the divine. Indeed, the poem presents the purpose of being in between as one of spiritual devotion: i.e., the poems assertion that "you are here to kneel" and take up the "conscious occupation" of prayer. Gardner insists that Little Gidding is a "place of dedication, to which people came with a purpose," and the poem shows that being suspended in time does indeed foster a deliberate spiritual purpose.¹⁷¹ When one exists in the temporal and seeks the eternal, prayer is the order of business. Although it might be argued that if Eliot intends an explicitly Christian message, he should have used liturgical language, the poem avoids overtly ecclesiastical language because it is concerned with the intuitive experience of time. In *Four Quartets*, prayer is not mere liturgical practice, but the intuitive awareness that in time the timeless resides. Eliot's description of prayer is remarkably like Bergson's language of intuition. In the act of intuition, the consciousness is isolated with a precise purpose of knowing in time and through that knowing being transformed.¹⁷² Such an exercise in conscious, intuitive connection is what *Four Quartets* associates with the purpose of prayer. It is through this purpose that temporal man

169. Eliot, "Little Gidding," lines 1–3.
170. Eliot, "Little Gidding," lines 45–48.
171. Garner, *The Art of T. S. Eliot*, 177. See also Walker's treatment, "T. S. Eliot: Poetry, Silence and the Vision of God," 98–101.
172. Bergson, *Time and Free Will*, 67–68.

can access the timeless moment of the incarnate logos. While the poem endorses this theological ascent of knowing the logos, it is ever mindful of the paradox of trying to experience the timeless while being in time: "Here, the intersection of the timeless moment / Is England and nowhere. Never and always."[173] Again "Little Gidding" situates experience with the timeless in time, while also demonstrating the interpenetrative implications for both on the other. In this in-between, the conscious prayer is spatially fixed and beyond fixity, missing from time and yet always in it.

Here at the end of *Four Quartets*, the eternal finally begins to overtake the temporal. Eternalized time arrests temporal designation ("Midwinter spring," line 1) and life in terms of spatial existence ("between pole and tropic," line 3), thus, creating an intersection through which the eternal may move ("here, the intersection of the timeless moment," line 53). Indeed, in "Little Gidding" there is no temporally identified "before and after," as the eternal erases the temporal signifier: "In concord at this intersection time / Of meeting nowhere, no before and after."[174] Furthermore, because prayer is a spiritual act of reaching for the logos (a movement along the *via positiva*), it is only possible because the temporal is overtaken by the eternal, because there is more than successive moments in conscious prayer. There is also the theological act of communing with the logos. In keeping with Eliot's theology of the present, the importance placed on the present moment increases in the poem's treatment of prayer. In "this intersection time" of the present, inattentive to notions of before and after, that purpose of prayer, which is accessing the eternal logos, is fulfilled.

The poem's theology of the present develops as "Little Gidding" progresses to its end. The poem dismisses past language and any meaning it might have had only to accentuate the always present: "For last year's words belong to last year's language / And next year's words await another voice. / . . . the passage *now* presents no hindrance."[175] In keeping with Bergsonian duration, which always has as its locus the present, the poem asserts that the past and future allow no access to spiritual meaning. But, the *now*, the present moment, expands temporal experience through durative transformation. The theology of the present in *Four Quartets* endorses the notion that because the Incarnation is by its very nature an act in time, God's transformative work in the individual only happens in time;

---

173. Eliot, "Little Gidding," lines 52–53.
174. Eliot, "Little Gidding," lines 105–6.
175. Eliot, "Little Gidding," lines 118–20.

thus, the poem fosters the "intersection time" through which individuals "become renewed, transfigured, in another pattern."[176] When looked at in the context of its preceding lines, the phrase "become renewed" becomes one of the most concentrated and important few lines about transformation through time in "Little Gidding":

> see, now they vanish
> The faces and places, with the self which, as it could, loved them,
> To become renewed, transfigured, in another pattern.[177]

Here the speaker reframes temporal experience through his increased theological perception of time, and the "always present" from earlier becomes the moment of renewal at this stage in the poem. The renewal mentioned here is only possible through the breach of the temporal by the eternal, which will become the prominent theme in the last stanzas of "Little Gidding." Because time houses the eternal, because it is Incarnate, all people and all experiences ("faces and places") are seen through the lens of eternal time. It is the task of time to redeem humanity. Through Eliot's theological framing of time, the temporal is transfigured through eternality. The Incarnate nature of theological time becomes "another pattern" by which the temporal is renewed. Through the lens of theological time, the temporal perception, even the temporal self, vanishes. Bergson writes of the transformation of consciousness as a result of rightly thinking about time. *Time and Free Will* warns that transformation through durative force only happens when time is not viewed superficially.[178] When flat, homogenized views of time prevail, then duration loses its force in the shaping of the consciousness. Conversely, when one perceives past temporality into duration's heterogeneous, dynamic, interpenetrative moments, then the consciousness undergoes a transformation so radical that all of life is viewed differently.[179]

The assertion that life is transfigured through redeemed time is sustained in the poem's last lines, as the tone of "Little Gidding" changes with the speaker's sense of spiritual awareness. Now that the speaker sees the temporal through the other pattern of Incarnate time, a new image of Incarnation enters the poem. In language reminiscent of Pentecost in the book of Acts, imagery of dynamic spirituality enters the poem's world of

---

176. Eliot, "Little Gidding," lines 105, 166.
177. Eliot, "Little Gidding," lines 163–65.
178. Eliot, "Little Gidding," lines 93–98.
179. Bergson, *Time and Free Will*, 95–96; *Creative Evolution*, 136–38.

time: "The dove descending breaks the air / With flame of incandescent terror."[180] There is a double meaning in this imagery. On the level of historical context, Eliot evokes images of WWII air raids. That historical reference is matched and even overshadowed by the image's second theological meaning. The language evokes biblical notions of spiritual awakening and temporal interruption.

The dove, an image of the Holy Spirit (cf. Luke 3:21–23), and the flame, an image of the Holy Spirit associated with the birth of the Christian church (cf. Acts 2:3), break into the poem's temporal world for the purpose of redemption. The terror mentioned here does not seem to collate with the tone of Acts 2. But it should be noted that Luke, the author of Acts, includes a prophecy from the Old Testament book of Joel. Acts 2:17–21 recounts the ominous, haunting words of Joel 2:28–32, "I will show wonders in the heavens above and signs on the earth below, blood and fire and billows of smoke. The sun will be turned to darkness and the moon to blood before the coming of the great and glorious day of the Lord." Eliot may have this Acts 2 passage in mind, when he describes the Incarnate moment as one of "terror." This reference to the dove breaking into the air is the poem's most vivid image of Incarnate divinity entering time. The result of this entrance is a newly spiritualized experience with time that leads to a salvation: "to be redeemed from fire by fire."[181] The speaker sees the fire of the Holy Spirit as protection from eternal damnation.

Some of the poem's final theological pronouncements recapitulate in even stronger theological language the theme of temporal redemption by the eternal. In a subtle reference to those mentioned in the prologue as having missed the logos and those in "East Coker" as having failed to see the theological nature of time, the speaker here declares that those who are unable to see time as Incarnate will miss redemption.

> A people without history
> Is not redeemed from time, for history is a pattern
> Of timeless moments.[182]

To be without history is to exist outside of time, and to exist outside of time is to miss God's presence in time through the Incarnation. Herein lies Eliot's ultimate theological agenda: to show that temporal, historical time is comprised of the "timeless moments" of eternal visitation. Again, the

---

180. Eliot, "Little Gidding," lines 200–201; cf. Acts 2:3.
181. Eliot, "Little Gidding," line 207.
182. Eliot, "Little Gidding," lines 233–35.

poem represents time as a conduit for the timeless. It has been a thematic constant through the poem to intimate that time and eternity can only be brought together at the cost of some paradox (cf. "and urge the mind to aftersight and foresight" line 128). And here at end of Eliot's theological articulation of time the poem ends with its central paradox. To experience the timeless, one must do so in time. Those with no theological view of temporal history will fail to see that the temporal is a pattern of timeless moments, and so they will fail to know the timeless.

The *Four Quartets* ends with an anticipation of eschatological time. The spiritual progression of the *Quartets* closes with a reaffirmation that time is when the eternal can be met, and it looks forward to a new dispensation of time, when, "And all shall be well and / All manner of thing shall be well / When the tongues of flame are in-folded / Into the crowned knot of fire / And the fire and rose are one."[183] The poem's closing consolation is that the work of Incarnate time will produce universal renewal. Again, with his fire imagery, Eliot likely has in mind the ongoing air raids as well as the theological meaning that the poem has fostered from its beginning. However, it is unlikely that Eliot has the Blitz primarily in mind, given that this fire occurs in conjunction with an eschatological consolation, "all manner of thing shall be well." Tongues of flame, Pentecostal images of the divinity that has broken into the temporal, are interwoven into time so that a transformation occurs—tongued flames becoming a crown.

In this state of theological transformation, the poem still insists on a duality of connected images. The fire and the rose are images of diversity becoming unity. The poem's last image recalls the rose garden in "Burnt Norton," where the speaker first contemplates the importance of the present moment. That present moment embodied here in the rose joins an image of Incarnate timelessness in the rose: "When the tongues of flame are in-folded / Into the crowned know of fire / And the fire and the rose are one."[184] The poem's prologue's logos common to all (the eternal Christ who indwells the "always present"), inhabiting every moment and animating the temporal with timelessness, is in its ultimate state when inhabiting temporal time.

---

183. Eliot, "Little Gidding," lines 155–59.
184. Eliot, "Little Gidding," lines 57–59.

Conclusion

As in Lewis's post-conversion work, the topic of time was of great importance for the post-conversion verse of Eliot, who believed that present time contained the eternal, the always present logos. Also like Lewis, Eliot appropriates Bergsonian ideas to create a theological poetic of time. Eliot's theology of time in *Four Quartets* partly originates from twentieth-century secular philosophy, without which he could not complete his theological articulation. In appropriating Bergsonian themes of durative force and conscious transformation in duration, Eliot creates a theological treatment of time. And Eliot's theology of time promotes the idea of transformation through duration. According to Eliot, this transformation is only possible because eternity intersects and animates the temporal. In his classic work on Eliot, *Reason and Imagination* (1960), R. L. Brett insists that the Christian doctrine of time operating in *Four Quartets* "sees history as the intersection of time and eternity, a series of what Eliot describes in *Four Quartets* as 'timeless moments.'"[185] Inherent in Eliot's theme of temporal time intersecting with the eternal are the assumptions that there are two kinds of time and that those times are interconnected. Eliot's theory of time coheres with no other philosophy in the twentieth century more strongly than that of Henri Bergson. As discussed in Chapter 1, and further demonstrated in my reading of the *Four Quartets*, Bergson held that there is both time and duration. Time is a superficial construct seen as the mere passing of successive moments. Duration is the force of consciousness as inner states succeed one another.[186] When Bergson speaks of the force of time he is speaking of the dynamic transformation of the individual's consciousness through time's influence. Though one lives in socially constructed time, the perceptive, intuitive mind sees beyond the veil of temporality into the timelessness of duration.

In duration, the present is the most important epoch of time because it is only in the present that consciousness is transformed through time. Therefore, in the present moment the timeless flow of consciousness meets the temporal individual and, thus, through time works to transform the individual's consciousness. My reading has demonstrated that Bergson's notion of the durative present is evidenced in Eliot's theology of the Incarnate present. In Eliot's *Four Quartets*, God only works in the present. Even past time as accessed through memory finds its transformative

---

185. Brett, *Reason and Imagination*, 120.
186. Bergson, *Time and Free Will*, 171.

force on the consciousness only when brought into the present moment. In the present moment, timelessness abides. In the temporal lies divinity. Anyone who would experience the Incarnate logos must first experience time. Those who will not recognize the logos in time are examples of those who Bergson describes as superficial selves. Bergson's fundamental self, by contrast, perceives in time a transformative power, accesses that power through consciousness, and is changed by the flow of time working in/on its inner states. The two spiritual experiences that *Four Quartets* poeticizes—one trapped in superficial perception of temporality and the other welcoming the power of the always present—are full endorsements of Bergson's theories of time.

5

W. H. Auden's Themes of Time and Dualism

The Bergsonian Theology of "Kairos and Logos"

In this last chapter I will look at Auden's "Kairos and Logos" in light of Bergson's notion of dualistic duration—the belief that there are two selves who experience time through different subjective experiences. Auden's connections with Bergson are not as well documented as Bergson's connections with Lewis and Eliot, and the philosopher's influence on Auden seems less apparent. However, a reading of Auden's poems on time in light of Bergson's theories reveals a remarkable ideological kinship.

There is no contesting that Auden's post-conversion verse is often concerned with the theme of time. Some of his most significant post-conversion poems, such as "For the Time Being," "Horae Canonicae," and "The Sea and the Mirror," all treat time from a theological standpoint. In Auden's work, time mediates man's perception and his experience of life and of God. I agree with the claim made by critic R. A. York concerning Auden's view of the nature of time—"For Auden, life is in time: he believes in change"—and I intend to investigate the poet's interest with the theme of time and its implications for his view of life, God, and man's relationship with the divine.[1] I want to show that the life that Auden believes exists in

---

1. York, "Auden's Study of Time." 221.

time is spiritual in nature and that the change that Auden believes in is akin to Bergson's belief in consciousness changing through time. To go beyond York's thesis, I intend to cover ground still largely unexplored by scholars of Auden and time. This chapter will show that Auden, a poet deeply interested in both secular and Christian philosophical systems of thought, constructs a poem strikingly Bergsonian in its depiction of human experience with God through time. I will also show the indebtedness in Auden's poetical theology of time to Bergson's dualistic notions of time and real duration. The ideological kinship between Bergson and Auden comes to light most fully when examining "Kairos and Logos" in terms of Bergson's dualistic theory of time and self. In his constructing a Bergsonian poem, Auden takes up the theological task of creating historical time and theological time, parsing two selves that inhabit both types of time, and privileging theological time as the conjoining force between human experience and Christian revelation.

Auden: Philosophical Poet for the Times

W. H. Auden is the most nebulous of the authors in this study. His conversion came a decade after Lewis's, over a decade after Eliot's, and did not translate into works as explicitly Christian as the bulk of Lewis's corpus, or works like Eliot's *Christianity and Culture* or *After Strange Gods*. Neither does Auden treat time the same as Lewis and Eliot do. For example, one does not find in Auden a fantasy realm where time carries with it the spiritual fate of each person, as does Lewis's *The Great Divorce*. And Auden's poetic articulation of time does not share the metaphors, tenor, or abstraction of Eliot's *Four Quartets*. But Auden's work is no less an example of a theology of time inspired by secular philosophy, and his view of time as "when the eternal can be met" is no less textually evident than in Lewis's or Eliot's work. After providing some context for Auden's pre-conversion career and tracing some of his most prominent theological motifs, I will focus on Auden's theological use of Bergsonian ideas in "Kairos and Logos."

Auden was born into a devout Anglo-Catholic family, though by 1922 at the age of fifteen (the same year he started writing poetry) he discovered that he had lost his faith.[2] The intermediate years between his teenage apostasy in 1922 and his return to the faith by 1940 were some of the most formative in the poet's life. Auden's years away from the faith were spent

---

2. Kirsch, *Auden and Christianity*, xii–xiii.

oscillating from interests in social theorists to mild adherence to various philosophical systems, all while writing some of the most innovative verse of the early twentieth century.[3] In the meantime, the tumultuous political events of the 1920s and 30s that provided the backdrop to Auden's emerging career helped create a new generation of poets.

Auden's emergence on the literary scene in the 1920s was shared by a generation of poets, for whom the greatest influence was that of T. S. Eliot. While Auden and fellow poets Stephen Spender, Cecil Day Lewis, and Louis MacNeice thought Eliot's faith to be a form of escapism, they drew heavily on his stylistic and formal innovations. As Stephen Spender testifies, "What attracted the young poets to *The Waste Land* was that rhythmically the language was so exciting . . . rhythmic excitement of the order of *The Waste Land* is rare in poetry . . ."[4] Not only were poets like Auden and Spender inspired by Eliot's stylistic innovations, but they were also influenced by poetry's new attention to the social. Indeed, Auden was caught in the currents of new thought, new ways of writing inspired by works like Eliot's *Waste Land*, and new world events that all culminated into what can be described as socio-literary upheaval.

The new type of poetry being written by authors like Eliot and Auden, with its emphasis on formal innovation and thematic concerns of the socio-political world as well as of myth, were reactions to the new European crises of the 1920s and 30s. As Mendelson asserts in the introduction to his *Early Auden*, "The poets of modernism devised their characteristic free verse as a response to the European disaster" and, indeed, the literary innovations that Auden and company found so attractive in Eliot were matched by the influence of political events.[5] The European tumults that left England so derelict were often the subjects that Auden found so appealing, reflecting man's place in society, the influence of politics on human relationships, and disillusionment caused by war. As generally understood by scholars like Mendelson, so strong was the tie between the poetic imagination and the social world that Auden understood England through Eliot's verse, taking England as the "unreal city" of Eliot's *Waste*

---

3. E.g., Auden's first published collection of poetry, *Poems*, appeared in 1930 and possessed remarkable emphasis on the relationship between the personal, social, and psychological. Auden's *The Orators: An English Study*, a formally unique mix of verse and prose, deals with forms of hero-worship in political life.

4. Spender, "Remembering Eliot," 50. For more on *The Waste Land*'s place in the history of literary modernism, see Levenson's chapter "The Waste Land" in *A Genealogy of Modernism*, 165–212.

5. Mendelson, *Early Auden*, xvii.

Land. For instance, Auden reported in 1940 that "the England of 1925 when [he] went up to Oxford was *The Waste Land* in character."[6] In "Address for a Prize-Day," from *The Orators* (1932), Auden rhetorically asks, "What do you think about England, this country of ours where nobody is well?"[7] In the vein of Eliot, Auden's socially conscious verse calls attention to current realities. But though Auden's attention to the social was no less concentrated than Eliot's, his approach was notably distinct from his predecessor. Where Eliot denigrated Western culture, Auden accepted and interwove the bleakness of his England into his poetic repertoire.[8] For example, in the chorus of his early *Paid on Both Sides* (1928), Auden speaks to the moral decay of his industrialized twentieth-century world:

> The Spring unsettles sleeping partnerships,
> Foundries improve their casting process, shops
> Open a further wing on credit till
> The winter. In summer boys grow tall
> With running races on the froth-wet sand,
> War is declared there, here a treaty signed;
> Here a scrum breaks up like a bomb, there troops
> Deploy like birds. But proudest into traps
> Have fallen. These gears which ran in oil for week
> By week, needing no look, now will not work.[9]

Auden portrays his modern world with images of entropy and decay. War interrupts the chorus's scene, disrupting the seasons of life. The machines that defined Auden's industrialized England have broken down. The social decay that Auden saw in post-Great War England is made a parable in *Paid on Both Sides*, as England is depicted and morally diagnosed but never explicitly mentioned.

Rather than transcendentally escaping the temporal world's problems, as Auden and poets like Spender accused Eliot of doing in his post-*Wasteland* work, Auden and fellow writers attempted to address them. Spender captures the precarious situation in which the new generation of poets wrote: "Instead of being horrified at the chaos of the *Waste Land* and contrasting it with a prodigious tradition of the past, instead of

---

6. From "Literary Transference," in *Southern Review VI*, 83. This passage is also quoted and discussed in Carpenter's biography, 57.

7. Mendelson, *English Auden*, 62.

8. See the chapter "Germany and England" in Buell's *W. H. Auden as Social Poet*, 77–117; see also Deane's "Auden's England," *Cambridge Companion to W. H. Auden*, 25–38.

9. Auden, *Completed Poems*, 11–12.

trying to cure and revolutionise it, they accepted it as the background of their lives, and allowed its rubbish and its plants to sprout through their poetry."[10] Here Spender likens Auden's acceptance of his social world to organic growth. Like weeds, the themes of social bleakness grew through the cracks of Auden's pre-conversion verse. The acceptance of the bleak modernist world was not a passive resignation, but was rather taken as a charge by Auden to write poetry fitting for the times. Beyond the inspiration that Auden took from Eliot's literary innovations, Auden's career was most shaped by the political upheavals of the 1930s. The force of such movements as Nazism and fascism, the ever-growing threat that Hitler posed to liberal democracy with his rise to power in 1933, and the outbreaks of such crises as the Spanish Civil War (1936–1939) helped shape Auden into a socially-conscious poet.[11]

Auden's concern for social issues was a staple in his work of the 1920s and 30s. Indeed, if there is one defining quality to pre-conversion Auden, it is his penchant for issues and systems larger than himself, whether they be the theological *topoi* of his Christian verse or the social and philosophical subjects of his pre-conversion years. As Auden critic Patrick Deane says in "Auden's England," the notion of writers having a social function in England was an orthodox one throughout the late 1920s and 1930s.[12] Deane also asserts that by the start of the Spanish Civil War, "it was indeed widely assumed that artists and writers *should* 'ransom' themselves, sacrificing their artistic aloofness in service to the communal good."[13] Auden fully subscribed to the charge to so "ransom" himself. His political interest in the Spanish Civil War culminated in the poem "Spain" (1937), a superb example of the poet's socially fueled poetic intensity. Auden decided that "the poet must have direct knowledge of the major political events," and he left to visit Spain sometime between January and March of 1937.[14] While in Spain, Auden intended to serve with a medical unit driving an ambulance, but this never happened; instead, the poet's exposure with the war's political forces—Auden was particularly affected by the anticlericalism of

---

10. Spender, *Life and Poet*, 105.

11. See Mendelson's *Early Auden* , see also McDiarmid excerpt "The Poet in Wartime: Yeats, Eliot, Auden" in Critical Essays on Auden, 97–106, and her larger mongraph, *Saving Civlization: Yeats, Eliot, and Auden Between the Wars*.

12. Deane, "Auden's England," 34.

13. Ibid.

14. Letter to E. R. Dodds on December 8, 1936, quoted in Fuller, *Commentary*, 283.

the communists—shaped his social conscience, which led to the poem's first manifestation, a somewhat propagandistic poetical pamphlet.[15]

"Spain" is a politically minded social commentary on the power of individual responsibility that contrasts the past and future, explores personal choice in a time of political risk, and probes the meaning of the present moment for the human will. It was also during this time that Auden began to seriously consider the truthfulness of the Christian faith, as "Spain" attests; the poem's political commentary is laced with religious language and Christian imagery.[16] From his time in Spain until his conversion in 1940, Auden's spiritual sensitivities heightened. "Spain" represents Auden's grander agenda of using larger ideals as poetic fodder, his penchant for philosophical issues, and his desire to address the turmoil of his twentieth-century world with art.

Art's ability to engage intellectual or philosophical paradigms was always important for Auden, as was the artist's role in that engagement. The role of art and the artist in society was a preoccupation that would carry into his Christian ideas of art. And with the dire circumstances facing Europe through his early career and into the first years of his post-conversion career, Auden acutely felt the importance of delineating the artist's role. In a birthday poem to friend, lover, and co-artist Christopher Isherwood in his *Look, Stranger!* (1936; published in the U.S. as *On This Island*, 1937) Auden captures the role of

> the artist in a society such as his own,[17]
> So in this hour of crisis and dismay,
> What better than your strict and adult pen
> Can warn us from the colours and the consolation;
> . . . .
> Make action urgent and its nature clear?
> Who give us nearer insight to resist
> The expanding fear, the savaging disaster.[18]

"What better than . . . strict and adult pen . . . [to] make action urgent" is Auden's charge to the artist in the "savaging disaster" that was the

---

15. For more on Auden's time in "Spain" and reaction to the anti-clericalism of the Communists, see Carpenter's biography, 206–16; see also Jenkins's "Auden and Spain," 88–93.

16. For more on religious language in "Spain," see Fuller's commentary, 282–88.

17. For more on the shaping of Auden's socio-political writing, see Mendelson's *Early Auden*, and Grass, "W. H. Auden, from Spain to Oxford," *South Atlantic Review* 66, 84–101.

18. Auden, *Look Stranger!*, lines 17–19, 22–24.

political turmoil of the 1930s. Here we get at a stance mostly unchanged throughout Auden's career and one that will similarly define his view of the poet and of writing theology: the only realm in which the poet has power is the realm of his own artistic creation. Early Auden struggled into this realization; the later theological Auden would fully realize that the power of art was inherent in itself. It would not be until the years immediately prior to Auden's conversion that he would fully "repent" of what early twentieth-century critic Julien Benda described as the "sin" of modernist artists. According to Benda, Auden is guilty of "the tendency to action, the thirst for immediate results, the exclusive preoccupation with the desired end."[19] In other words, early Auden desired to change society. What began as a socially active voice would become a theological voice, as Auden's attention turned to theological concerns. And as it did so, his already high opinion of art increased even more. It is important to recognize Auden's exalted opinion of art if one is to understand Auden's post-conversion verse. According to Auden, it is the artist's highest task to use his art to engage the social and ideological world, to "make action urgent" through "strict and adult pen."

In the context of the desperate events of the early to mid-twentieth century, Auden's attitude toward art is part a reaction to a society bereft of humanity, peace, and religious belief.[20] Thus, to Auden's thinking, it is in art, not in society, that the poet has power and influence:

> Follow, poet, follow right
> To the bottom of the night,
> With your unconstraining voice
> Still persuade us to rejoice;
>
> With the farming of a verse
> Make a vineyard of the curse,
> Sing of human unsuccess
> In a rapture of distress;
>
> In the deserts of the heart
> Let the healing fountain start,
> In the prison of his days
> Teach the free man how to praise.[21]

19. Benda, *The Treason of Intellectuals*, 46.

20. For more on early to mid twentieth-century poet's engagement with society through art, see Benda's *The Treason of the Intellectuals*, and McDiarmid's "The Poet in Wartime: Yeats, Eliot, Auden," 97–106.

21. Auden, "In Memory of W. B. Yeats," lines 13–24.

Though the outer world is bereft of meaning, Auden cultivates a theme of hope in art. Drawing on Edenic biblical imagery for "vineyard" and "curse," Auden sees art's role as redemptive, a "farming of verse" that irrigates the human's distressed heart. Auden scholar Lucy McDiarmid comments that in this passage "the imperatives directed at the poet require him not to make the dark cold surroundings disappear, or to transform them magically, but to face them and act in spite of them.... The poet persuades with full awareness of his context. In the act of persuading ... in spite of circumstances, the poet creates his own world."[22] McDiarmid hits upon an important quality in Auden's work, that the poeticizing early awareness of art's role within society but its inability to change society will carry into his post-conversion verse.

Indeed, Auden was keenly aware of what poetry tried to convey. According to Auden, poetry is a transmitter of the experiential. It is to evoke an experience common to everyone, but relative to the individual reader. In his late post-conversion theoretical work, *Secondary Worlds*, Auden explains his view of poetry's role as a harbinger of experience through the analogy of the relationship between the biblical Adam and Eve. Auden explains:

> In so far as one can speak of poetry as conveying knowledge, it is the kind of knowledge implied by the Biblical phrase—That Adam knew Eve his wife—knowing is inseparable from being known. To say that poetry is ultimately concerned only with human persons does not, of course, mean that it is always overtly about them ... to say that a poem is a personal utterance does not mean that it is an act of self-expression. The experience a poet endeavors to embody in a poem is an experience of a reality common to all men; it is only his in that this reality is perceived from a perspective which nobody but he can occupy.[23]

Auden's allusion to the biblical concept of "knowing" is related to his belief that poetry engages the world by conveying experience. A poem might not be an act of self-expression, nor should it aim to be, for the poet's job is to transmit experience common to all. This concern for a common experience will be especially apparent in "Kairos and Logos," as Auden compares two very different experiences of time. In that poem, the desire to convey experience—a reality common to all men—becomes a matter of conveying the one reality most common to all men: time. How one

22. McDiarmid, "The Poet in Wartime," 105.
23. Auden, *On Secondary Worlds*, 131.

experiences time, and by extension how one experiences God, becomes an existential problem in the poem.

Auden's affinity for the philosophical along with his high view of art and its role as a conveyer of experience often translated into highly allusive, philosophical, and theological verse. Indeed, the theological was even integral to Auden's pre-conversion verse, and while he remained an apostate from the Christian faith until 1940, Auden retained strong interest in biblical knowledge and religious rituals.[24] Many of Auden's pre-conversion poems are as concerned with religious motifs as they are with the socially mindful philosophical abstractions for which they are famously known. Auden's pre-conversion religious interest is highlighted in the frequent biblical allusions throughout the obscure blend of prose and verse in *The Orators* (1932), the evocation of communal Eucharistic worship in the imagery of "A Summer Night" (1933), and the assertions of blessing along with the allusions to portions of Isaiah 40 in "As I Walked Out One Evening" (1938).[25] Auden's return to the Anglican faith of his youth in 1940 was preceded by years of philosophical wanderings, religious skepticism, and poetic innovation.

Not only did Auden's pre-conversion poetry express religious themes, but it did so in a distinctly twentieth-century philosophical manner, creating the morally ambiguous feel of a poet searching for answers to the pervasive social problems that colored modernism. And it is in his addresses to the crises of his modernist readers that Auden's poetry is most distinctly characterized by traits of philosophical searching and morally unresolved ambiguity. In *Early Auden*, Mendelson notes how some of Auden's most well-known earlier works, like *The Orators* (1932) and *The Ascent of F6* (1936), attempt to make no moral judgment on his twentieth-century context, no coherent diagnosis of twentieth-century morality, and impose no sense of personal or social wholeness on his twentieth-century audience. Rather, his early verse takes up social problems by sharing in the pervasive, seemingly irreparable divisions of his time.[26] The details of these poems' moral ambiguity is not nearly as important as the poet's greater inclination to treat philosophically difficult topics, likely a reason for the Bergsonian tenor of "Kairos and Logos," as it is the type of difficult

---

24. See Kirsch's treatment of Auden's early years in *Auden and Christianity*, 1–23.

25. Cf. "As I Walked Out One Evening": "For in my arms I hold" (lines 18) and Isa 40:11: "He gathers the lambs in his arms." "As I Walked Out One Evening": "O plunge your hands in water" (line 37) and Isa. 40:12: "Who has measured the waters in the hollow of his hand . . ."

26. Mendelson, *Early Auden*, 10.

philosophical system with which Auden liked to work. Like the social poetry that marked his early career, his progressively philosophical bent shares the same ambitious intention to convey notions of reality common to all.

Before turning to Auden's attempt to take on the Bergsonian philosophy of experienced time, I want to emphasize the poet's willingness to absorb philosophical systems. If Auden's early social poetry suffered from a lack of ideological certainty in its refusal to offer prescriptive answers, and if his more philosophical verse leaned toward the morally ambiguous, it is partly because Auden himself was so ideologically promiscuous before converting to the Christian faith, never fully ascribing to any one philosophical system, as will be demonstrated below. Indeed, it is Auden's penchant for the philosophical that will carry beyond his conversion and define his theological treatment of time.

One need only look back on Auden's biography to help explain his poetry's philosophical range. From his maturation as a socially engaged "public poet" in 1929, to toying with the idea of becoming a Communist in 1932 and 1933, to engaging in 1934 with the Oxford Group Movement, an aristocratic Christian sect, Auden constantly engaged philosophical paradigms.[27] Indeed, Auden's pre-conversion poetics were nurtured by social subjects and philosophical theories in much the same way that his post–conversion poetry was nurtured by the theological tropes of the Christian faith. His post-conversion verse shares the same philosophically inclusive quality. For example, in his "Letter to Lord Byron," Auden contemplates the poet's role and the poet's pondering of philosophical issues:

> It is a commonplace that's hardly worth
> A poet's while to make profound or terse,
> That now the sun does not go round the earth,
> That man's no centre of the universe;
> And working in an office makes it worse.
> The humblest is acquiring with facility
> A Universal-Complex sensibility.[28]

Here Auden alludes to the outdated geocentric view of the universe and subtly references humanistic philosophy, which values man as the highest arbiter of truth, the "centre." Auden dismisses this man-as-center

---

27. For more on Auden's engagement with diverse philosophical paradigms, see Mendelson's chapters "Trickster and Tribe," 84–116, "Private Places," 117–36, and "Looking for Land," 137–56 in the authoritative volume *Early Auden*.

28. Auden, "Letter to Lord Byron," lines 658–65.

doctrine, as he questions the worth of a poet's doing philosophy. This question of the poet-philosopher is ironic given that Auden's "Letter to Lord Byron" reads like a catalogue of philosophers and influential thinkers, including names like Milton, Wordsworth, Einstein, Eddington, Rousseau, and Plato. Because of Auden's extensive interest in philosophical thought, Ursula Niebuhr, wife of Protestant theologian Reinhold Niebuhr, described Auden's Christianity as too exploratory and too capacious to be narrowed by association with one denominational tradition.[29] Even Auden's ecclesiastical devotion resisted any monolithic expression, as he capriciously picked up and discarded doctrines espoused by those thinkers most influential to him. For example, Auden accepted ideas like Kierkegaard's existentialism and Charles Williams's doctrine of free will, championed individualistic faith rather than stressing the importance of community, and shifted his denominational affiliation for most of his Christian life, moving back and forth between Anglicanism and Catholicism but often participating in both.[30]

Despite these inconsistencies, Auden was most certainly a theological poet, whose post-conversion works were attempts to affix the doctrines of the Christian faith with his twentieth-century world. As Kirsch insists, Auden's Christian works like "For the Time Being" and "Horae Canonicae" are "a consummate representation at once of sacred history and twentieth-century experience."[31] Kirsch remarks that Auden's recurrent marrying of traditional theological tenets and his twentieth-century world makes up the "underlying balance" of Auden's work.[32] Similar to Kirsch's notion of balance in Auden's work is Auden scholar Alfred Corn's claim that the poet's post-conversion verse acted "as an endorsement of whatever new certainties the poet found to replace previous convictions and serve as a counterweight" to his pre-Christian ideologies that "offered little or no reassurance."[33] For the Christian Auden, much as for Eliot and Lewis, writing literature was not only a turning away from something, and thereby only rejection of twentieth-century ideals, but also a turn to something, a new converted poetic ideal that held that literature should convey theology.

---

29. Kirsch, *Auden and Christianity*, 109.
30. Ibid., 110.
31. Ibid., 112.
32. Ibid.
33. Corn, "For the Time Being: A Relocation of the Poet," 79.

The development of this new poetic ideal, like the growth of his social awareness and philosophical affinity, originated in some of the early- to mid-twentieth-century's most influential thinkers. Perhaps more than Lewis or Eliot, Auden's career can most fully be ascribed to the influence of early twentieth-century philosophers, particularly religious ones. That Auden exposed himself to diverse theologies before coming to the Christian faith has been noted by critics. For example, Arthur Kirsch's work *Auden and Christianity* (2005) considers Auden's post-conversion "Horae Canonicae" in light of his influence by twentieth-century theologians Karl Barth, Paul Tillich, and Reinhold Neibuhr.[34] I should mention that while there are apparent connections between Auden's thinking and Paul Tillich's theory of time, no scholar has explored the similarities of Bergson's philosophy of time to that of Auden's poem, "Kairos and Logos." But before turning to the presence of Bergson's influence in Auden's work I want to look at some of the thinkers most formative to Auden's religious sensibilities. Of the Christian thinkers especially important to Auden, particularly around the time of his conversion, some of the most influential were Charles Williams, Søren Kierkegaard, and Reinhold Niebuhr.

Already growing in his sensitivity to the theological, Auden's incidental meeting with Charles Williams significantly shaped the poet's spiritual life. Charles Williams, Christian novelist and member of C. S. Lewis and J. R. R. Tolkien's writing group, the "Inklings," first met Auden in the summer of 1937. This was the same year of Auden's important trip to Spain and arguably one of the poet's most ideologically formative years. Auden met Williams at Oxford University Press, for which Auden was editing the *Oxford Book of Light Verse*. His encounter with Williams would be of inestimable importance to Auden's pre-conversion years. About the meeting, Auden testified,

> Shortly afterwards, in a publisher's office, I met an Anglican layman, and for the first time in my life felt myself in the presence of personal sanctity. I had met many people who made me feel ashamed of my own shortcomings, but in the presence of this man—we never discussed anything but literary business—I did not feel ashamed. I felt transformed into a person who was incapable of doing or thinking anything base or unloving.[35]

---

34. Kirsch, *Auden and Christianity*, 109–12.

35. Pike, quoted in untitled essay in *Modern Canterbury Pilgrims*, 41. For more of Auden's comments about Williams, see *The Complete Works of W. H. Auden*, 4: 25, 197.

Auden and Williams seemingly found an intellectual kinship, and it is only the significant impact that Williams had on Auden that is relevant for this study. In Williams, Auden saw the embodiment of personal holiness. Williams awakened a sense of sanctification in Auden that never weakened in those few years before his conversion. William's impact on Auden also went beyond the personal. Ideologically, Williams demonstrated for Auden a model of theologized literature meant for a twentieth-century audience. One theme that Auden noticed in Williams's books is a "doctrine of exchange and substitution."[36] Auden defines Williams's doctrine of exchange: "the first law of the spiritual universe, the Real City, is that nobody can carry his own burden; he only can, and therefore he must, carry someone else's."[37] Williams projects a theological position, which furthers the scriptural mandate to "love your neighbor as yourself" (cf. Mark 12:31), by proposing that every person must bear the burdens of his neighbor. The important thing to note in this study of Auden is that Williams conveyed this doctrine through his fiction, rather than writing a work of systematic theology. In Williams, Auden found a model for a writer of theologized literature.

Like Williams's fictionalization of a doctrine of substitution, Auden formulates a theology of time in "Kairos and Logos" that demonstrates the same quality that Auden so admired in Williams's work, an *orthodoxy of his imagination*, or a use of the imagination for theological purposes. Auden also describes this orthodoxy of imagination as transcendence of the "life of the body and its finite existence in time," a means of transcending finitude in order that the theological be made manifest.[38] Auden asserts that in the works of Williams, especially like his theological novel *Descent into Hell* and his creative history of the Christian church, *The Descent of the Dove*, one finds an answer to the often bleak reaction literary artists have toward their twentieth-century culture. Auden says most contemporary writers "show a Manichean bias," that is to say, "an emphasis on the drab and sordid."[39] Others, like materialists, concentrate their artistic expressions on the external world, while Christians typically imagine the road to salvation from the modern world as the Negative Way (*via negativa*), or a theology built on what cannot be said about God, rather than theological affirmations. But in Williams, one sees an imagination that coheres with

---

36. Auden, *Complete Works: Prose*, 25.
37. Auden, *Complete Works: Prose*, 25.
38. Auden, *Complete Works: Prose*, 29.
39. Auden, *Complete Works: Prose*, 29.

the Christian faith and sees the world through lens of the faith, akin to a *via positiva*. Williams depicts the temporal world through this orthodoxy of imagination by creating fictional worlds that convey Christian truths in the bleak twentieth-century context. Indeed, in Williams one finds this theological thread of transcendence, as Williams uses the creative to depict the theological, and it is from Williams that Auden learned the effectiveness of communicating theological themes through creative works.

Particularly important in Williams's influence of Auden's own communication of theology is Williams's view of the Incarnation. Auden admired Williams's ability to retain the theological complexity of the Incarnation by emphasizing the paradox of the eternal inhabiting the temporal, while not retreating from the task of conveying that complexity. Auden says of Williams that his greatest virtue as an apologist is "that he never pretends the orthodox view is easy to believe."[40] According to Williams, and then later to Auden, communicating a doctrine as difficult and complex as the Incarnation was the theological writer's task. Williams saw the Incarnation as the paradoxical union of the divine and human through which God's justice and man's guiltiness meet to produce the salfivic act of the Crucifixion.[41] According to Williams, to know God and to gain an understanding of how He relates to man requires an acceptance of the Incarnate Christ. At the Incarnation, the finite world meets the infinite God. "Kairos and Logos" will testify to the importance that Auden places on the Incarnation, as the poem continues Williams's practice of communicating complex theological doctrine through creative media.

Williams's creative account of church history *The Descent of the Dove: A Short History of the Holy Spirit in the Church*, published in 1939, a year before Auden's conversion, also helped initiate Auden into theology. Auden insists that before *The Descent of the Dove*, he had never read "a history of the church so completely imbued with ecumenical passion."[42] In *Descent of the Dove* Auden found a creative articulation of distinctly Christian content, a textual medium for the theological. One aspect of *Descent of the Dove* that Auden found so convincing was Williams's imaginative use of theology. In an introduction to the 1956 reprint of this text, Auden praises Williams's "orthodoxy of imagination," an artistic sensibility that was masterfully applied to his writing of theology, though different

---

40. Auden, *Complete Works*, 4.199.
41. Auden, *Complete Works: Prose*, 199.
42. Auden, *Complete Works*, 4.29.

from the specifics of a belief.[43] Williams's ability to imaginatively construct the theological certainly influenced Auden, whose post-conversion works share the same tendencies.

For example, in *Descent of the Dove*, Williams conceives the idea that God has ordained the whole of man's history and that the model of the Christian church is an equally ordained pattern for all of society. In other words, God decrees all of history, and the church, as the entity that exists in submission to God, is the model for a good society. According to Williams, the role of free will is integral to God's providential ordering of both society and church.[44] Thus, there are two economies at play under God: the free and the sovereign. Freedom is man's ability to make decisions that pertain to any area of life, even if that decision is a rejection of God. Sovereignty is God's ability to have complete lordship over man, despite this freedom. God ordains absolutely, but man lives freely, and these two doctrines work together mutually in that freedom exists under sovereignty, and God uses both to achieve His will. Williams deals with sovereignty and freedom by depicting apparently different realms of activity, though God controls both: that which man experiences and that which God controls. Auden's "Kairos and Logos" reflects this notion by depicting man's experience with time as dualistically polarized by his perception of God's activity. Drawing from a Bergsonesque model, Auden writes a tale of two times: man's existential time spent in ignorance of God's activity and theological time in which man understands God's involvement.

Another Christian thinker important for Auden's spiritual development is the Christian existentialist Søren Kierkegaard. In an article entitled "Auden's Religious Leap," literary critic and Auden scholar Justin Replogle traces the philosophy of Auden's poetry from the writings of Marx and Freud to the writings of Kierkegaard. Replogle emphasizes Auden's perennial tendency to appropriate philosophical ideology and in particular the poet's "move from one current in the existentialist stream to another."[45] According to Replogle, what Auden found most attractive in Kierkegaard's

---

43. Auden, *Complete Works*, 4.29.

44. As Williams explains the role free will plays in God's sovereign economy, "No . . . dogma has ever been satisfactory to the Church that does not involve free lives mutually co-inhering. . . . In the Crucifixion of Messiah necessity and freedom had mutually crucified each other, and both (as if in an exchanged life) have risen again. Freedom existed then because it must; necessity because it could," *The Descent of the Dove*, 174–75.

45. Replogle, "Auden's Religious Leap," 52.

thinking was his emphasis on personal freedom grounded in subjectivism. For Kierkegaard, truth was found in subjective human experience,

> When the question of truth is raised in an objective manner, reflection is directed objectively to the truth, as an object to which the knower is related. Reflection is not focused upon the relationship, however, but upon the question of whether it is the truth to which the knower is related. . . . When the question of truth is raised subjectively, reflection is directed subjectively to the nature of the individual's relationship; if only the mode of this relationship is in the truth; the individual is in the truth . . .[46]

Kierkegaard's notion of truth is associated with the subjective stance of the knower and in the relationship between the knower and the thing known. Subjective truth is opposed to objective truth, which is defined by the object of truth itself, e.g., objects like an idea, proposition, or a doctrine. Subjective truth is found in the relationship between the knower and the object of truth; therefore, the relationship itself becomes an object of truth. Replogle actually mentions Bergson as a figure who stands under the existentialist umbrella along with Kierkegaard, though he makes no strong connection between Auden and Bergson.[47]

According to Replogle, because of Auden's conversion to the philosophy of the Christian faith, he is most fruitfully depicted as a poetic voice for Kierkegaardian ideals.[48] While Replogle's claim that Auden should be located in a Kierkegaardian tradition may be true concerning other topics in other poems, it is not true on the issue of time in "Kairos and Logos."[49] The tradition that Auden's thinking in "Kairos and Logos" most closely resembles is Bergson's.

Considering his theological employment of Bergsonian philosophy in "Kairos and Logos," demonstrated below, and considering how interested Auden was in philosophical systems, one could argue that Auden's theological interests are a continuation of the intellectual interest present

---

46. Kierkegaard, *Concluding Unscientific Postscript*, 178.

47. Replogle, "Auden's Religious Leap," 49.

48. Ibid., 54–74. For more on Kierkegaard's influence on Auden, see Pandey's chapter "The Shaping of the Religious Sensibilty," 12–31; and Mendelson's chapter "Imaginary Saints" in *Later Auden*, 148–73.

49. Some traces of Kierkegaardian thought in Auden's poems are Kierkegaard's epistemology of the double man in Auden's "New Year Letter," the Kiekegaardian idea of disparity between art and life in Auden's "The Sea and the Mirror," and Kiekegaardian anxiety in *The Age of Anxiety*.

in his earlier verse, when Auden took interest in a variety of philosophical and social systems. For example, even in works as early as "1929," Auden demonstrates a keen interest in the role of theology to inform poetry. The poem begins, "It was Easter as I walked in the public gardens."[50] The explicitly stated setting immediately evokes the Christian holiday of Easter and its most closely associated theme of resurrection, as well as evoking the biblical scene in which Mary Magdalene encounters the resurrected Christ in the garden but incorrectly identifies him as the gardener (John 20:15).[51] The poem then moves from resurrection into the "public gardens" that foster the poem's theological themes of newness and spiritual dynamism. In this garden,

> lovers and writers find
> An altering speech for altering things,
> An emphasis on new names, on the arm
> A fresh hand with fresh power.[52]

Commentators have missed the biblical allusion here, but Auden is drawing on the biblical idea of rebirth and renewal revealed through "new names." There is one verse in the Bible that especially speaks to the theological significance of names and renaming. Revelation 2:17 refers to God's giving new names to those believers who overcome temporal persecution.[53] It is significant, then, that Auden chooses this line, which evokes both naming and the suggestion of the new name on the arm, "An emphasis on new names, on the arm."[54] The poem's biblical allusion help foster its emphasis on theological rebirth and renewal, a theme that Auden weaves through the poem's nine stanzas. The poem, "1929," demonstrates that Auden's writings on Christianity furthered a career already devoted to an intense engagement with ideological systems, particularly theological systems. In his attempt to amalgamate the theological with the mod-

---

50. Auden, "1929," line 1.

51. "Woman," he said, "why are you crying? Who is it you are looking for?" Thinking he was the gardener, she said, "Sir, if you have carried him away, tell me where you have put him, and I will get him."

52. Auden, "1929," lines 5–8.

53. "He who has an ear, let him hear what the Spirit says to the churches. To him who overcomes, I will give some of the hidden manna. I will also give him a white stone with a new name written on it, known only to him who receives it." Though not explicitly referring to giving new names, Isa. 49:16 says that God has engraved the names of his people on the palms of his hands: "See, I have engraved you on the palms of my hands. . . ."

54. Auden, "1929," line 7.

ern, Auden drew heavily on philosophies that shaped the early twentieth century.

One other Christian thinker whose contribution to Auden's theological ideals is Reinhold Niebuhr. Auden dedicated his book of poetry *Nones* (1951) to Niebuhr as way to show his appreciation for the influence the Protestant theologian had on him. Particularly important to Auden and particularly relevant to my study is Niebuhr's view of man as spirit and finite creature caught in the flux of temporal existence. In a review of Neibuhr's *Christianity and Power Politics* (1940), Auden confided that from Niebuhr he learned that "the issue of Biblical religion is not primarily the problem of how finite man can know God but how sinful is to be reconciled to God and how history is to overcome the tragic consequence of its false eternals."[55] Here Auden boils the Christian faith down to a relationship with God in time.

From Niebuhr, Auden not only learned that the faith must be lived in the temporality of history, but that history itself as a correlative to faith must be seen to have the power to overcome the consequences of the Fall, described in "Tract for the Times" as false eternals, i.e., eternal states of fallenness and damnation. Faith and history have this potential because God indwells both. The idea that Auden inherited from Niebuhr is that because God has entered historical time, as Lewis, Eliot, and Auden all attest, history itself can have redemptive agency. The poet's absorption of Niebuhr's ideas superbly demonstrates the importance of philosophical systems in his verse. Auden is, above all else, a philosophical poet for whose work large ideological systems and issues are paramount. A common thread that runs throughout Auden's pre- and post-conversion career is the absorption and poeticization of philosophical systems. Auden's desire to engage larger systems, from the social issues of his early career to Kierkegaardian existentialism and Niebuhr's thinking, attempts to communicate common experience from philosophical topoi. "Kairos and Logos" will communicate the experience of time while taking up the philosophical intricacies of a Bergsonian inspired, Christian view of time.

"Kairos and Logos" exemplifies the position that God actively enters history, which is the root of Auden's theology of time. This position Auden arrived at from both theological and philosophical sources. And as evidenced below, in Auden's philosophical thinking, like Lewis and Eliot, time was the realm of the theological. Thus, to write about time, to convey experience in time, was to approach the heart of one's experience with

---

55. Auden, "Tract for the Times," lines 24–25.

God. Indeed, the importance that Auden placed on time shows through in other works beside "Kairos and Logos." The most significant example of Auden's emphasis on time is the Christmas oratorio, "For the Time Being" (published in a volume of the same name in 1944). "For the Time Being" is a collection of monologues spoken by characters from the biblical Christmas story (e.g., Joseph, Mary, Wise Men, and Shepherds), as well as choruses and a narrator. The poem is divided into nine episodes, each comprising some of the following elements: a chorus, narration, dialogue, song, and meditation. In part, the poem deals with the theological significance of the time between Christmas and Easter, between the Incarnation and the Crucifixion. In its celebration of Christmas and the Incarnation, the poem celebrates the theological significance of the physical body. In fact, what defines both Christmas and Easter in the play is the physicality of the spiritual acts: the physical birth of Christ and his physical sacrifice.

"For the Time Being" further shows the importance Auden placed on the Incarnation, as the poem celebrates the theological concept of divinity manifesting itself through the body in temporal time. There is a Herculean struggle in the poem's presentation of Incarnation theology between believing in the Incarnation and anxiety and doubt that God could appear in temporal time. The poem seems to be built on its question, "How could the Eternal do a temporal act, / The Infinite become a finite fact?"[56] The poem's doubt that such a theological phenomenon could occur is accompanied with the demand for such an act as the Incarnation: "Nothing can save us that is possible / We who must die demand a miracle."[57] Temporal humanity's lament can only be effectively answered with the miraculous act of the Incarnation.

The poem's interest in the Incarnation is obviously a theological concern but is also ultimately a concern for the nature of time, because the Incarnation has no meaning apart from the time in which it occurs. The theme of time pervades the work, always fostering the poem's theology. For example, the poem's first major section, Advent—which in the liturgical calendar is the season preceding Christmas and thus the time leading up to the Incarnation—privileges the idea of transformation. Transformation is likely a poetic expression of Auden's own spiritual maturation, akin to a changing ontology as the demigod aspires to become a god, i.e., a reverse type of Incarnation.[58] The poem questions if transformation can

---

56. Auden, "For the Time Being," lines 138–39.
57. Auden, "For the Time Being," lines 140–41.
58. Corn, "For the Time Being: A Relocation of the Poet," 83.

occur, "Can Hercules keep his / Extraordinary promise / To reinvigorate the Empire?"[59] Here the poem first evokes the dual idea of divinity and time and the ontological transformation that occurs when the two meet. Hercules, who in his deity while seeking immortality is a metaphoric figure for divine transformation, represents a semi-divine entity who was subjected to the temporal while seeking to transcend it by becoming fully a god. Auden uses this metaphor to suggest that the divine can and, indeed, does inhabit time and that transformation occurs through that inhabitation.[60]

The pagan figure of Hercules demonstrates that the poem's consideration of time is not only confined to a Christian paradigm. In fact, the poem also reflects a pre-Christian understanding of time as circular, a perpetual cycle without definitive teleology. For example, the refrain "As winter completes an age, . . . Winter completes an age" evokes a seasonal time that functions in repetitive cycles.[61] Another example is *For the Time Being*'s recurring images of the clock and the mirror (ideas of time and space, though only time is significant to this study), which serve Auden's preoccupation with the theology of time which culminate in the poem's commentary on the Nativity. While the Nativity's theological role in time is important to Auden, it was not what he deemed the most important theological event in history. Partly because of the influence of thinkers like Niebuhr and Williams, Auden viewed the Incarnation as the most important theological event in history. In the doctrine of the Incarnation Auden found a belief that he adopted and employed in his own theological poetry: that it is in history that God is known, and that time reveals eternity. Indeed, as the poet's devotion to the theme in "For the Time Being" and "Kairos and Logos" show, according to Auden, the Incarnation comprises history's most important theological moment, and it is at the heart of Auden's theology time.

M. S. Pandey, an Auden scholar who focuses on the poet's religious writings, insists that Auden "looked upon Incarnation as an answer to the

---

59. Auden, "For the Time Being," lines 15–17.

60. E.g., "Let number and weight rejoice / In this hour of their translation / Into conscious happiness: For the whole in every part, / The truth at the proper centre / (There's a Way. There's a Voice.) . . . "The rich and the lovely have seen / For an infinitesimal moment / (There's a Way. There's a Voice.)" (book 4, lines 1–6, 13–15). "The Meditation of Simeon": "Because in Him the Word is united to the Flesh without loss of perfection, Reason is redeemed from incestuous fixation on her own Logic" (*Collected Poems* 389).

61. Auden, "For the Time Being," lines 34–42.

problem, not of the finiteness [temporal existence] of man but of his sin, not his involvement in the flux of nature, but his abortive effort to escape the flux."[62] Pandey is commenting on an important theological problem for Auden, partly demonstrated by the quote from "For the Time Being" that serves as the poem's central concern, "how could the Eternal do a temporal act?"[63] Pandey's point is that finiteness in and of itself is not at the heart of the theological problem, but rather man's sinfulness in finiteness. Neither was temporality ("flux of nature") the wedge between God and man, but rather man's discontent in his temporal state, which implies, for Auden, a discontent in God's economy. To be in time is to be potentially receptive of the Incarnation. Apart from time man cannot experience the Incarnate. Therefore, discontent with time, for Auden, is discontent with God's plan of the Incarnation.

As the doctrine's elevated status in "Kairos and Logos" testifies, Auden believed the Incarnation to be the one event in history through which man's depravity could be overcome by means of a breach of the temporal by the eternal. In a short poem, "The Means of Grace," Auden declares "The significance of the doctrine of the Incarnation is twofold. In the first place it asserts that at an actual moment in historical time, the Word was actually made Flesh, the possibility of the union of the finite with the infinite made a fact."[64] It is this belief that in the Incarnation the finite and infinite met in the temporal that will lead Auden to write "Kairos and Logos." Like Eliot, Auden saw the Incarnation as the most defining moment in time for the Christian. Also like Eliot, who made the Incarnation the core of his theology of time, Auden views time through the lens of the Incarnation. "Kairos and Logos" will depict a Bergsonian duality of times, which are brought together and further polarized by the Incarnation.

"Kairos and Logos": The Theology of Two Times for Two Selves

"Kairos and Logos" has attracted very little comment. Apart from the readings of the few major Auden scholars (notably Mendelson, Fuller, and Pandey), there is only one remarkable reading devoted solely to "Kairos

---

62. Pandey, *The Religious Poetry of W. H. Auden*, 21.
63. Auden, "For the Time Being," lines 138.
64. Auden, *Complete Works*, 2.132.

and Logos," Bruce Redford's "I Believe Again: Auden's 'Kairos and Logos' in the Context of Christianity Regained" (1980), which I will engage at some length.

Redford's reading is significant to my own work because of his theological approach. Redford notes the difficulty in the poem's imagery, even comparing it to Eliot's abstract work on time *Four Quartets*. As with my own argument of Auden, Redford's argument considers Auden's philosophical influences: "The poet betrays no one, least of all himself. Auden's immersion in Kierkegaard, who shares a dialectical view of history with Marx, goes far toward accounting for the poet's shift in intellectual allegiance."[65] Redford emphasizes Kierkegaard's influence on Auden's thinking while also discussing Auden's experience with the Spanish Civil War and the poet's encounter with Christian writer Charles Williams.[66] After establishing Auden as a poet preoccupied with philosophy, Redford approaches Auden's "Kairos and Logos" intertextually by drawing from the essays Auden published between 1939 and 1944.

But Redford does not explore why Auden theologized the theme of time, despite Redford's performing an exhaustively close reading of the poem that draws connections between elements in each sestina to the works of Kierkegaard and to Auden's prose. Nor does Redford situate Auden's work on time in its twentieth-century context. While Redford argues that each of the four sestinas that comprise the poem are four different ways of approaching the Incarnation, I will argue that each sestina depicts different experiences of the eternal through the temporal: a superficial and a fundamental experience, to use Bergson's terms. An important dimension related to these different experiences of the eternal is that some of them are depicted pejoratively. For example, the later part of the second sestina and all of the third depict a shallow experience with time had by those who fail to see the eternal behind the temporal, or what Bergson calls a superficial experience with duration.

While Redford acknowledges the poem's commentary that those obsessed by temporality (i.e., a superficial experience) are apt to miss the eternal, he offers no coherent frame of reference from which Auden is working. Rather, Redford patches together Christian influences from St. Ambrose and St. Augustine to Charles Williams, but gives no rationale as to why Auden chose those authors or how (or why) their notions of time

65. Redford, "'I Believe Again': Auden's 'Kairos and Logos' in the Context of Christianity Regained," 395.

66. Redford, "'I Believe Again': Auden's 'Kairos and Logos' in the Context of Christianity Regained," 395–96.

might be articulated to a twentieth-century audience. For example, in the span of just two pages, Redford mentions Italian theologian Jacopone da Todi, writer E. M. Forster, theologian Paul Tillich, theological writer Charles Williams, theologian Charles Cochran, and author Franz Kafka, among others, all as possible sources for the first two stanzas of the poem. But the question of why Auden would choose such an array of authors to articulate his theology of time is never addressed. While Redford's reading is helpful in understanding the depth of Auden's intellectual appetite and his affinity for employing the ideas of other thinkers, it does not account for the remarkable similarities between Auden's ideas and those of Bergson, whose ideas so significantly influenced twentieth-century thinking about time.

As with my reading of Lewis and Eliot, I intend to show Auden to be a theological thinker whose ideas about time were modeled on the philosophies of twentieth-century thinker Henri Bergson, who gave Auden a philosophical system on which to build a relevant, twentieth-century theology of time. Bergson provided a philosophy of time that both endorsed a Christian theology due to its emphasis on metaphysical experience and that dealt with the paradoxical problem of experiencing the eternal when experiencing the temporal. No other thinker, Christian or not, provided more material than Bergson for such an understanding of time as Auden depicts in "Kairos and Logos." My argument will privilege the theme of the Incarnation, as Redford does, but it will also consider how Auden constructs his theology and why that theology would be relevant to a twentieth-century readership.

"Kairos and Logos" is one of Auden's most underrated works, especially among his early post-conversion poems. Written not long after his conversion in early 1941, dropped by the poet in the 1960s, and then reclaimed at the end of his life for its theological value, "Kairos and Logos" emerges as one of Auden's most important theological productions. The theological themes in "Kairos and Logos" include what Mendelson calls a "transformation of personal abandonment into love" and a Christian view of history comprised by the injection of the Christian logos into historical time (*kairos*).[67] The implementation of those themes is enabled through a Bersgonian model of time. Like Lewis and Eliot, who both borrowed the Bergsonian ideas of durative duality and dichotomized experience in

---

67. Mendelson, *Later Auden*, 48. For a full treatment of these dual theological concepts, see Carey's *Kairos and Logos: Studies in the Roots and Implications of Tillich's Theology*.

time, Auden creates a world in which some perceive time as spiritually meaningful and some are blind to time's theological nature.

The title establishes a theme of duality that divides both time and experience of time. *Kairos* is Greek for "the right moment" or "the supreme moment." According to Gerhard Kittel's exhaustive lexical entry, the "linguistic development of the term clearly suggests that the basic sense is that of the 'decisive or crucial place or point.'"[68] In the Greek version of the Old Testament known as the Septuagint, *kairos* means "the decisive point of time" and is often used to connote a point in time ordained by God.[69] In the New Testament, *kairos* is used to mean the "fateful and decisive point," and the use of the term often has "strong emphasis on the fact that it is ordained by God."[70] In the Christian tradition, in which Auden is working, *logos* is the all-creating Word of John's gospel (1:1). John 1:1 ascribes complete deity to the logos: "In the beginning was the Word (logos), and the Word was with God, and the Word was God." The first chapter of the gospel of John goes on to Christologize the logos, equating the Word of John 1:1 with the Incarnate Christ: "The Word became flesh and dwelt among us" (John 1:14).[71] Given the meanings of these two terms, then, the title expresses such a meaning as "the right time for the Word." Already in the title Auden has connected time with theology, specifically with the Incarnation.

Not only does the title allude to the Johannine logos, which fellow Christian poet Eliot found so important for his poetry, but Auden draws on another text as the poem's titular source: theologian Paul's Tillich's treatment of kairos and logos, *The Interpretation of History* (1936). In *Interpretation*, Tillich identifies *kairos* to be the opportune historical moment in which the dynamic work of God is manifested. According to Tillich,

> While time remains insignificant in that static type of thinking in terms of form, and even history presents only the unfolding of the possibilities and laws of the Gestalt "Man," in this dynamic thinking in terms of creation, time is all-decisive, not empty time, pure expiration; not the mere duration either, but rather

---

68. Kittel, *Theological Dictionary*, 3: 455.

69. E.g., Job 39:18, Numbers 23:23, and Daniel 2:21. Kittel, *Theological Dictionary*, 3: 458–59.

70. E.g., Luke 12:54, 56, Mark 1:15, Acts 24:25. Kittel, *Theological Dictionary*, 3: 459–62.

71. For more textual analysis of the Incarnation in John, see Carson, *The Gospel According to John*.

qualitatively fulfilled time, the moment that is creation and fate. We call this fulfilled time, the moment of time approaching us as fate and decision, *Kairos*.[72]

One can see in Tillich a view of time almost as exalted as Bergson's. Indeed, like Bergson, Tillich holds to a dual perception of time, the seemingly insignificantly static (*chronos*) and the all-decisive spiritually fulfilled creative time (*kairos*). Tillich holds "fulfilled time" as that which contains creative spiritual force of inseparable consequence for a person's personal life (fate and decision). God inhabits historical moments in the individual's life as Christ inhabited time at the Incarnation. According to Tillich, this inhabitation of the divine is no less than the Kingdom of God breaking into history.[73] The form of time—its temporal nature, or *chronos*—and time's mere durative passing are insignificant for the whole man, but the spiritually fulfilled moment approaches the individual as fate by altering his course through divine intervention. These moments of spiritual visitation (*kairoi*) are cyclical, occurring repeatedly throughout history since the Incarnation of Christ and subsequent birth of the church.[74]

While clearly influenced by Tillich's work, Auden does not write a thoroughly Tillichian poem. Indeed, in "Kairos and Logos," Auden adopts Tillich's terminology (the terms *kairos* and *logos* that were themselves first used in modern theology by Tillich), theological categories (theology and history), and dualistic presentation of time (spiritual time versus mere chronological time), but Auden also depicts theological time in remarkably Bergsonian terms. Rather than being a rewrite in verse of Tillich's theology on time or an adoption of Tillich's ideological framework, Auden's "Kairos and Logos" is best seen as a theo-creative adaptation of Bergsonian dualism in terms of both kinds of time and human experience. The strongest Bergsonian themes in Auden's work are Bergson's notion of "time" and a deeper duration, the notions of two modes of experience in duration, and the belief that time has transformative meaning for the individual.

The four sestinas that comprise "Kairos and Logos" depict different dispensations of theological activity. The first sestina takes place in the time of the early Christians in the Roman Empire. The second depicts an allegorical history of the Christian faith through the images of fantastic,

---

72. Tillich, *Interpretation*, 128.

73. For Tillich's full treatment of *kairos*, see his chapter "The Kingdom of God Within History," *Systematic Theology*, 3.362–93.

74. Tillich, *Systematic Theology*, 3.362–77.

fairytale-esque imagery. The third deals with the relationship between truth and language in a narrative with some features of the modern short story, and the fourth sestina portrays the result of human history, which intimates a sense of a missed spiritual moment brought about by abandoning God but culminates in salvation.

The first sestina begins with a curious phrase that calls attention to the poem's leitmotif of dualistic time, "around them boomed the rhetoric of time." The phrase "rhetoric of time" distinguishes two experiences of time that Auden is playing with: between the thing itself (i.e., time) and the representation of that thing. The opening lines provide some commentary on this distinction.

> Around them boomed the rhetoric of time,
> The smells and furniture of the known world
> Where conscience worshipped an aesthetic order
> And what was unsuccessful was condemned . . .[75]

It is not the thing itself (i.e., time) being experienced in the "rhetoric of time" but a representation of that thing. Between the representation and the thing stands the "rhetoric," the poem's figurative way of connoting a fabricated removal from time itself. What initially "booms" in the poem is not true time itself, nor is it the annunciation of the divine. True time, *kairos*, is inhabited by the logos by nature of God's constant interaction into time. The rhetoric of time is merely the chronological shell of kairos. The boom originates in the temporality that engulfs human existence, "the smells and furniture of the known world." Here Auden's desire to convey experience common to all men is apparent, as the opening of the poem depicts temporal existence in a material world through this material, un-theological language, the "furniture of the known world." The "them" in the opening line is important and the first instance of dichotomized experience. The "them" refers to those who perceive nothing more than the "known world," where conscience worships aesthetics. This is also a utilitarian world that only sees value in the material and pragmatic, an "aesthetic order" in which everything proves to be "unsuccessful" by the standard of the fixtures of temporality.

In his attempt to explain the two modes of subjective experience possible in time and duration, Bergson delineates two types of people, two selves: the superficial and the fundamental. Bergson says the superficial self is a "phantom" not in touch with ultimate reality through duration and

---

75. Auden, "Kairos and Logos," lines 1–4.

whose life unfolds in the materiality of space. The problem with the phantom self is that it "only touches the external world by its surface."[76] The superficial self only touches the external world because the "external . . . social life has more practical importance" than inner experience.[77] Already Auden is constructing his theology through a Bergsonian framework, which holds that time must be experienced through human inner states (intensities), if duration's force will be known. The poet begins the poem with a depiction of the common temporal experience had by "them"—by those who only value practical externality.

Auden provides the example of Caesar, "with his pleasures, dreading death," to epitomize this kind of Bergsonian phantom self. Caesar can stand as a metaphor for ultimate social, material, and external living. Because of the trappings of his political life, his leading society, and his implicated role in the death of Christ, who is the logos, Caesar embodies the superficial self. This type of self has a distorted view of time and thus lives in a confused spiritual state. The temporality minded "them" do not enjoy life through lived time, nor do they experience time meaningfully; rather, their temporality translates into an anxiety living in time. Thus, the dread of death is described as,

> Transferring its obsession onto time,
> Besieged the body and cuckolded love;
> Puzzling the boys of an athletic world,
> These only feared another kind of Death
> To which the time-obsessed are all condemned.[78]

The temporal minded only toil about in futility, the poem implies. Auden paints the "time-obsessed" in some of the poem's harshest strokes here, announcing that they are "condemned" to both bodily and spiritual death. Here the poem introduces an antithesis to the "them" with a "they." Though the same pronoun, the poem switches to a different antecedent, a transition marked by a description of how the group of people relates to temporal time. The poem's "them" are "time-obsessed" and so condemned to a life lived in fear of death. The "they" renounce the world, realizing that the temporal is merely a conduit of the eternal. Turning to another group of people, who will experience time much differently than the time-obsessed, the speaker says that, "They, to enjoy it [time], must renounce

---

76. Bergson, *Time and Free Will*, 93.

77. Ibid., 97.

78. Auden, "Kairos and Logos," lines 8–12.

the world."[79] Given the poem's logocentric theology and that its setting of the first sestina is the Roman Empire, it follows that this second group represents the Christians from the church's earliest days under Roman rule.

> They came to life within a dying order;
> Outside the sunshine of its civil world
> Barbarians waited their appointed time[80]

Here called barbarians because of their refusal to subscribe to the mores of secular Rome, the Christians were converted ("came to life") within the dying order of the temporal world. Auden introduces a group that Bergson would describe as being representative of the "fundamental self." Contrary to the superficial self's preoccupation with externality and temporality, the fundamental self "feels" time (by "feels" Bergson means intuitive consciousness). Through this intuitive knowledge of time the fundamental self returns a temporal moment back to a "state of quality."[81] This qualitative time is akin to the idea behind Auden's *kairos* in that time experienced as a state of quality is spiritually more than a chronological moment, the *kairos* represents *the* right moment, the "appointed time." What separates the time-obsessed from the Christians in the poem is their perception of the nature of time. Where the time-obsessed conflate time with temporal superficial experience, the Christians see time as a divine gift and enjoy it as such. While Bergson never goes so far as to equate the fundamental self with Christian theology (though he comes very close in his *Introduction to Metaphysics*, as seen from some of the quotes used throughout this work), he does place a great deal of importance on the inner states' development through time. Both Auden and Bergson see time as having special meaning for those who perceive it rightly.

Implied in the two types of self are the two types of time, the temporal and the theological. While the "obsessed" are entrapped in chronological time's fixtures, the Christians in Auden's poem believe theological time is salvational and represents a renouncing of the temporal world. The poem recounts the Incarnational moment that caused the Christians to see time as theologically endowed:

> Through them, had witnessed, when predestined love
> Fell like a daring meteor into time,
> The condescension of eternal order.[82]

79. Auden, "Kairos and Logos," lines 18.
80. Auden, "Kairos and Logos," lines 22–24.
81. Bergson, *Time and Free Will*, 93–94.
82. Auden, "Kairos and Logos," lines 28–30.

The poem has been discussing the Christians of the first-century church, and continues to do so here by continuing to contrast them with the unbelieving Roman Empire, the speaker says that the early believers had experienced the transformative power of the Incarnation. It is thoroughly Bergsonian that Auden's terms for the early Christian's spiritual states are time related. Bergson speaks of durative time as a causal agent in the temporal. In life, Bergson asserts, "duration seems to act as a cause" creating dynamic events in the human conscious.[83] Likewise, Auden imagines time as a causal agent, creating a new spiritual understanding for those who perceive the Incarnation. By "condescension" of the eternal, Auden is here referring to the superiority of the eternal with its lesser counterpart, the temporal. Auden's notion of this act is not merely his own, but has theological precedent in the Christian tradition. The Apostle Paul in his letter to the Philippians discusses the Incarnation as the ultimate act of lowering from one greater ontology to a lesser.[84] For the eternal to enter the temporal, according to Auden's theological construction, a divine act of condescension had to occur. God had to lower himself to know man through the temporal. The condescension of the Incarnation led to a movement of theological belief (adherence to the Christian faith) that "Broke out spontaneously all over time," or throughout history, through numerous conversions.[85]

Like Eliot's *Four Quartets*, "Kairos and Logos" depicts time as the door through which the eternal may enter the temporal. The "condescension" (a term Christian reformer Martin Luther also used for the Incarnation) of eternal order is the force of logos entering into time.[86] Like Eliot's use of "another pattern" in *Quartets*, the Incarnate act brings with it another type of time.[87] And unlike the first type of time associated with the superficial self, whose occupation was the furniture of a temporally dying world, the Christians are defined by their exposure to the eternal through the temporal.

---

83. Bergson, *Time and Free Will*, 115.

84. See Phil. 2:6–8, "[Christ] Who, being in very nature God, did not consider equality with God something to be used to his own advantage, rather, he made himself nothing by taking the very nature of a servant, being made in human likeness. And being found in appearance as a man, he humbled himself by becoming obedient to death—even death on a cross!"

85. Auden, "Kairos and Logos," line 33.

86. See Mendelson's comments about Auden's use of this Lutheran term in *Later Auden*, 169.

87. Auden, "Kairos and Logos," line 30.

In the first sestina lies the heart of Auden's Bergsonian theology of time: that there are two selves that experience time in two ways and from that experience are spiritually defined. And the second sestina explores the break between two times and two selves that was created in the first sestina through the diction and imagery of fairy tale. Auden creates a fairy tale world in which a girl's dreams seem real and she is self-convinced that her dreams are the real world. Explicit in the second sestina is the Bergsonian paradigm of two parallel worlds that are both accessed by consciousness. The girl accesses another state of consciousness and time through dream. The dream is consciously actualized as the girl inhabits the world:

> Quite suddenly her dream became a word:
> There stood the unicorn, declaring—"Child. . . ."[88]

Bergson says that dreams detach the self from superficial thinking and place the individual into intuitive duration. In dreams, according to Bergson, "we no longer measure duration [i.e., think mistakenly about time], we feel it."[89] This feeling allows one to experience the heterogeneous, interpenetrative nature of duration, and in experiencing, to be changed by it at the level of deep consciousness.[90] Auden draws on this concept and couples it with his own that time can be spiritually known through conscious connection.

The dreaming girl creates an imaginative world in which reality works intuitively. What she thinks comes to be: "She piled up stones, pretending they were Home, / Called the wild roses that she picked 'My Garden.'"[91] The dream world is unfettered, generative, and in dynamic connection with the girl's consciousness. This dream world is a figure of duration, an imaginative realm that shows how durative time can work. In this world the girl feels, acts, and thinks freely. Thus, her experience is closest to what Bergson describes as a "time of becoming," when one experiences the freedom of durative force and is separated from temporal entrapments. And this experience of freedom in duration is "like a fruit, which has become too ripe," a spiritual ripening that exceeds a shallow experience with the temporal.[92] The girl is existentially flourishing through her dream state and has been separated from the world of the "time-obsessed." Most sig-

---

88. Auden, "Kairos and Logos," lines 40–41.
89. Bergson, *Time and Free Will*, 94.
90. Ibid., 95–96.
91. Auden, "Kairos and Logos," 59–60.
92. Bergson, *Time and Free Will*, 132.

nificant in the second sestina's treatment of time is that the girl's dream-induced imaginative state is linked to the Incarnate logos:

> Talked to herself as to a doll, a child
> Whose mother-magic knew the Magic Word.[93]

Auden plays on the word "Word" and its association with the logos. The girl is here described as an imaginative child who "talked to herself as to a doll," and whose mother possesses a kind of magic connected to the logos. Auden's notion of exercising imagination has a theological connotation, for in this stanza the imagination is exercised in relation to a knowledge of the logos. Auden was not the first twentieth-century Christian writer to associate the imaginative act with the theological. In discussing what constitutes a Christian poetic, Auden's contemporary Dorothy Sayers states that "there is the Creative Energy [or Activity] begotten of that idea [God, the Father, or what Sayers calls the "Creative Idea"], working in time from the beginning to the end, with sweat and passion, being incarnate in the bonds of matter: and this is the image of the Word."[94] Here Sayers depicts the creative energy of imaginative activity with an articulation of the divine Word. To exercise imagination, according to Sayers, is to participate in a theological articulation of the divine Word. Imagination, therefore, is partly an expression of the Word. I think Auden, who was fully aware of Sayers's ideas, is working under this idea of imagination and logos. His own theology centers on the image of the "Word" (logos) and promotes an Incarnate leitmotif that controls his work.

The second sestina of "Kairos and Logos" is thoroughly incarnational. Indeed, the imaginative fairy tale world is a seemingly perfect synthesis of durative connection through dreams, existential freedom through duration, and spiritual life through the logos. But like the juxtaposition of the first sestina's two types of time, the ideal fairy tale world is interrupted by the antithetically opposite temporal world. As will be shown below, this second sestina depicts a turn from a deep conscious connection to duration through imagination to a self-centered knowledge of time, which Bergson calls "superficial." The poem uses natural imagery to show the intrusion of temporality on the fairy tale figure of duration: "Till the day came the children of the forest / Ceased to regard or treat her as a child"[95]; "Of course the forest overran her garden, / Yet, though, like everyone,

93. Auden, "Kairos and Logos," lines 62–63.
94. Sayers, *The Mind of the Maker*, 37.
95. Auden, "Kairos and Logos," lines 65–66.

she lost her home, / The Word still nursed Its motherhood, Its child."[96] Here the temporal world of the sestina closes in on the imaginative act. A change in the girl's relationship to the imaginative world occurs in the last three stanzas, as the girl goes from exercising her imagination to taking her imaginative world for granted, "took the earth for granted as her garden."[97] The girl matures and so loses the imaginative ability that the sestina endorsed at its beginning.

Auden's use of the child figure to aid his theology of time is reminiscent of Bergson's use of the child to aid his theory of intuitive consciousness. Bergson insists that to "penetrate into the depths of consciousness" is to take on a childlike state of intuitive thinking.[98] Dreams, the imagination, and intuitive thinking are "like childhood back again," Bergson asserts. Auden's child figure in "Kairos and Logos" is a Bergsonian figure that represents intuitive thinking in time, a figure who through her use of intuitive imagination accesses the eternal Word.

The girl moves from an intuitive knowledge of time naturally mediated by her imagination to a knowledge of time that only seeks to conform to the girl's self. As it speaks to the theme of time, the fairy tale analogizes how one moves from an intuitive, conscious connection with duration to a superficial, shallow, self-centered relationship of time. The sestina ends in tension, as temporality has undone the dream figure of duration. The durative world with which the girl once lived in harmony has been disturbed because of the girl's change in consciousness, a change that disturbed her intuitive dream and so her relationship to duration. Even in this temporal disturbance, the poem reaffirms its incarnational leitmotif, facilitating a logocentric relationship between the Word and "its child." The overall message of the sestina is that even when temporal confusion breaks durative experience, the Word remains a knowable constant.

In the third sestina, Auden adopts a poetic mode that Mendelson describes as a modernist short story (*Later Auden*, "The third sestina is a modern short story, told with knowing and laconic dryness, about an adult temptation that mirrors the child's temptation").[99] Of course, Mendelson's claim is problematic, as the third sestina is still, in fact, a sestina, but his argument about the third sestina's terseness and "adult" theme are helpful to understanding this section of the poem. The sestina narrates the

---

96. Auden, "Kairos and Logos," lines 76–78.
97. Auden, "Kairos and Logos," line 164.
98. Bergson, *Time and Free Will*, 50.
99. Mendelson, *Later Auden*, 169.

adult temptations of a man to see the world as purely material, arbitrarily ordered, and personally meaningless. The sestina's main character is in a personal state of flux produced and exasperated by temporality's state of flux. The man sees neither meaning in his present moment nor meaning in any notion of truth:

> If one could name the father of these things,
> They would not happen to decide one's fate
> He woke one morning and the verbal truth
> He went to bed with was no longer there . . .[100]

The man in the third sestina embodies a type of thinking in his myopic focus on mundane events that Bergson describes as distinct multiplicity. The man rationalizes the ordinary, events of life in the temporal world as having no greater power behind them ("the father of these things . . . would not happen to decide one's fate"). The man with the rationalistic "twentieth-century intelligence" believes in no truth, waking up holding to a belief and abandoning it before sleeping.[101] Susan Guerlac describes distinct multiplicity as a mode of thinking which is manipulated by external thinking and "pertains to the world of things that exist in space."[102] Ideologically juxtaposed to the imaginative girl from the second sestina but comparable to Bergson's distinct multiplicity, the modern man discovers his own truth through an episteme of empiricism: "The bright and brutal surface of things / Awaited the decision of his eyes"[103]; "One notices, if one will trust one's eyes, / The shadow cast by language upon truth."[104] Awaiting the decision of his eyes, the man judges truth through pragmatic ways of thinking.

Allowing faith in nothing but that which his eyes will create, the man affirms the "the shadow cast by language" rather than the truth it shadows. Bergson criticized this very issue in language, arguing that language's reductive nature veils full, true expression of inner states, thus reducing true durative experience. Indeed, Bergson said that the constant temptation of man experiencing time is to confuse language for the actual inner state.[105] In this confusion, inner states are suppressed and supplanted by language.

100. Auden, "Kairos and Logos," lines 79–82.
101. Mendelson, *Later Auden*, 169.
102. Guerlac, *Thinking in Time*, 62.
103. Auden, "Kairos and Logos," lines 86–88.
104. Auden, "Kairos and Logos," lines 92–93.
105. Bergson, *Time and Free Will*, 97.

In Auden's "Kairos and Logos," the modern man's worldview represents a kind of Bergsonian reduction of meaning through language fixed in the material and temporal world: "the power of decision lay with *things*"; "In walls, catastrophes, sins, poems, things / Whose possibilities excluded truth"; "instead of earth / His fatherless creation."[106] Denying any theological operation behind time, the modern man attempts to create meaning in temporality but instead finds spiritual exile. The language of the poem turns increasingly bleak as the sestina goes on. Unlike the mirrored opposite world of the imagination, dream and the Word at the beginning of the second sestina, this third sestina is more of a cautionary tale that ends in an experience of time without the logos. The man is described as a . . . fatherless creation . . . that saw himself there with an exile's eyes, / Missing his Father, a thing of earth / On whose decision hung the fate of truth."[107] The spiritual diagnosis is bleak as the man maintains a self-perception that isolates him from relationships, ancestry, and ability to know Incarnate truth. Unlike the girl in the second sestina, who despite having been invaded by the temporal has maintained the parentage of the Word, this man is left orphaned. The reason for the different spiritual states is that the girl experienced duration and saw ultimate meaning in it, while this modern man toils in temporality and is cut-off from the logos by unbelief. The girl experiences *kairos*, the empowered moment, while the man only knows *chronos*.

Auden's Bergsonian dichotomy of time reaches its culmination in the poem's fourth and final sestina. Much like Eliot's "Little Gidding," which completed the overarching spiritual journey in the *Four Quartets*, the fourth sestina brings "Kairos and Logos" to a theological conclusion about what these two experiences of time ultimately mean. The sestina begins by continuing the third sestina's bleak spiritual tone. But instead of the third sestina's individualized depiction of time, the fourth sestina universalizes a temporal void of theological perception:

> Castle and crown are faded clean away,
> . . . .
> We are imprisoned in unbounded spaces,
> Defined by an indefinite confusion.[108]

---

106. Auden, "Kairos and Logos," lines 24, 29–30, 34–35.
107. Auden, "Kairos and Logos," lines 115–18.
108. Auden, "Kairos and Logos," lines 119, 122–23.

Auden's description in spatial terms of the bleakness of temporally confined thinking is another thoroughly Bergsonian element in "Kairos and Logos." This critique of temporal thinking is the entirety of Bergson's agenda in *Time and Free Will*, where Bergson says that spatially thinking about time, an "unfurling of time into space," leads to the loss of inner feeling.[109] "Then," Bergson concludes, "we are left with only the shadow of ourselves."[110] This loss of inner, spiritual feeling is the note on which Auden concludes his discussion of temporality without theology. The theologically void temporal leaves the individual in a state of "indefinite confusion." The image of the fading castle and crown recalls the imaginative fairy tale world of the second sestina. To show the full effects of temporality without Incarnate theology, those images have vanished, leaving the speaker to lament moments gone by when the logos could have been known:

> We should have wept before for these occasions,
> We should have given what is snatched away. . .[111]

Because of missing the eternal Word in the temporal, and so wasting life lived in the time's purpose of experiencing the eternal, what was snatched away was temporal life. Snatching away temporal life is here contrasted with the phrase, "we should have given," which refers to the Christian notion of sacrificially spending your life in allegiance to the Word. The idea of giving life away is a biblical one. For example, Jesus makes a clear distinction between giving life away and having it taken in John 10:18: "No one takes it from me, but I lay it down of my own accord. I have authority to lay it down and authority to take it up again." And in his Epistle to the Romans, Paul admonishes his readers: "Do not offer the parts of your body to sin, as instruments of wickedness, but rather give yourselves to God, as those who have been brought from death to life; and offer the parts of your body to him as instruments of righteousness."[112] Auden draws on this sacrificial paradigm of giving one's life to the logos and contrasts it with the "time obsessed" life, which the poem declares will be snatched away because of its failure to meet the eternal. This is the poem's sobering conclusion about temporality without theology: that though time is when the eternal can be met, it can also be where the eternal can be

---

109. Bergson, *Time and Free Will*, 98.
110. Ibid., 98–99.
111. Auden, "Kairos and Logos," lines 124–25.
112. Romans 6:13.

missed. Time is eventually snatched away and then can only be wept over. At this point of temporal bleakness, the poem takes an ideological turn and ends at a theological crossroads. Auden has depicted the problem of temporal thinking as an existentially superficial life. To remain temporal in one's thinking is to remain in a state of "indefinite confusion." The poem laments that fixtures of the external world, temporality with eternity, and superficial thinking have contributed to,

> our confusion;
> We are at loggerheads with our own lives.[113]

The vital impulse of life has been blocked by purely superficial thinking, as the confusion of temporal thinking has neglected the inner states of consciousness (the diminished "inner regimen"), and so lessened the meaning of the eternal for the individual.[114] Thus, the speaker cries, "Our inner regimen has given way" (and has led to the spiritual void which the poem calls "eternal silence."[115] Again, a Bersgonian paradigm is at work here. Bergson makes the analogy that the life trapped by the social, meaning the purely external, is like a dead leaf on a pond.[116] When becoming trapped in temporality and social construction, "we distance ourselves from the deeper layers of the self," and "these states of consciousness take on an inert mode of being."[117] This inertness characterizes the spiritual apathy of the "time-obsessed" in "Kairos and Logos," as they remain consciously stagnant because of their superficial thinking. And the poem seems to bury its hope for Incarnate visitation in increasingly bleaker descriptions of temporal confusion:

> Where the historic routes, the great occasions?
> Laurel and language wither into silence;
> The nymphs and oracles have fled away.
> And cold and absence echo in our lives.[118]

The poem's field of vision is skewed and misguided. History has lost meaning. Human expression has been silenced. The fantastic other that inhabited the durative dream of the second sestina has fled. And personal experience has been reduced to the level of Bergson's phantom self.

113. Auden, "Kairos and Logos," lines 128–29.
114. Auden, "Kairos and Logos," lines 133.
115. Auden, "Kairos and Logos," lines 133, 135.
116. Bergson, *Time and Free Will*, 101.
117. Ibid., 101.
118. Auden, "Kairos and Logos," lines 148–51.

Then, just at the end and like the Incarnate's meteoric entrance into time from the first sestina, the speaker considers the theology behind temporality, concluding, "reproach, though, is a blessing."[119] The speaker begins to recall the Incarnate behind the temporal and perceiving past time realizes that

> We are not lost but only run away
> The authors and the powers of confusion;
> We are the promise of unborn occasions . . .[120]

This last contemplation is durative thinking in that the consciousness perceives the significance in time's shaping individual personal experience. Rather than being permanently alienated from the Word, mankind is only run away, prodigals in time. And while humans are agents of confusion, whose proclivity for temporal futility has been well attested in the poem, they are also a part of God's divine activity in time. Even before birth ("unborn occasions"), the same "predestined love" mentioned in the first sestina and embodied in the Incarnation has also promised mankind's theological role in time. The durative force of time is the poem's only imagined sphere of theological resolution. Just as the Incarnation only finds its full meaning in time, so the promise of mankind can only find fulfillment in time.

The poem ends in a particularly Bergsonian way by offering a hope that what will ultimately guide human experience without confusion will be "the flora" of life, here an organic metaphor meaning life's dynamic, organic nature. The image is one of vital impulse, a central tenet in Bergson's vitalistic philosophy:

> The flora of our lives could guide occasions
> Without confusion on their frisking way
> Through all the silences and all the spaces.[121]

That by "flora," the poem means more than vegetative life is clear from the hope placed in the image. Here flora is used in a genitive construction and is possessed by human, individual life. The speaker hopes that the flora of life will guide the individual "without confusion," a Bergsonian allusion that speaks to a fundamental connection to time, already detailed in this dissertation. According to Bergson, durative experience is marked by an "intimate fusion" between time, consciousness, and the

---

119. Auden, "Kairos and Logos," lines 148.
120. Auden, "Kairos and Logos," lines 150–52.
121. Auden, "Kairos and Logos," lines 154–56.

vital impulse of life.[122] Auden's "Kairos and Logos" endorses a Bergsonian model of vitalism and furthers Bergsonian ideas in its construction of theology of time. In Auden's theology of time, not only is durative living a matter of theological perception and a subsequent acceptance of the Incarnation, but it is also a matter of dynamic life experience lived through the power of durative force. In other words, to exist in duration with theological awareness is to be transformed by time on the level of consciousness, reaching into the individual's deepest inner states. The navigation of temporal existence's "silences and . . . spaces" will be done through the power of time's Incarnate Word and the animation the Word brings to human experience.

Conclusion

A connection with Bergson has not been as well attested in Auden's biography as has that with Lewis and Eliot, who both recorded their impressions of Bergsonism, even admitting points of intersection and influence in their own work. I admit that Auden chronicles no such intersections. For a poet whose affinity for contemporary philosophers is so well chronicled, Auden's lack of recorded exposure to Bergson is curious. However, while Auden does not share the biographical interactions with Bergson that Lewis and Eliot do, his work demonstrates Bergson's influence just as strongly.

I would like to conclude this chapter differently than those on Lewis and Eliot by recruiting two other of Auden's post-conversion works that bear a Bergsonian influence. Because Auden's biographical connections with Bergson are not nearly as well documented as those of Lewis and Eliot, and because Auden's theology of time could feasibly be attributed to thinkers like Niebuhr or Tillich, it could be argued that the resemblance between "Kairos and Logos" and Bergson's theories of time is merely a coincidence. Thus, to further strengthen my argument that Auden's theology of time was influenced by the secular philosophy of Bergson, I will demonstrate Bergsonian ideas in two of Auden's most important works: the theological "New Year Letter" and the aforementioned "For the Time Being." Time was of great interest to Auden, and the poet often turned to the subject; for example, *Another Time* (1940), *The Double Man* (1941),

---

122. Bergson, *Time and Free Will*, 101.

The Age of Anxiety (1947), and *Nones* (1951) are all collections that privilege the theme of time.

Time is also the subject of Auden's "New Year Letter." The poem focuses on the significance of events of human history, the emergence of philosophical ideas, personal contemplation of those ideas, including of ontology, of theological belief, and of how personal experience are manifest in time. As with "Kairos and Logos," Auden's "New Year Letter" is replete with Bergsonian motifs. "New Year Letter" is about the development of personal experience and individual thought throughout time. The first part of the poem delves into the emergence of ideas during the last few centuries of Western human history, surveying the contributions of thinkers ("great masters," line 106), such as Blake, Voltaire, Rimbaud, Tennyson, Rilke, and Kipling. Each thinker influenced human history and so animated time, creating in it a philosophical current, a force, that shapes subsequent thinkers. Auden traces this ideological history in the first two parts of "New Year Letter," but in the third part turns to more theologically motivated reflection. The poem's initial theme of historical progression of ideas throughout time is a precursor to the later theme of spiritual progression in time. In part three, Auden considers the development of human history in relationship to God's divine economy, asserting that God enters human life and controls human destiny:

> But perfect Being has ordained
> It [human life] must be lost to be regained,
> And in its orchards grow the tree
> And fruit of human destiny.[123]

God possesses agency in the events of human destiny. And in language reminiscent of the line "we should have given what is snatched away," Auden claims that God has so ordained life that it must be given away (here termed "lost") in order for it to be salvifically regained.[124] In the orchard of this temporal existence given to the divinely perfect Being grows human destiny. This abstract portion of theologized contemplation becomes a reflection of eternal states, both heaven and hell. The poem is more interested in how these two eternal states are reached in time than in the two states themselves. The poem asserts that a denial of divine Being and acceptance of existential "becoming" is the path to hell:

---

123. Auden, "New Year Letter," 3. lines 45–48.
124. Auden, "Kairos and Logos," line 25.

> Hell is the being of the lie
> That we become if we deny
> The laws of consciousness and claim
> Becoming and Being are the same.[125]

The poem asserts that to miss the "Being" because one has conflated it with the "Becoming" is a damnable path. In "New Year Letter," this path is inseparable from temporal existence, as it is in time that one either comes or fails to know the Being. Those who come to know the divine Being are those who perceive the spiritual beyond their life in time, which is their temporal process of becoming. And those who miss the Being will "lie / Time-conscious for eternity," or in other words, will spend their eternal state in a regressive temporal state of consciousness.[126] This temporally confined thinking binds those who adhere it for eternity, comprising what the poem depicts as hell (cf. "Kairos and Logos": "which the time-obsessed are all condemned").[127]

Like the way to hell, the way to heaven is depicted as a spiritual journey in time, a climbing up the "purgatorial hill" to eternity through time.[128] Here the poem reveals a Bergsonian thread as it asserts that Time is the realm in which decisions with eternal consequences are made. Time is both finite man's spiritual problem and cure:

> But Time is sin and can forgive;
> Time is the life with which we live.[129]

Much like "Kairos and Logos" in its declaration that while in time humanity is "not lost but only run away" (line 150), "New Year Letter" associates time with mankind's fallenness ("Time is sin") while simultaneously declaring that while humanity is in time, and thus in sin, it is subject to forgiveness. Thus, in time one can move from sinfulness associated with temporality to forgiveness facilitated through temporality. In other words, only in time can time be forgiven (cf. *Four Quartets*, "Burnt Norton": "only through time time is conquered," line 90). The Bergsonian thread that runs throughout this portion of "New Year Letter" is the agency given to time in shaping man's inner states.

---

125. Auden, "New Year Letter," 3. lines 63–66.
126. Auden, "New Year Letter," 3. lines 63–66.
127. Auden, Auden, "New Year Letter," 3. line 78. Auden, "Kairos and Logos," line 12.
128. Auden, "New Year Letter," 3. line 94.
129. Auden, "New Year Letter," 3. line 91–92.

In *Matter and Memory*, Bergson describes man's biggest metaphysical problem as one of duration and consciousness. In order for humanity to experience metaphysical reality, it must place itself "back in duration, whose flow is continuous, and where one passes, by minute gradations, from one state to another: a truly lived continuity."[130] By placing oneself back into duration, one experiences change at the level of consciousness resulting in transformed inner states.[131] Giving time agency in the transformation of inner states is also one prominent theme in *Time and Free Will*, as I discussed at length in chapter 2. Like Auden's assertion that "time can forgive," Bergson's assertion is that time can transform. Upon Bergson's influential idea that in duration human inner states can change, Auden constructs a theology of time that promotes spiritual change through time.

The agency that "New Year Letter" gives to time is one of the primary Bergsonian themes from which Auden draws to create his theology of time. It is a theme that runs through "Kairos and Logos," the third part of "New Year Letter," and Auden's post-conversion "For the Time Being," which I have mentioned several times already in this chapter. "For the Time Being" is perhaps one of Auden's most theological interpretations of time's force to mediate spiritual transformation. The force of time in "For the Time Being" finds its source in the Incarnation, which has been discussed frequently throughout this work. Each character and voice in the poem provides commentary on some aspect of the Incarnation, each from his or her point of view. In the section of the poem entitled "The Summons," one of the wise men provides his point of view on the Incarnate act in time, speaking these remarkably Bergsonian words,

> My faith that in Time's constant
> Flow lay real assurance.[132]

The wise man adds that his faith in Time's constancy has been broken by the insecurities of temporal living. After reflecting on life in time, the wise man concludes that,

> At any given instant
> All solids dissolve, no wheels revolve,
> And facts have no endurance.[133]

130. Bergson, *Matter and Memory*, 207.
131. Ibid., 219.
132. Auden, "For the Time Being," lines 31–32.
133. Auden, "For the Time Being," lines 34–36.

The wise man's reflection on life in time has led to disillusionment. There is nothing left to cling to for meaning, the wise man intimates. Because he has yet to experience time's deeper significance, which is manifest in the Incarnation of the eternal, the wise man finds temporal existence meaningless. Thus, to find meaning in temporal existence, the wise man he has set out to follow the Nativity star, to encounter the eternal,

> To discover how to be living now
> Is the reason I follow this star.[134]

The wise man's faith in time's constant flow has been temporarily interrupted by the disillusionment of temporal living, but the poem suggests that faith in the meaning of time's flow will be restored once he encounters the eternal. There are two Bergsonian themes at play in this portion of "For the Time Being": the notion of durative flow and temporal disillusionment. Auden's phrase "in Time's constant Flow" is from Bergson, who expresses his theory of durative flow as an anti-theory of conservation in that time always flows, always effects change, and always transforms those who experience it.[135] For the conscious being, the flow of time "is a gain" in that the realm of consciousness is ever affected.[136] According to Bergson, because of durative flow, one can experience new modes of consciousness and new revelations about the nature of life in time, much like the wise man of "For the Time Being." According to Bergson, human consciousness moves with time's flow, and time's immutable law is that "the same does not remain the same."[137]

Not only does "For the Time Being" promote a Bergsonian understanding of durative flow, but the poem also captures what Bergson called superficial temporal thinking which I have discussed several times throughout this work. The wise man in "The Summons" is experiencing a sort of existential crisis brought on by his temporal existence. He has reflected on life and on his life lived in time, has become disillusioned, and so wonders if,

> ... the Present destroys its inherited self-importance?[138]

---

134. Auden, "For the Time Being," lines 41–42.
135. Auden, "For the Time Being," lines 31–32.
136. Bergson, *Time and Free Will*, 116.
137. Bergson, *Time and Free Will*, 115.
138. Auden, "For the Time Being," line 38.

The wise man thinks that the Present has possibly destroyed its own importance not because of anything innate in the nature of time, but because of the subjective, experiential meaning that man brings to time,

> With envy, terror, rage, regret,
> We anticipate or remember but never are.[139]

Here the wise man describes humanity's common experience with time in much the same way Bergson describes one's superficial experience with time. The wise man laments that mankind often allows unbridled emotion to disrupt experience with the Present. Mankind often anticipates, which is here meant as a worrying for the future, or remembers, which is a preoccupation with the past, but rarely experiences the meaning of consciously connecting to and being ("but never *are*," emphasis mine) in the Present. Bergson says precisely the same thing about mankind's common error in its experience with time: that the importance of the present is lost due to anxiety over the future or preoccupation over the past, and that these erroneous types of thinking lead to frustrated, superficial inner states.[140] Bergson asserts, "we confuse the feeling itself [an inner state], which is in a perpetual mode of becoming [transformation through durative flow]" with a mistaken thinking about time, which leads to a "shadow of the self... refracted and subdivided."[141] The wise man is describing what Bergson calls a "superficial psychological life," a confused experience with time caused by attentiveness to emotional fluctuation rather than durative force.[142] By focusing on his own emotional states ("confuse the feeling"; "envy, terror, rage, regret"), which in and of themselves are disturbed, rather than focusing on present time, which has the power to transform the consciousness into a better state, the wise man is exemplifying Bergson's "superficial" psychology.[143]

Had I more time I would further demonstrate Bergson's influence on Auden's poetry, which is far more extensive than indicated by the examples I have here set forth. But the examples just discussed certainly demonstrate that the Bergsonian presence in "Kairos and Logos" is no coincidence. Even more explicitly than "New Year Letter" and "For the Time Being," the poem "Kairos and Logos" promotes Bergsonian paradigms, particularly

139. Auden, "For the Time Being," lines 39–40.
140. Bergson, *Time and Free Will*, 97.
141. Ibid., 95–95.
142. Ibid., 93.
143. Auden, "For the Time Being," line 39.

those of dualistic time and dualistic experience of time. Also important to the poem is the theme of life's vital impulse simultaneously working in the individual's experience with time. Throughout the poem's matrix of Bersgonian ideas, Auden employs his own distinct theology of Incarnate time. As in Lewis and Eliot's theologies of time, Auden's theology of time finds its cumulative identity in Christian theology and Bergson's ideas. Using a Bergsonian model of duration, Auden takes up the philosophical issue of time, inserting a theology of Incarnate time that promotes human experience in time as a way of knowing the logos, the logos as that which makes temporal moments (kairoi) theologically meaningful and duration as the only time when the eternal can be met.

Conclusion

Immersed in the ideologies of their day, C. S. Lewis, T. S. Eliot, and W. H. Auden came to the Christian faith in a time of marked social, political, and moral upheavals. In this context of two World Wars and a post-World War society, a decline in Christian belief, and the emergence of Bergsonian and other philosophical ideas, fellow Christian writers Lewis, Eliot, and Auden wrote theologies of time. These three prominent literary figures converted to the Christian faith in a little over a decade of each other. And upon their conversions, they all turned to the theme of time. Other than man's relationship with God in general, the three authors took up no other common theological topic besides time in their post-conversion writing. For instance, Lewis often emphasized a personal relationship with God and how that relationship is expressed in an individual's daily life, while the application of the Christian faith on a personal level is largely missing from Eliot and Auden's post-conversion productions. Eliot wrote about Christian conversion in the most abstract of ways, while Lewis's treatment of salvation was explicit and Auden rarely dealt with the subject. And Auden devoted much of his post-conversion writings to the theological role of art, often treating theological topics with abstract metaphor and complex allusion, a treatment that chiefly served his interest in art as theological expression. Unlike Auden, whose emphasis on the nature of art thus rivaled his emphasis on theology, Lewis and Eliot were more interested in explicating the theological topic itself rather the artistic medium through which that topic was conveyed. But time was one theme that each author wrote about in remarkably similar fashion. It is safe to say that each author saw time as being of great theological importance. Dorothy Sayers, whose work I looked at in chapter 1 when considering the idea of theologized literature, captures the theological importance of time:

> Time is so intimately the mode of our own existence that it is equally difficult to conceive of Time apart from Being or of Being apart from Time. Perhaps this means that we ought not to try to conceive of them separately: for scientists frequently warn us that questions which produce meaningless answers usually turn out to have been meaningless questions. It may be more fruitful to consider Time as a part of creation, or perhaps that Time is necessarily associated with Being in Activity—that is, not with God the Father but with God the Son; with the Energy and not with the Idea.[1]

Sayers connects time to three important ideas here: human existence, ontology, and God's creative activity in history. For Sayers, time is the approach to each of these issues. Simply put, what one understands about time will inevitably affect what one understands about man's relationship with God. The theological import that Sayers places on time is not limited to theology proper but always reaches into one's definition of human nature and experience. As this work has demonstrated, Lewis's *The Great Divorce*, Eliot's *Four Quartets*, and Auden's "Kairos and Logos" share Sayers's view of time as both a revealer of God and an interpreter of man's experience. Lewis, Eliot, and Auden shared no formal community and together compiled no uniform Christian theory of writing, yet each devoted some of his most significant post-conversion work to the theme of time.

I have argued that in their treatments of time, Lewis, Eliot, and Auden's work should be seen as theologies informed by the secular philosophy of Henri Bergson. Depending upon and employing the twentieth-century's common currency of Bergsonian ideas, each author created a theology of time that would be most relevant to a twentieth-century audience. From Bergson's philosophy, each author constructed his own Christian treatment of time that shared a common emphasis on the importance of time for revealing God to man. Lewis's *The Great Divorce* promotes a theology of the present as the moment when God meets man. In that present, moral decisions and spiritual states dictate how one experiences God. Likewise, Eliot's *Four Quartets* advances a theology of the present but through the doctrine of the Incarnation, which resides in every present moment, so that in every present moment man can experience divine timelessness. Like Eliot's *Four Quartets*, Auden's "Kairos and Logos," places great theological importance on the Incarnation. But, while important, the Incarnation can be missed by thinking in terms of temporality without theology.

---

1. Sayers, *The Mind of the Maker*, 100.

Conclusion

All three authors saw theology as available for absorption by poetry, and each demonstrated that a Christian poetics of time must also be a theological poetics of time.

Beyond working with a theological theme, each author also displays a uniquely twentieth-century component in his theologized works: Bergsonism. I have argued throughout this study that what makes a theology of time characteristically twentieth-century is the use of thinking that is specifically twentieth-century in its nature. To execute my argument, I have done what no scholar before me has done: I have read the works of Lewis, Eliot, and Auden together in light of Bersgon's theories about time. Although other scholars have written on the connection between Bergson and Lewis, or between Bergson and Eliot, no other scholar that I have been able to find has written on the connection between Bergson and Auden, and certainly none have written on Lewis, Eliot, and Auden together in terms of Bergson's philosophy.

The appeal that Bergson had to each author was Bergson's assumption that time had deep metaphysical connections to human consciousness and that through time, transformation can occur. It was Bergson's notions of dynamism, of the vital impulse of life, of the force of time in the individual's life, and of two selves in two kinds of time that provided Lewis, Eliot, and Auden with the philosophical ideas necessary to construct contemporary theological treatments of time. Indeed, Bergson provided Lewis, Eliot, and Auden with a middle way between a twentieth-century secular philosophy and the Christianity to which they all converted. Bergson's ideals, while not considered Christian yet birthed in twentieth-century philosophical inquiries, assume the presence of a reality beyond the physically apparent. Bergson's ideas of intuition, duration, and the divided self with its two subjective modes of experience are all modernist ideas that provided Lewis, Eliot, and Auden with philosophical frameworks through which to construct Christian theologies of time. And while the three authors did not convene to articulate a theory of Christian literature, and did not have the same conversion experience from unbelief to Christianity, and did not assimilate or deploy Bergson's theories in the same way, they all saw in Bergson a way to approach the intersection of secular philosophy and the Christian faith.

Bergson's theories that are so generative of theological ideas can most broadly be described as dynamism, dualism, and durative force. Bergson's entire philosophy begins and ends in dynamism. For Bergson, all organic life is dynamic, time is dynamic, memory is dynamic, consciousness is dynamic, and human experience is dynamic. This philosophical belief supported a theological concept in Lewis, Eliot, and Auden, all of whom believed that God's animation of time dynamically empowered time.

Bergson's belief in dualistic categories pervades his thinking so thoroughly that rarely does he propose one view without offering its polar opposite. In Bergson's thinking, there are two selves, two types of time, two ways of viewing time, two types of subjective experience in time, and two types of knowing. Bergson's dualistic thinking is one of his philosophy's most distinctive qualities. By thinking in polarized concepts of time and human experience in time, Bergson creates a philosophical framework through which he can capture the nuanced multi-dimensionality of existing in time. It is also through his dualistic categories that Bergson qualifies types of conscious states in duration, whether they are superficially or intuitively connected with durative force. Bergsonian dualism is employed by each author in my study, as Lewis, Eliot, and Auden each create a theology predicated on choice, divergent temporal and spiritual perception, and the dualistic doctrine of the eternal operating in relationship with the temporal.

Durative force is Bergson's belief that time is a force that works on the consciousness in such a way that the individual's inner states are dynamically transformed. Time is force for Bergson. Any human experience fostered by intuitive connection with duration will share time's powerful property. Lewis, Eliot, and Auden predicate their entire theologies of time on this Bergonsian concept of durative force. Each author sees God working through time. Therefore time, as an agent of the eternal, carries imputed dynamic qualities. If God operates in time, then time is filled with His power. The theologies that Lewis, Eliot, and Auden construct all pronounce that God is how time possesses its force.

Bergson's idea operates in each author's work in different yet equally significant ways to help compose a theology of time. Indeed, the theologies of C. S. Lewis's *The Great Divorce*, T. S. Eliot's *Four Quartets*, and W. H. Auden's "Kairos and Logos" are unmistakably Bergsonian. If what makes Lewis, Eliot, and Auden's articulations of time into twentieth-century projects is their merging of the theological with the philosophically secular, then their common employment of Bergson demonstrates twentieth-century theologized literature as effectively as any other body of Christian work. In their recruitment of the Bergsonian themes of dynamism, dualism, and durative force and in their consistent view of time as when the eternal can be met, Lewis, Eliot, and Auden created a body of work on the

Conclusion

common theme of time that can not only lead to new understandings of how each author constructed his theology, and to new understandings of the commonalities in the post-conversion works of each author, but also to a new understanding of how secular philosophy and Christian theology cooperate to produce some of the twentieth-century's most important literature.

Bibliography

Ackroyd, Peter. *T. S. Eliot: A Life*. New York: Simon & Schuster, 1985.
Alexander, Samuel. *Space, Time and Deity: The Gifford Lectures at Glasgow, 1916–1918*. 2 vols. London: Macmillan, 1920.
Alighieri, Dante. *The Divine Comedy*. Edited by David Higgins. Translated by C. H. Sisson. Oxford: Oxford University Press, 2008.
Aquinas, Thomas. *The Summa Theologica*. 5 vols. Edited by John Fearns. Translated by Francis Spellman. New York: Benziger, 1948.
Asher, Kenneth. *T. S. Eliot and Ideology*. Cambridge: Cambridge University Press, 1998.
Auden, W. H. *The Age of Anxiety: A Baroque Eclogue*. Princeton, NJ: Princeton University Press, 2011.
———. *Another Time*. New York: Random House, 1940.
———. "As I Walked Out One Evening." In *Collected Poems*, edited by Edward Mendelson, 133–34. New York: Vintage, 1976.
———. *Collected Poems*. Edited by Edward Mendelson. New York: Vintage, 1976.
———. *The Complete Works of W. H. Auden: Prose*. 4 vols. Edited by Edward Mendelson. Princeton, NJ: Princeton University Press, 1997–2012.
———. *The Double Man*. Westport, CT: Greenwood, 1941.
———. *The Dyer's Hand*. New York: Vintage, 1989.
———. *English Auden*. Edited by Edward Mendelson. New York: Faber, 1988.
———. "For the Time Being." In *Collected Poems*, edited by Edward Mendelson, 347–400. New York: Vintage, 1976.
———. "Horae Canonicae." In *Collected Poems*, edited by Edward Mendelson, 627–41. New York: Vintage, 1976.
———. "In Memory of W. B. Yeats." In *Collected Poems*, edited by Edward Mendelson, 247–48. New York: Vintage, 1976.
———. "Insignificant Elephants." In *Collected Poems*, edited by Edward Mendelson, 807–8. New York: Vintage, 1976.
———. "Kairos and Logos." In *Collected Poems*, edited by Edward Mendelson, 305–9. New York: Vintage, 1976.
———. "Letter to Lord Byron." In *Collected Poems*, edited by Edward Mendelson, 79–116. New York: Vintage, 1976.
———. "Literary Transference." *Southern Review* 6 (1940) 78–86.
———. *Look Stranger!* New York: Faber, 1946.
———. "The Means of Grace." In *The Complete Works of W. H. Auden: Prose*, edited by Edward Mendelson, 2:132. Princeton, NJ: Princeton University Press, 1997–2012.
———. "The Meditation of Simeon." In *Collected Poems*, edited by Edward Mendelson, 385–90. New York: Vintage, 1976.
———. "New Year Letter." In *Collected Poems*, edited by Edward Mendelson, 197–246. New York: Vintage, 1976.

Bibliography

———. "1929." In *Collected Poems*, edited by Edward Mendelson, 45–49. New York: Vintage, 1976.
———. *Nones*. New York: Random House, 1951.
———. *On Secondary Worlds*. New York: Random House, 1968.
———. *The Orators: An English Study*. New York: Random House, 1932.
———. "Paid on Both Sides" In *Collected Poems*, edited by Edward Mendelson, 1–28. New York: Vintage, 1976.
———. *Poems*. New York: Faber, 1930.
———. *Preface to "Paradise Lost."* Oxford: Oxford University Press, 1942.
———. *The Prolific and the Devourer*. Hopewell, NJ: Ecco, 1976.
———. "The Sea and the Mirror." In *Collected Poems*, edited by Edward Mendelson, 401–46. New York: Vintage, 1976.
———. *Spain*. New York: Faber & Faber, 1937.
———. "Spain." In *Collected Poems*, edited by Edward Mendelson, 54–57. New York: Vintage, 1976.
———. "A Summer Night." In *Collected Poems*, edited by Edward Mendelson, 117–18. New York: Vintage, 1976.
———. *The Table Talk of W. H. Auden*. Edited by Nicholas Jenkins. London: Faber, 1990.
———. "Tract for the Times." *The Nation* 152 (1941) 24–25.
Baggett, David J., et al. *C. S. Lewis as Philosopher: Truth, Goodness and Beauty*. Downers Grove, IL: InterVarsity, 2008.
Barfield, Owen. "Either : Or: Coleridge, Lewis, and Romantic Theology." In *Owen Barfield on C. S. Lewis*, 36–63. Oxford: Barfield, 2011.
———. "Some Reflections on *The Great Divorce*." In *Owen Barfield on On C. S. Lewis*, 83–91. Oxford: Barfield, 2011.
Barth, Karl. *Barmen Declaration*. In *The Church's Confession Under Hitler*, edited by Arthur Cochrane, 237–42. Philadelphia: Westminster, 1962.
———. *Church Dogmatics*. 14 vols. Translated by T. H. L. Parker. Edinburgh: T. & T. Clark, 1961.
———. *The Epistle to the Romans*. Translated by Edwyn Hoskyns. Oxford: Oxford University Press, 1919.
Basillie, D. "Prof. Bergson on Time and Free Will." *Mind* 20 (1911) 357–78.
Bazarnik, Katarzyna. *James Joyce and After: Writer and Time*. Cambridge: Cambridge Scholars, 2010.
Beckett, Samuel. *Waiting for Godot*. New York: Grove, 1954.
Benda, Julien. *The Treason of Intellectuals*. New York: Beacon, 1955.
Benjamin, Walter. "Theses on the Philosophy of History." In *Illuminations: Essays and Reflections*, edited by Hannah Arendt, 253–64. New York: Harcourt, 1940.
Bergson, Henri. *Creative Evolution*. Translated by Arthur Mitchell. New York: Dover, 1998.
———. *The Creative Mind*. Translated by Mabelle L. Andison. New York: Citadel, 1992.
———. *Laughter: An Essay on the Meaning of the Comic*. Translated by Cloudesley Brereton and Fred Rothwell. New York: MacMillan, 1914.
———. *An Introduction to Metaphysics*. Translated by T. E. Hulme. Indianapolis: Hackett, 1999.
———. *Matter and Memory*. Translated by Nancy Margaret Paul and W. Scott Palmer. New York: Zone, 1994.

———. *Time and Free Will*. Translated by R. L. Pogson. New York: Harper, 1960.
Bergsten, Staffan. *Time and Eternity: A Study in the Structure and Symbolism of T. S. Eliot's Four Quartets*. Lund, Sweden: Scandinavian University Books, 1960.
Berkoff, Lois. *Systematic Theology*. Grand Rapids: Eerdmans, 1932.
Bistis, Marguerite. "Managing Bergson's Crowd: Professionalism and the Mondain at the College de France." *Historical Reflections/Réflexions Historiques* 22/2 (1996) 389–406.
Bonhoeffer, Dietrich. *The Cost of Discipleship*. New York: Touchstone, 1937.
Bradbury, Malcolm, and James McFarlane, eds. *Modernism: A Guide to European Literature, 1890–1930*. London: Penguin, 1991.
Brett, R. L. *Reason and Imagination: A Study of Form and Meaning in Four Poems*. London: Oxford University Press, 1960.
Brooker, Jewel Spears. "Substitutes for Religion in the Early Poetry of T. S. Eliot." In *The Placing of T. S. Eliot*, edited by Jewel Spears Brooker, 11–26. Columbia: University of Missouri Press, 1991.
Brooks, Cleanth. *The Hidden God*. New Haven, CT: Yale University Press, 1963.
Brueggemann, Walter. *Old Testament Theology*. Minneapolis: Augsburg, 2001.
Brunner, Emil. *Man in Revolt*. Louisville: Westminster John Knox, 1979.
Buell, Frederick. *W. H. Auden as a Social Poet*. Ithaca, NY: Cornell University Press, 1973.
Bunyan, John. *Pilgrim's Progress*. Edited by W. R. Owens. Oxford: Oxford University Press, 2009.
Bush, Ronald, ed. *T. S. Eliot: The Modernist in History*. Cambridge: Cambridge University Press, 1991.
Calinescu, Matei. *Five Faces of Modernity*. Durham, NC: Duke University Press, 1987.
Capek, Milic. *Bergson and Modern Physics: A Reinterpretation and Re-Evaluation*. Dordrecht: Nijhoff, 1971.
Carpenter, Humphrey. *The Brideshead Generation: Evelyn Waugh and His Friends*. London: Faber, 1990.
———. *W. H. Auden: A Biography*. New York: Faber & Faber, 2011.
Carson, D. A. *The Gospel According to John*. Grand Rapids: Eerdmans, 1991.
Carey, John Jesse. *Kairos and Logos: Studies in the Roots and Implications of Tillich's Theology*. Macon, GA: Mercer University Press, 1984.
Clubb, Merrel D. "The Heraclitean Element in Eliot's *Four Quartets*." *Philological Quarterly* 40 (1961) 19–33.
Como, James. *Branches of Heaven*. Dallas: Spence, 2008.
Comte, Auguste. *General View of Positivism*. Translated by J. H. Bridges. New York: Speller, 1957.
Conrad, Joseph. *The Secret Agent*. Greensboro, NC: Empire, 1907.
Cooper, John Xiros. *T. S. Eliot and the Ideology of Four Quartets*. Cambridge: Cambridge University Press, 1995.
Corn, Alfred. "For the Time Being: A Relocation of the Poet." In *Atlas: Selected Essays, 1998–2007*, 78–88. Ann Arbor: University of Michigan Press, 2008.
Cowley, Malcolm. *Exile's Return*. 2nd ed. New York: Viking, 1951.
Craig, William Lane. *Time and Eternity: Exploring God's Relationship to Time*. Wheaton, IL: Crossway, 2001.
Crane, J. K. "Golding and Bergson: The Free Fall of Free Will." *The Bulletin of the Rocky Mountain Modern Language Association* 26 (1972) 136–41.

Bibliography

Cuddy, Lois. *Making a Space in Time: T. S. Eliot, Evolution, and the* Four Quartets. Lund, Sweden: Lund University Press, 1994.

Davies, Paul. *The Mind of God*. New York: Simon & Schuster, 1992.

Deane, Patrick. "Auden's England." In *The Cambridge Companion to W. H. Auden*, edited by Stan Smith, 25–38. Cambridge: Cambridge University Press, 2004.

Deleuze, Gilles. *Bergsonism*. Translated by Hugh Tomlinson and Barbara Habberjam. New York: Zone, 1991.

Dieks, Dennis. "Space-Time Relationism in Newtonian and Relativistic Physics." *International Studies in the Philosophy of Science* 15 (2001) 5–17.

Douglass, Paul. *Bergson, Eliot, and American Literature*. Louisville: University Press of Kentucky, 1986.

Downing, David. *The Most Reluctant Convert: C. S. Lewis's Journey to Faith*. Downers Grove, IL: InterVarsity, 2006.

———. *Planets in Peril: A Critical Study of C. S. Lewis's Ransom Trilogy*. Amherst: University of Massachusetts Press, 1992.

Edwards, Bruce. *Further Up and Further In: Understanding C. S. Lewis's* The Lion, the Witch and the Wardrobe. Nashville: Broadman & Holman, 2005.

Edwards, Michael. "Rewriting *The Waste Land*." In *European Literature and Theology in the Twentieth Century*, edited by David Jasper and Colin Crowder, 70–85. Eugene, OR: Wipf & Stock, 1999.

———. *Towards a Christian Poetics*. Grand Rapids: Eerdmans, 1984.

Einstein, Albert. *Relativity: The Special and the General Theory*. Greensboro, NC: Empire, 1917.

Eliot, T. S. *After Strange Gods*. New York: Harcourt & Brace, 1934.

———. *American Literature and the American Language*. St. Louis: Washington University Press, 1953.

———. "Burnt Norton." In *The Complete Poems and Plays: 1909–1950*, 117–22. New York: Harcourt & Brace, 1950.

———. *Christianity and Culture*. San Diego: Harcourt, 1948.

———. *The Complete Poems and Plays: 1909–1950*. New York: Harcourt & Brace, 1950.

———. "The Dry Salvages." In *The Complete Poems and Plays: 1909–1950*, 130–37. New York: Harcourt & Brace, 1950.

———. "East Coker." In *The Complete Poems and Plays: 1909–1950*, 123–29. New York: Harcourt & Brace, 1950.

———. "Journey of the Magi." In *The Complete Poems and Plays: 1909–1950*, 68. New York: Harcourt & Brace, 1950.

———. "Little Gidding." In *The Complete Poems and Plays: 1909–1950*, 138–48. New York: Harcourt & Brace, 1950.

———. "Mr. Middleton Murry's Synthesis." *Criterion* 6 (1927) 340–47.

———. "Religion and Literature." In *Selected Prose of T. S. Eliot*, edited by Frank Kermode, 97–106. New York: Harvest, 1975.

———. *The Sacred Wood and Major Early Essays*. Mineola, NY: Dover, 1997.

———. *To Criticize the Critic and Other Writings*. Lincoln: University of Nebraska Press, 1991.

———. "Tradition and the Individual Talent." In *Selected Prose of T. S. Eliot*, edited by Frank Kermode, 37-44. New York: Harvest, 1975.

———. *The Waste Land*. Edited by Michael North. New York: Norton, 2001.

———. "The Writer as Artist." *The Listener* 24 (1940) 773.

Fabian, Johannes. *Time and the Other*. New York: Columbia University Press, 2002.
Flinn, Anthony. *Approaching Authority: Transpersonal Gestures in the Poetry of Yeats, Eliot, and Williams*. Lewisburg, PA: Bucknell University Press, 1997.
Forster, E. M. *A Passage to India*. Orlando: Harcourt Brace, 1924.
Fuller, John. *W. H. Auden: A Commentary*. London: Faber, 1998.
Gardner, Helen. *The Art of T. S. Eliot*. London: Faber, 1949.
Gillies, Mary Ann. "Bergsonism: 'Time Out of Mind.'" In *A Concise Companion to Modernism*, 95–115. Oxford: Blackwell, 2003.
———. *Henri Bergson and British Modernism*. Montreal: McGill-Queen's University Press, 1996.
Gish, Nancy K. *Time in the Poetry of T. S. Eliot: A Study in Structure and Theme*. Totowa, NJ: Barnes & Noble, 1981.
Glover, Donald. *C. S. Lewis: The Art of Enchantment*. Columbus: The Ohio State University Press, 1981.
Glyer, Diana. *The Company They Keep: C. S. Lewis and J. R. R. Tolkien as Writers in Community*. Kent, OH: Kent State University Press, 2008.
Gordon, Lyndall. *Eliot's Early Years*. Oxford: Oxford University Press, 1977.
———. *Eliot's New Life*. New York: Noonday, 1988.
———. *T. S. Eliot: An Imperfect Life*. New York: Norton, 1998.
Gourmont, Remy de. *Selected Writings*. Ann Arbor: University of Michigan Press, 1966.
Grass, Sean. "W. H. Auden, from Spain to Oxford." *South Atlantic Review* 66 (2001) 84–101.
Guerlac, Suzanne. *Thinking in Time: An Introduction to Henri Bergson*. Ithaca, NY: Cornell University Press, 2006.
Hawking, Stephen. *A Brief History of Time*. New York: Bantam, 1998.
Healey, Richard. *Reduction, Time, and Reality*. Cambridge: Cambridge University Press, 2010.
Heidegger, Martin. *Being and Time*. Translated by John MacQuarrie and Edward Robinson. New York: Harper, 1962.
Hemingway, Ernest. *A Farewell to Arms*. New York: Scribner, 1929.
Hinlicky, Paul. *Divine Complexity: The Rise of Creedal Christianity*. Minneapolis: Fortress, 2010.
Hoefer, Carl. "Absolute Versus Relational Spacetime: For Better Or Worse, the Debate Goes On." *British Journal for the Philosophy of Science* 49 (1998) 451–67.
Hugel, Friedrich von. *Essays and Addresses on the Philosophy of Religion*. Eugene, OR: Wipf & Stock, 2001.
———. *Eternal Life: A Study of Its Implications and Applications*. Berkeley: University of California Press, 1912.
Hugget, Nick, and Carl Hoefer. "Absolute and Relational Theories of Space and Motion." In *The Stanford Encyclopedia of Philosophy*, edited by Edward Zalta. April 30, 2012. http://plato.stanford.edu/archives/fall2009/entries/spacetime-theories.
Hurnard, Hannah. *Hinds' Feet on High Places*. Blacksburg, VA: Wilder, 1955.
Hurtado, Larry. *Lord Jesus Christ: Devotion to Jesus in Earliest Christianity*. Grand Rapids: Eerdmans, 2003.
Jacobs, Alan. *The Narnian: The Life and Imagination of C. S. Lewis*. San Francisco: Harper, 2005.
James, William. *The Varieties of Religious Experience*. Oxford: Oxford University Press, 2012.

Bibliography

Jasper, David, and Colin Crowder, eds. *European Literature and Theology in the Twentieth Century*. Eugene, OR: Wipf & Stock, 1999.

Jeffrey, David. *Christianity and Literature*. Downers Grove, IL: InterVarsity, 2011.

Jenkins, Nicholas. "Auden and Spain." In *W. H. Auden: "The Map of All My Youth": Early Works, Friends and Influences*, edited by Katherine Bucknell and Nicholas Jenkins, 88–93. Oxford: Clarendon, 1990.

Johnson, D. H. "Logos." In *Dictionary of Jesus and the Gospels*, edited by Joel Green, Scot McKnight, and I. Howard Marshall, 481–84. Downers Grove, IL: InterVarsity, 1992.

Joyce, James. *Ulysses*. Eastford, CT: Martino, 1922.

Kant, Immanuel. *Critique of Pure Reason*. Translated by Paul Guyer and Allen Wood. Cambridge: Cambridge University Press, 1998.

Kierkegaard, Soren. *Concluding Unscientific Postscript*. Princeton, NJ: Princeton University Press, 1941.

Kilby, Clyde. *The Christian World of C. S. Lewis*. Grand Rapids: Eerdmans, 1964.

Kirsch, Arthur. *Auden and Christianity*. New Haven, CT: Yale University Press, 2005.

Kittel, Gerhard, ed. *Theological Dictionary of the New Testament*. 10 vols. Translated and edited Geoffrey Bromiley. Grand Rapids: Eerdmans, 1965–1986.

Kramer, Kenneth Paul. *Redeeming Time: T. S. Eliot's Four Quartets*. Lanham, MD: Cowley, 2007.

Kumar, Shiv. *Bergson and the Stream of Consciousness*. New York: New York University Press, 1963.

Lawrence, D. H. "The Rocking Horse Winner." In *Complete Short Stories*, 530–39. Pickering, UK: Blackthorn, 2007.

———. *Women in Love*. Edited by Charles Ross. New York: Penguin, 1982.

Le Brun, Philip. "T. S. Eliot and Henri Bergson." *The Review of English Studies* 18 (1967) 149–61.

Lewis, C. S. *The Abolition of Man*. San Francisco: Harper, 1944.

———. "Apology." In *Spirits in Bondage: A Cycle of Lyrics*, edited by Walter Hooper, 12. New York: Harcourt, 1984.

———. *Christian Reflections*. Edited by Walter Hooper. Grand Rapids: Eerdmans, 1968.

———. *The Collected Letters of C. S. Lewis*. 3 vols. Edited by Walter Hooper. San Francisco: Harper, 2004.

———. "De Profundis." In *Spirits in Bondage: A Cycle of Lyrics*, edited by Walter Hooper, 20–21. New York: Harcourt, 1984.

———. *An Experiment in Criticism*. Cambridge: Cambridge University Press, 1961.

———. *The Four Loves*. New York: Harcourt, 1960.

———. *God in the Dock*. Grand Rapids: Eerdmans, 1970.

———. *The Great Divorce*. San Francisco: Harper, 1945.

———. *The Last Battle*. New York: HarperCollins, 1956.

———. *Mere Christianity*. San Francisco: Harper, 1940.

———. *Miracles*. New York: HarperCollins, 1947.

———. *On Stories and Other Essays on Literature*. San Diego: Harcourt, 1966.

———. *Perelandra*. London: Bodley Head, 1943.

———. *The Pilgrim's Regress*. Grand Rapids: Eerdmans, 1992.

———. *The Problem of Pain*. San Francisco: Harper, 1940.

———. *Rehabilitations and Other Essays*. Oxford, Oxford University Press, 1939.

———. *The Screwtape Letters*. San Francisco: Harper, 2001.

———. *Spirits in Bondage: A Cycle of Lyrics*. Edited by Walter Hooper. New York: Harcourt, 1984.
———. *Surprised by Joy: The Shape of My Early Life*. New York: Harcourt, 1955.
———. *They Asked for a Paper*. London: Bles, 1962.
———. *Till They Have Faces: A Myth Retold*. New York: Harcourt, 1956.
———. *The Weight of Glory*. San Francisco: Harper, 1949.
———. *The World's Last Night and Other Essays*. New York: Harcourt, 1960.
Lewis, Wyndham. *Time and Western Man*. Boston: Beacon, 1957.
Levenson, Michael. *A Genealogy of Modernism: A Study of English Literary Doctrine, 1908–1922*. Cambridge: Cambridge University Press, 1984.
Lobb, Edward. "Limitation and Transcendence in 'East Coker.'" In *Words in Time: New Essays on Eliot's Four Quartets*, 28. Ann Arbor: University of Michigan Press, 1993.
Longenbach, James. "Ara Vos Prec: Eliot's Negotiation of Satire and Suffering." In *T. S. Eliot: The Modernist in History*, edited by Ronald Bush, 41–66. Cambridge: Cambridge University Press, 1991.
———. "'Mature Poets Steal': Eliot's Allusive Practice." In *The Cambridge Companion to T. S. Eliot*, edited by A. David Moody, 176–88. Cambridge: Cambridge University Press, 1994.
Lucas, James. *The Religious Dimension of Twentieth-Century British and American Literature*. Washington: University Press of America, 1982.
Magny, Claude Edmonde. "A Double Note on T. S. Eliot and James Joyce." In *T. S. Eliot: Symposium*, edited by Richard March, 213–15. Translated by Sonia Brownwell. Chicago: Kessinger, 1949.
Manlove, Colin. *The Literary Achievement of C. S. Lewis*. San Francisco: Winged Lion, 2010.
Markos, Louis. *Lewis Agonistes: How C. S. Lewis Can Train Us to Wrestle with the Modern and Postmodern World*. Nashville: Broadman, 2003.
———. *Restoring Beauty: The Good, the True, and the Beautiful in the Writings of C. S. Lewis*. Colorado Springs: Biblica, 2010.
Marshall, I. Howard. *New Testament Theology*. Downers Grove, IL: InterVarsity, 2004.
Matthews, T. S. *Great Tom: Notes Toward the Definition of T. S. Eliot*. San Francisco: Harper & Row, 1973.
Matthiessen, F. O. *The Achievement of T. S. Eliot*. Boston: Houghton, 1935.
McClure, Roger. *Philosophy of Time*. New York: Routledge, 2005.
McDiarmid, Lucy. "The Poet in Wartime: Yeats, Eliot, Auden." In *Critical Essays on Auden*, edited by George W. Bahlke, 97–106. New York: Hall, 1991.
———. *Saving Civlization: Yeats, Eliot, and Auden Between the Wars*. New York: Cambridge University Press, 1984.
McFarlane, James. "The Mind of Modernism." In *Modernism: A Guide to European Literature, 1890–1930*, edited by Malcolm Bradbury and James McFarlane, 71–104. London: Penguin, 1991.
Mendelson, Edward. *Early Auden*. New York: Farrar, 1981.
———. "Early Auden (Look Stranger!)." In *Critical Essays on W. H. Auden*, edited by George Bahlke, 70–79. New York: Hall, 1991.
———. *English Auden: Poems, Essays, and Dramatic Writings, 1927–1939*. London: Faber & Faber, 1988.
———. "The European Auden." In *The Cambridge Companion to W. H. Auden*, edited by Stan Smith, 55–67. Cambridge: Cambridge University Press, 2004.

Bibliography

———. *Later Auden*. New York: Farrar, 1999.

Moody, A. David. "*Four Quartets*: Music, Word, Meaning and Value." In *The Cambridge Companion to T. S. Eliot*, edited by A. David Moody, 142–57. Cambridge: Cambridge University Press, 1994.

———. *Thomas Stearns Eliot: Poet*. Cambridge: Cambridge University Press, 1995.

Myers, Doris T. *C. S. Lewis in Context*. Kent, OH: Kent State University Press, 1994.

Neilson, Brett. "At the Frontiers of Metaphysics: Time and History in T. S. Eliot and Walter Benjamin." In *T. S. Eliot and the Concept of Tradition*, edited by Giovanni Cianci and Jason Harding, 201–14. Cambridge: Cambridge University Press, 2007.

New American Standard Bible. La Habra, CA: Lockman Foundation, 1960.

Niebuhr, Reinhold. *Christianity and Power Politics*. New York: Scribner's, 1940.

———. *Faith and History*. New York: Scribner's, 1949.

Newton, Isaac. *Philosophiae Naturalis Principia Mathematica*. Translated by Andrew Motte. Berkeley: University of California Press, 1934.

Nott, Kathleen. *The Emperor's Clothes: An Attack on the Dogmatic Orthodoxy of T. S. Eliot, Graham Greene, Dorothy Sayers, C. S. Lewis and Others*. Bloomington: Indiana University Press, 1954.

Oser, Lee. *The Return of Christian Humanism: Chesterton, Eliot, Tolkien, and the Romance of History*. Columbia: University Press of Missouri, 2007.

Pandey, M. S. *The Religious Poetry of W. H. Auden*. Jaipur, India: Pointer, 1990.

Pascal, Blaise. *Pensées*. Translated by W. F. Trotter. New York: Dutton, 1932.

Pearce, Joseph. *C. S. Lewis and the Catholic Church*. San Francisco: Ignatius, 2003.

Pike, James, ed. *Modern Canterbury Pilgrims*. New York: Morehouse-Gorham, 1956.

Pilkington, A. E. *Bergson and His Influence: A Reassessment*. Cambridge: Cambridge University Press, 1976.

Pinion, F. B. *A T. S. Eliot Companion*. Totowa, NJ: Barnes & Noble, 1986.

Quirk, Tom. *Bergson and American Culture*. Chapel Hill: University of North Carolina Press, 1990.

Rabate, Jean-Michel. *1913: The Cradle of Modernism*. Oxford: Blackwell, 2007.

Radmacher, Rebecca. "'Nothing Said Clearly Can Be Said Truly': Modernism in C. S. Lewis's *Till We Have Faces*." PhD diss., Arizona State University, 1997.

Raiger, Michael. "The Place of the Self in C. S. Lewis's *The Great Divorce*: A Marriage of the 'Two Lewises.'" *Logos: A Journal of Catholic Thought and Culture* 13 (Spring 2010) 109–31.

Reibetanz, Julia. *A Reading of the Four Quartets*. Ann Arbor: University of Michigan Press, 1983.

Redford, Bruce B. "'I Believe Again': Auden's 'Kairos and Logos' in the Context of Christianity Regained." *Thought: A Review of Culture and Idea* 55 (1980) 393–411.

Renan, Ernest. *The Future of Science*. London: Chapman & Hall, 1891.

Reeves, Gareth. "Auden and Religion." In *The Cambridge Companion to W. H. Auden*, edited by Stan Smith, 188–99. Cambridge: Cambridge University Press, 2004.

Replogle, Justin. "Auden's Religious Leap." *Wisconsin Studies in Contemporary Literature* 7 (Winter 1966) 47–75.

Richards, I. A. "A Background in Contemporary Poetry." *The Criterion* 3 (1925) 520.

Rilke, Rainer Maria. *Duino Elegies*. New York: Random House, 1922.

Sayers, Dorothy. *The Mind of the Maker*. New York: Harcourt, 1941.

Schwartz, Sanford. "Bergson and the Politics of Vitalism." In *The Crisis in Modernism: Bergson and the Vitalist Controversy*, edited by Frederick Burwick and Paul Douglass, 277–305. Cambridge: Cambridge University Press, 1992.

———. *C. S. Lewis on the Final Frontier: Science and the Supernatural in the Space Trilogy*. Oxford: Oxford University Press, 2009.

———. *Matrix of Modernism: Pound, Eliot and Early Twentieth-Century Thought*. Princeton, NJ: Princeton University Press, 1985.

———. "Paradise Reframed: Lewis, Bergson, and Changing Times on Perelandra." *Christianity and Literature* 51 (Summer 2002) 569–602.

Sheppard, Richard. "The Problematics of European Modernism." In *Theorizing Modernism*, edited by Steve Giles, 1–51. London: Routledge, 1993.

Shopenhauer, Arthur. *The World as Will and Representation*. Vol. 1. Trans. E. F. J. Payne. Mineola, NY: Dover, 1966.

Sicari, Stephen. "In Dante's Wake: T. S. Eliot's Art of Memory." *Cross Currents* 38 (Winter 1988–89) 413–34.

Smart, James. *The Divided Mind of Modern Theology: Karl Barth and Rudolph Bultmann, 1908–1933*. Philadelphia: Westminster, 1967.

Smith, Grover. *T. S. Eliot's Poetry and Plays: A Study in Sources and Meaning*. Chicago: University of Chicago Press, 1956.

Spencer, Herbert. *Progress: Its Law and Cause*. Ann Arbor: University of Michigan Press, 1891.

Spender, Stephen. *Life and the Poet*. San Francisco: Haskell, 1974.

———. "Remembering Eliot." In *T. S. Eliot: The Man and His Work*, edited by Allen Tate, 50. Harmondsworth, UK: Penguin, 1967.

———. *The Struggle of the Modern*. London: Hamilton, 1963.

Spurr, Barry. *"Anglo-Catholic in Religion": T. S. Eliot and Christianity*. Cambridge: Lutterworth, 2010.

Stein, Howard, "On Einstein-Minkowski Space-Time." *Journal of Philosophy* 65 (1968) 5–23.

———. "A Note on Time and Relativity Theory." *Journal of Philosophy* 67 (1970) 289–94.

Stirner, Max. *The Ego and Its Own*. Mineola, NY: Dover, 2005.

Tate, Allen. *The Poetry Reviews of Allen Tate: 1924-1944*. Baton Rouge: Louisiana State University Press, 1983.

Taylor, Charles. *A Secular Age*. Cambridge, MA: Belknap, 2007.

———. *Sources of the Self: The Making of the Modern Identity*. Cambridge, MA: Harvard University Press, 1989.

Tetreault, James. "Parallel Lines: C. S. Lewis and T. S. Eliot." *Renascence* 38 (1986) 256–69.

Thomas, George F. "The Method and Structure of Tillich's Theology." In *Theology of Tillich*, edited by Kegley and Bretall, 85–106. New York: Macmillan, 1952.

Tillich, Paul. *The Dynamics of Faith*. New York: Harper, 1958.

———. *The Interpretation of History*. New York: Scribner's, 1936.

———. *Systematic Theology*. 3 vols. Chicago: Chicago University Press, 1967.

Todorov, Tzvetan. *The Fantastic: A Structural Approach to a Literary Genre*. Ithaca, NY: Cornell University Press, 1975.

Valéry, Paul. *The Collected Works*. 7 vols. Edited by Jackson Matthews. Princeton, NJ: Princeton University Press, 1989.

Bibliography

Vanhoozer, Kevin. *The Drama of Doctrine: A Canonical Linguistic Approach to Christian Doctrine.* Louisville: Westminster John Knox, 2005.

Walker, Peter. "T. S. Eliot: Poetry, Silence and the Vision of God." In *European Literature and Theology in the Twentieth Century*, edited by David Jasper and Colin Crowder, 86–104. Eugene, OR: Wipf & Stock, 1999.

Ward, Michael. *Planet Narnia: The Seven Heavens in the Imagination of C. S. Lewis.* Oxford: Oxford University Press, 2008.

Weitz, Morris. "T. S. Eliot: Time as a Mode of Salvation." *The Sewanee Review* 60 (1952) 48–64.

Whitehead, Alfred North. *Adventures of Ideas.* New York: Simon & Schuster, 1933.

———. *Process and Reality.* New York: Free Press, 1978.

Whitworth, Michael. *Einstein's Wake: Relativity, Metaphor, and Modernist Literature.* Oxford: Oxford University Press, 2002.

Wilcox, Donald. *The Measure of Time Past: Pre-Newtonian Chronologies and the Rhetoric of Relative Time.* Chicago: Chicago University Press, 1989.

Williams, Charles. *Descent into Hell.* London: Longman, 1937.

———. *The Descent of the Dove: A Short History of the Holy Spirit in the Church.* London: Longman, 1939.

Williams, Donald. *Mere Humanity: G. K. Chesterton, C. S. Lewis, and J. R. R. Tolkien on the Human Condition.* Nashville: Broadman & Holman, 2006.

Wilson, A. N. *C. S. Lewis: A Biography.* New York: Norton, 2002.

Wood, Ralph. "The Baptized Imagination: C. S. Lewis's Fictional Apologetics." *Christian Century* 112 (1995) 812–15.

———. *Literature and Theology.* Nashville: Abingdon, 2008.

Young, R. V. "Withered Stumps of Time: *The Waste Land* and Mythic Disillusion." *Intercollegiate Review* 38 (Spring–Summer 2003) 24–32.

York, R. A. "Auden's Study of Time." *Orbis Litterarum* 54 (1999) 220–38.

www.ingramcontent.com/pod-product-compliance
Lightning Source LLC
Chambersburg PA
CBHW062022220426
43662CB00010B/1433